THE PREDATORY PARADOX

The Predatory Paradox

Ethics, Politics, and Practices in Contemporary Scholarly Publishing

*Amy Koerber, Jesse C. Starkey,
Karin Ardon-Dryer, R. Glenn Cummins,
Lyombe Eko, and Kerk F. Kee*

https://www.openbookpublishers.com

©2023 Amy Koerber, Jesse C. Starkey, Karin Ardon-Dryer, R. Glenn Cummins, Lyombe Eko, and Kerk F. Kee

This work is licensed under an Attribution-NonCommercial 4.0 International (CC BY-NC 4.0). This license allows you to share, copy, distribute and transmit the text; to adapt the text for non-commercial purposes of the text providing attribution is made to the authors (but not in any way that suggests that they endorse you or your use of the work). Attribution should include the following information:

Amy Koerber, Jesse C. Starkey, Karin Ardon-Dryer, R. Glenn Cummins, Lyombe Eko, and Kerk F. Kee, *The Predatory Paradox: Ethics, Politics, and Practices in Contemporary Scholarly Publishing*. Cambridge, UK: Open Book Publishers, 2023, https://doi.org/10.11647/OBP.0364

Copyright and permissions for the reuse of many of the images included in this publication differ from the above. This information is provided in the captions and in the list of illustrations. Every effort has been made to identify and contact copyright holders and any omission or error will be corrected if notification is made to the publisher.

Further details about CC BY-NC licenses are available at
http://creativecommons.org/licenses/by-nc/4.0/

All external links were active at the time of publication unless otherwise stated and have been archived via the Internet Archive Wayback Machine at https://archive.org/web

Digital material and resources associated with this volume are available at
https://doi.org/10.11647/OBP.0364#resources

ISBN Paperback: 978-1-80511-134-4
ISBN Hardback: 978-1-80511-135-1
ISBN Digital (PDF): 978-1-80511-136-8
ISBN Digital ebook (epub): 978-1-80511-137-5
ISBN XML: 978-1-80511-139-9
ISBN HTML: 978-1-80511-140-5

DOI: 10.11647/OBP.0364

Cover image: Trinity College Library, Dublin, Ireland. Photo by Lyombe Eko (2021), CC BY-NC. Cover design: Jeevanjot Kaur Nagpal

Contents

Author Information	1
Acknowledgements	5
Introduction	7
Chapter Contents	27
References	33
1. Ethical, Legal, and Policy Issues in the Knowledge Creation Paradigm: The Case of OMICS International, Open Access, and 'Predatory' Publishing	37
Key Takeaways	64
Discussion Questions	65
Activities	67
References	69
2. Open Science, Open Data: The 'Open' Movement in Scholarly Publishing	73
Key Takeaways	94
Discussion Questions	95
Activities	96
References	99
3. Research Quality: Understanding Definitions of and Challenges to Quality in the Knowledge Production Process	103
Key Takeaways	130
Discussion Questions	131
Activity	131
References	133

4. Scientific Hoaxes and the Predatory Paradox: Past, Present, and Future — 137
    Key Takeaways — 159
    Discussion Questions — 159
    Activities — 160
    References — 162

5. Avoiding the Pitfalls of Predatory Publishing: Guidance for Graduate Students and Junior Scholars — 169
    Key Takeaways — 191
    Discussion Questions — 193
    Journal Assessment Activity — 194
    Discussion Questions — 195
    References — 197

6. What's Being Taught about Predatory Publishing? A Systematic Review of University Resources — 201
    Key Takeaways — 228
    Discussion Questions — 229
    Activities — 229
    References — 231

7. Predatory Paradoxes: What Comes Next? — 237
    References — 261

Index — 265

Author Information

First author Amy Koerber and second author Jesse C. Starkey were major contributors to all content and played a significant role in compiling and editing all chapters, in addition to authoring or co-authoring their own chapters. The remaining four authors (Ardon-Dryer, Cummins, Eko, and Kee) are listed in alphabetical order by last name; each of these four authors is primarily responsible for the content of one chapter in the book and made equivalent contributions to the overall manuscript.

Amy Koerber
https://orcid.org/0000-0002-6926-5520
Amy Koerber, Ph.D., is Professor in Communication Studies and Associate Dean for Administration & Finance in the College of Media & Communication at Texas Tech University. Dr. Koerber's research agenda explores how experts make effective arguments in contexts of health, science, and medicine. Toward this end, she employs multiple research methods, including textual analysis as well as interviews and focus groups. Although her doctoral training is based in classical rhetoric, her current research employs a wide variety of theoretical frameworks, and she is especially interested in scholarly approaches that facilitate interdisciplinary collaboration and knowledge-making. Dr. Koerber's last book, *From Hysteria to Hormones: A Rhetorical History*, was published by Penn State University Press in April 2018 and was awarded the President's Book Award at Texas Tech University.

Jesse C. Starkey
https://orcid.org/0000-0001-7063-3397
Jesse C. Starkey, Ph.D. is an independent grant writer and strategic communication consultant, serving clients in the academic, private, and non-profit sectors who are seeking to make positive social change in their communities. She has a Master's degree in Higher Education

Administration from Sam Houston State University and a Ph.D. in Media and Communication from Texas Tech University. Her experience bridges the academic and industry worlds, and her research examines communication in areas of social change, including scholarly knowledge production, social movements, and mental health. Dr. Starkey served as a research assistant for the STEPP project during her Ph.D. program, assisting with all aspects of the research design, data collection and analysis, and report writing. She continued working with the research team after graduation as an editor and project manager.

Karin Ardon-Dryer
https://orcid.org/0000-0002-0383-1905
Karin Ardon-Dryer, Ph.D., is a faculty member in the Department of Geosciences at the Atmospheric Science Group at Texas Tech University. Before joining TTU she was a Postdoctoral Associate in the Department of Earth, Atmosphere, and Planetary Sciences (EAPS) at the Massachusetts Institute of Technology (MIT); and later a Postdoctoral Fellow in the Department of System Biology at Harvard Medical School at Harvard University. Dr. Ardon-Dryer received her Ph.D. in Atmospheric Science from the Department of Geophysics, Atmospheric and Planetary Science, and the Porter School of Environmental Studies at Tel Aviv University in Israel. Dr. Ardon-Dryer's main research is on the effect that aerosols (mainly dust particles) have on climate, the environment, and our health. In particular, she takes an interdisciplinary approach and combines field and laboratory work to investigate the interaction between humans and climate (e.g., the impact dust storms have on human health) in the short and long term. As part of her role as Co-PI in the STEPP project, Ardon-Dryer was responsible for the STEM topic as well as the early-career aspects of the project.

R. Glenn Cummins
https://orcid.org/0000-0001-9626-0453
R. Glenn Cummins, Ph.D., is a professor of Journalism and Creative Media Industries at Texas Tech University. His research interests fall under the umbrella of media psychology and examine audience response to and processing of media as a function of message content, structure, and individual characteristics. His research has employed a variety of novel measurement approaches to studying individual

cognitive and emotional processing of media messages, including psychophysiology, eye tracking, continuous response measurement, and more. He formerly served as Associate Dean for Research and Grants in the College of Media & Communication at Texas Tech where he helped grow the College's sponsored research goals and facilitate interdisciplinary collaborations between communication scholars and partners across and beyond the university. He has been part of research teams sponsored by the NSF and USDA.

Lyombe Eko
https://orcid.org/0000-0002-6080-4727
Lyombe Eko, Ph.D., is a professor in the College of Media & Communication, Texas Tech University. His areas of research and teaching are comparative and international communication studies, as well as comparative information and communication technology law, policy, and ethics, with a focus on Africa, the European Union, the United States, France and the UK. He also studies visual communication, human rights, and freedom of expression. He has published award-winning books on comparative international communication law and policy. He has also published numerous, widely cited articles in international law review and media studies journals. He has been an associate professor, Director of Graduate Studies, and Director of the African Studies Program at the University of Iowa. He has also taught at the University of Maine, Orono. He earned his Ph.D. in Journalism from Southern Illinois University at Carbondale. Before his academic career, he was a journalist at Cameroon Radio and Television (CRTV), and an editor/translator, at the African Broadcasting Union (URTNA) in Nairobi, Kenya.

Kerk F. Kee
https://orcid.org/0000-0002-0543-5009
Kerk F. Kee, Ph.D., is Professor in the College of Media & Communication at Texas Tech University. His research primarily focuses on information diffusion and innovation adoption in scientific organizations, and secondarily in health communities and pro-environmental societies. Broadly speaking, his research interests lie at the intersection of information dissemination, technology use, and scientific work. Besides the National Science Foundation (NSF) funded research co-authored

with colleagues in this book on predatory publishing, he is also working on an NSF project looking at designing an AI-driven platform and chatbot with algorithms to filter COVID-19 related publications based on different levels of evidence (e.g., meta-analyses vs. randomized controlled trials vs. editorials/expert opinions without empirical support), in order to help clinicians and medical professionals screen and rank a large amount of (mis/dis)information on COVID-19, a data deluge problem that became overwhelming during the pandemic. Kee received his Ph.D. in organizational communication from the University of Texas at Austin.

Acknowledgements

The authors are grateful for an award from the National Science Foundation that made this project possible (Grant #1926348), and we are grateful for the expertise and support provided by Mr. Tyler Myatt, grant writer in the College of Media & Communication, in the early phases of the project. The authors are also grateful to the forty-eight individuals who participated in interviews as part of this research. In the final phases of the research, we have been especially grateful to Dr. Alessandra Tosi, co-founder and Managing Director of Open Book Publishers (OBP), as well as the entire OBP staff. Dr. Tosi's enthusiasm for the project and her team's support at every step along the way have been integral to the success of this book.

Introduction

Academic life is a lot like a reality television show. In reality television, we get an insider's perspective on people interacting with each other, working toward a goal that may or may not be seen as important to anyone other than the contestants in the show. Sometimes these contestants collaborate with each other, and they often compete against each other. Quite frequently, they do all they can to make sure someone else loses so they can win. The contest is subject to rules that should be followed but do not always have to be followed. For those who accumulate the right allies, such rules can also become contingent on the whims of those who wield the power to enforce them. When it comes time to make a final judgment about the outcome of the contest, there is a vote — either anonymous or not — with results that can be impacted by preexisting alliances, political motivations, and manipulation of the process. In both reality television and academic knowledge production, we have those who participate in the process (contestants and researchers), we have those who profit from the process (producers and publishers), and we have consumers (viewers and readers). In short, reality television exposes all the messiness, beauty, complexity, elegance, and ugliness that is inherent in any endeavor that involves multiple human beings — academic life being no exception.

Most of us involved in the pursuit of scholarly knowledge — whether as publishing professionals, teachers, researchers, editors, or some other professional title — aim to produce knowledge for the betterment of society. We tend to conceive our motives as loftier than those at play in reality television. In opening with this analogy, our intention is not to deny any of these loftier motives. We do not mean to imply that we should trust academic knowledge any less than we ever have; nor is it our intention to diminish bedrock institutions such as tenure and promotion and peer review, or to devalue these mechanisms in any way.

Rather, opening with an analogy to reality television is meant to open some new perspectives on the 'ivory tower' that we often idealize as the place where scholarly knowledge is produced. It is a reminder that scholarly communication is not, and never has been, a pure, unfettered product of scientific advancement or progress. Academic knowledge is created by humans and is, therefore, fraught with the same uncertainties, idiosyncrasies, complexities, and nuances as any other human endeavor. And like any other human endeavor, academic knowledge production is to some extent a game, or contest.

The Predatory Paradox: Ethics, Politics, and Practices in Contemporary Scholarly Publishing is an open access book designed to prepare researchers, academic administrators, publishing professionals, and other stakeholders to be ethical and successful players in this game. Our premise in this book is that to succeed, these stakeholders need to know how to navigate a rapidly evolving landscape that presents more options than ever before, but also a greater number and type of pitfalls. The knowledge and expertise that is offered in this book is meant to benefit not only these individuals but all of us who live in a society that depends on scholarly communication to continue as a successful enterprise for generations to come.

Although the game of academic knowledge production is continually evolving in new and interesting ways, the game itself is nothing new. At least as long as the scientific method has been in place as a trusted means for producing knowledge, we can safely say this game has existed. It existed, for example, in 1953 when James D. Watson and Francis H.C. Crick (Watson and Crick 1953) published an article in *Nature* that established their double-helix model of DNA as the one that would be accepted as scientific fact for generations to come. In so doing, Watson and Crick won a big victory over other 'contestants' in the game, including Oswald Avery and two coauthors, who had published a paper nine years earlier, in which they were the first to argue for the existence of DNA (Avery and others 1944). At the time it was published, Avery and his coauthors' paper received far less attention than Watson and Crick's. However, it is not so much that Watson and Crick 'won the game' because their science was superior to Avery's. Rather, a complex array of factors was at play, including timing, or *kairos*. As explained by Carolyn R. Miller (1994), Avery and colleagues' article was written in a style of 'cautious skepticism' (p. 311). Although this may be one reason why it did not receive as much attention as Watson and Crick's, the explanation is not quite this simple. Rather, Miller (1994) asserts, the more cautious style used in Avery and colleagues' article was necessary because they were presenting an idea that the scientific community was not yet ready to accept when their article was published: the idea that DNA was something other than a protein. So even though Avery and his colleagues' findings were widely accepted many years later, they received little attention when they were published in 1944. In terms more familiar to us today, we might say Avery and his colleagues' article had far less *impact* than the article published nine years later by Watson and Crick. However, as is often the case today, the lesser impact of Avery and his colleagues' findings had little to do with the quality of their science and much to do with a wide array of other factors beyond the scientists' immediate control — factors such as audience reception, historical context, and timing.

Of course, many of the rules have changed since Watson and Crick published their double-helix model of DNA in 1953, and we now have a wider variety of media available for disseminating scientific knowledge. However, we are still playing this game today, almost a century later. For example, researchers across the globe have been competing to find answers to the many unknowns that the scientific community faces regarding COVID-19 — disagreeing, sometimes vehemently, on the level and duration of immunity offered by various vaccines, the length of immunity after vaccination or infection with the virus, the value of face masks as a protective measure, and many other topics. Someday we will be able to look back and identify winners and losers in this game, but for now all we can do is be grateful that the game exists; without it, we would have little hope.

Scholarly publishing has long been a crucial component of this game — scientific knowledge that is not published cannot be said to exist. However, as this book will explore, the mechanisms that regulate the production and sharing of scientific knowledge are facing new threats. Specifically, the emergence of unethical and sometimes illegal variants of scholarly publishing — such as so-called 'predatory publishing' — are posing new problems for the integrity of the scholarly research and publication paradigm.

In setting out to provide the skills and expertise that researchers and other stakeholders need to succeed in today's academy, this book extends the work that individuals and organizations have already undertaken to offer guidance on so-called 'predatory publishing' and related phenomena that are emerging as potential threats to the integrity of scholarly communication. In addition to addressing the historical, political, and economic aspects of scholarly publishing that have culminated in the present situation, each chapter also offers practical advice on how to navigate this complex and contradictory situation. Based on National Science Foundation-funded research[1] that has included interviews, case studies, legal and policy analysis, and content analysis, *The Predatory Paradox* aims to provide readers with a comprehensive, systematic, and accessible resource on predatory publishing and the academic trends associated with it.

What is Predatory Publishing?

A relatively recent addition to the game of academic publishing, predatory publishers and journals first caught the attention of the scientific community in 2008 when Jeffrey Beall, a librarian at the University of Colorado-Denver, coined the term to characterize a small number of open access journals and publishers that he included on a 'blacklist'[2] he had published on his website. Along with its many benefits, the transition to open access has also introduced new practices, such as the 'article processing charge' or APC, whereby the cost of an article's publication is shifted partially or fully to authors to enable open access via the publisher. Beall (2012) used the word *predatory* to characterize journals and publishers that he believed were exploiting this publishing model to accept a greater number of articles, purely for the sake of increasing profits, often without adequate peer review. He started his list to help scholarly authors make informed decisions in the context of this rapidly changing publishing landscape.

---

1   Award#1926348.https://www.nsf.gov/awardsearch/showAward?AWD_ID=1926348
2   'Blacklist' was the term that Beall used, and it was widely used at the time. In recent years, the terminology has changed to avoid the racial symbolism implied by the terms 'black' and 'white' (Bisaccio, 2020).

When it first appeared in 2008, Beall's list included a handful of journals and publishers that he identified as predatory. However, as the list grew, so did the controversy that surrounded it. The controversy flared when Beall [@Jeffrey_Beall] tweeted on 18 October 2015, that he had added a journal called *Frontiers* to his list of predatory journals (Beall 2015). A *Frontiers* associate editor [@Lakens] immediately tweeted back: 'Frontiers being added to Beall's list reveals the big weakness of Beall's list: it's not based on solid data, but on Beall's intuition' (Bloudoff-Indelicato 2015; Crawford 2014; Teixeira da Silva 2020).

Beall took his list offline in 2017, amidst controversy and accusations that it was too reliant on anecdotal evidence and personal judgment (Bloudoff-Indelicato 2015; Crawford 2014). As an indication of the intensity of the controversy that surrounded Beall's list, when he took it offline, he offered the following explanation: 'In January 2017, facing intense pressure from my employer, the University of Colorado Denver, and fearing for my job, I shut down the blog and removed all its content from the blog platform' (Beall 2017: para. 1).

However, many years after the demise of Beall's list, predatory practices continue to be a concern for scholars, policymakers, research funders, and the public. In fact, a report by the National Academies of Sciences, Engineering, and Medicine identified predatory journals as one of the 'new forms of detrimental research practices' that currently threaten research integrity ('Fostering Integrity' 2017: 2). Although most stakeholders agree on the seriousness of this problem, there is widespread disagreement on many issues related to it. For instance, experts disagree on the inherent value of open access publishing as a sustainable publishing model and even on how to define *predatory* (Roberts 2017; Teixeira da Silva and others 2019). Some groups are developing consensus around agreed-upon definitions (Grudniewicz and others 2019; 'Predatory Publishing' 2019), whereas others have argued for abandoning the term altogether and replacing it with another term such as *deceptive* (Anderson 2018).

Some recent books on publishing have paid attention to predatory publishing, often situating it in the context of other twenty-first century trends in scholarly publishing. One is *Gaming the Metrics: Misconduct and Manipulation in Academic Research*, published in 2020 by Massachusetts Institute of Technology Press (Biagioli and Lippman 2020). This edited collection's focus is the academy's current obsession with metrics such as impact factor that are being used to offer a numeric evaluation of a publication's value independent from considering the quality of its actual content. Predatory publishing is presented as a product of this evaluation system: 'While light-years away from high impact journals like *Science*, *Nature*, or *Cell*, these 'predatory journals' may be simply the other side, or perhaps the bottom, of the same metrics economy' (Biagioli and Lippman 2020: 9). Thus, predatory journals are situated as one of many current practices that, the editors contend, require us to expand our understanding of academic misconduct to account for the many new forms of illegitimate scholarly activity that can occur as researchers and other stakeholders in academic publishing develop new ways to 'game' the system in a 'metrics economy'.

Another book that offers significant coverage of predatory publishing is *Scholarly Communication: What Everyone Needs to Know* (Anderson 2018). This book is intended as a guide for scholarly authors and other audiences who want to understand various aspects of publishing in the present time. The book offers definitions of key terms and concepts that are central to scholarly publishing, as well as some historical coverage to show how current trends and practices have come to exist as we know them today. The author's statement of purpose in the introduction echoes that indicated by the title; he aims to provide coverage of 'things about scholarly communication that everyone (or most people anyway) would benefit from knowing' (Anderson 2018: 1). To a greater extent than most other recent books on scholarly publishing, this author considers predatory publishing part of that content. For example, a chapter titled 'Problems and Controversies in Scholarly Publishing' devotes significant coverage to topics such as 'What is predatory publishing?' and 'What is the difference between predatory publishing and vanity or subsidy publishing?' In a writing style that is clear and accessible, this book succeeds at explaining these basic concepts to a broad audience that extends beyond the academy.

In recent years, two books devoted exclusively to predatory publishing have been published. The first was published by Routledge (Xia 2021). In this book, Xia offers an overview of predatory practices and examines how these practices have impacted scholarly communication. Xia cites Beall (2013) as a source for a definition of predatory publishing as 'an exploitative business model in the scholarly publishing market that is devised solely for financial gain' (p. 1) and claims that 'predatory publishing has become an epidemic practice over the last two decades' (p. 2). In addition to introducing readers to the various practices that can be considered 'predatory', Xia also summarizes various initiatives underway to combat predatory publishing and provides readers with some advice on how to avoid falling prey.

The second recent book on predatory publishing is Simon Linacre's (2022) open access book published by Against the Grain Media. Linacre says his aim in this book is 'to shed light on the dark arts of predatory journals' (p. 4). He aims to provide both 'contextual information' and 'practical guidance' on predatory publishing. Along these lines, Linacre offers a comprehensive history of the term, an overview of key events such as the origins and demise of Beall's list, and some analysis of key journals that have come to be known as predatory. An important contribution of Linacre's book is his insightful analysis of the different reasons why scholars submit their work to predatory journals — a more complex set of reasons than we might expect. In his final chapters, he also leaves readers with some creative suggestions for moving forward, including steps that individuals can take to avoid falling prey to predatory publishing practices as well as systemic changes we might consider as members of the larger scholarly community.

In *The Predatory Paradox*, we aim to expand on the groundbreaking research of Xia (2021), Linacre (2022), and other authors who have addressed predatory publishing in recent years. We offer a scholarly explication of key terms and concepts that goes beyond the basic introductory explanations that general audiences need to understand scholarly communication, and we offer recommendations to a wide array of stakeholders, including academic authors as well as publishing professionals, academic administrators, policymakers, and science journalists. The recommendations we offer in the book are based on extensive interview research with a wide array of stakeholders in scholarly publishing and on various forms of textual inquiry that we have used to follow up on questions posed by these interviews. Thus, we are equipped in this book to extend the scholarly conversation on predatory publishing in new directions and, hopefully, to set the agenda for future researchers who will investigate this problem for years to come. Our research has found that any attempt to create a list, or any other mechanism, that makes clear-cut distinctions between journals, publishers, or publishing practices that are predatory and those that are not will be incomplete, subject to dispute, and out-of-date from the moment it is conceptualized. This is partly because of the extent to which predatory publishing is changing and growing every day. In short, we argue in this book, defining *predatory publishing* is far from a simple task. Although some have argued we should abandon the term altogether, in this book we aim to achieve a more robust understanding of the word *predatory* by embracing the many paradoxes — 'contradictory yet interrelated elements that exist simultaneously and persist over time' (Smith and Lewis 2011: 382) — that arise from it. In so doing, we use predatory publishing as a window into the complex and fascinating world that is scholarly publishing in the twenty-first century.

By conducting interviews with forty-eight individuals who are involved in scholarly publishing in various capacities, from multiple disciplines, and a diverse set of geographic locations, we sought to gain a deeper understanding of this term and of the ways in which it impacts diverse stakeholders.[3] From these interviews, we have learned that the term itself, 'predatory publishing', is the product of a desire to find simple solutions and understandings to what is inherently a complex problem.

When authors receive emails inviting them to submit their work to a journal far afield from their own discipline, they often have good reason to suspect that these email solicitations are fraudulent. This can happen, for example, when a communication scholar who conducts research in health communication or science communication publishes articles with titles and key words that turn up in searches to identify potential authors for medical journals. If the editors of a peer-reviewed medical journal invite a communication scholar to submit a research article to their journal, this is clearly fraudulent, and the author is likely not qualified to submit their work to a medical journal. But in many cases, it is far less straightforward.

---

3   Our Texas Data Repository Dataverse includes a table showing participant demographic information. See https://doi.org/10.18738/T8/QUBMLI ('Participant Occupation and Regional Demographics Table').

The Multidisciplinary Digital Publishing Institute (MDPI) presents us with one such case. This publisher was added to Beall's list in 2014 but was removed on 28 October 2015 after a successful appeal by MDPI. However, as explained in a recent blog post by Paolo Crosetto (2021), determining whether MDPI should be considered predatory is not at all straightforward:

> So, is MDPI predatory or not? I think it has elements of both. I would name their methods aggressive rent extracting, rather than predatory. And I also think that their current methods & growth rate are more likely to make them shift towards more predatory over time. (para. 3, original emphasis)

Crosetto goes on to argue that depending on how one views MDPI, they could be seen as world leaders in a new model of academic publishing, or as a quintessential example of how predatory practices can infiltrate commercial publishing on the largest scale possible.

Regardless of which perspective one adopts toward MDPI, the publisher is remarkable for the pace of its growth: they published 36,000 articles in 2017 and 167,000 in 2020 — more than a four-fold increase in only three years. In fact, one recent blog post predicts that MDPI will soon move ahead of Taylor & Francis to become the '4th largest publisher in the world', and that MDPI is already, as of 2019, the largest open access publisher, having overtaken Springer (Petrou 2020). The author of this blog post, Christos Petrou, reports the following response from an interview he conducted with Delia Mihaila, CEO of MDPI, when he asked her about the publisher's remarkable growth and whether they have sacrificed quality of publication for speed and quantity:

> Delia attributes MDPI's fast performance to getting the headcount and task allocation right. She said that large, in-house teams (as many as 70–80 FTEs for one of the large journals) take over the tedious part of the work of the academic editors. The in-house team pushes and negotiates with the other stakeholders (editors, reviewers, authors) to meet strict deadlines as well as possible. Delia said that adhering to such deadlines may sometimes lead to complaints, but MDPI always shows flexibility. She added that ultimately there is common understanding that a rapid process serves everyone's interests.
>
> I asked Delia whether, in addition to working fast, MDPI takes any editorial risks. She said that given its ascent, MDPI is in the spotlight and as result 'we are very, very careful in everything we do, and we must

always have evidence of a rigorous peer review process. Open Access publishers are always under the suspicion of skipping the peer review just for the sake of making money. We cannot afford to not conduct the peer review properly or to act unethically.' (Petrou 2020: 27–28)

Authors like MDPI for their fast turn-around time, and on some markers of quality, MDPI journals have been successful. For example, seventy-four of their journals currently have an impact factor, and eighteen of these have an impact factor above four (Crosetto 2021).

In addition to these business successes, the publisher also emphasizes the social benefits that their publishing practices offer:

> MDPI's focus on offering the best service to the scientific communities of the world remains unchanged. The past year once again proved that making research results freely and immediately available to as wide an audience as possible is of the utmost importance. This strengthened our efforts and reaffirmed our commitment to serve researchers by delivering important scientific insights faster than was ever previously possible. ('Annual Report' 2020: 1)

Along these lines, the publisher reports that the 'median time from submission to first decision remains short, at around three weeks' ('Annual Report' 2020: 1). Even while maintaining this rapid turnaround time, though, the publisher claims that they uphold the highest standards of peer review and that 57% of articles submitted in 2020 were rejected.

Despite these successes, MDPI is still subject to intense criticism, such as that expressed in a blog post titled 'Why not to publish in "Sustainability" (and you're welcome to share this post')' (Fischer 2020). *Sustainability* is one of MDPI's titles, and the author of this blog post complains about receiving repeated spam emails encouraging him to submit articles to special issues of the journal or to guest edit a special issue:

> If you do accept to guest edit a special issue, you become one of now more than 1800 editorial board members (!). (I won't link this to the journal's website, but you can find that information easily on the journal website.) Hardly much of an achievement or distinction, given the predatory process with which the journal recruits people who are willing to run special issues. (Fischer 2020: para. 3)

What further complicates any effort to assess MDPI is that other publishers who are more well established are starting to mimic the practices that have led to MDPI's growth and success. For example, Springer Nature recently announced its *Discover* journal series, which is intended not only to expand open access options but to offer authors many of the same benefits that have made MDPI so successful in recent years. Specifically, the new series will include 'up to 40 new titles' in various disciplines. Through this initiative, the publisher is promising 'a new streamlined OA publishing experience, extending Springer Nature's commitment to OA by supporting quick access to high quality research to aid the advancement of scientific discovery' ('Springer Nature Continues to Drive OA' 2020: para. 11). This move by Springer reminds us that publishing, even when carried out by an entity not named as 'predatory', can be a commercial endeavor. And publishers — whether 'predatory' or not — do not always operate with purely altruistic motives.

Springer makes some claims about the *Discover* series that suggest the publisher is adopting the same practices that have made MDPI attractive to authors. For example, the Springer Nature Group website claims, 'The series puts the author at the heart of the publication process and aims to publish manuscripts 7–10 weeks from submission — whilst maintaining the high levels of research integrity expected of any Springer Nature title' (para. 2). Putting the author 'at the heart of the publication process' (para. 2) clearly means a promise of fast turnaround times, but the Springer Nature brand is invoked to assure authors that research integrity will be maintained. Emphasizing the benefits to the author is an interesting twist on the typical rationale for open access, which tends to emphasize benefits to the public — suggesting the publisher is, at least in part, motivated by a need to compete with publishers such as MDPI. But it is also worth noting the *Discover* series is adopting open science principles, not just open access: 'The *Discover* series will also seek to address the issue of reproducibility and negative publication bias by introducing Registered Reports (1) across the portfolio for authors conducting hypothesis-driven research' ('Springer Nature Continues to Drive OA' 2020: para. 2).

Sage Open is another example of a publishing initiative adopting strategies that, in many ways, resemble those employed by MDPI. This journal's promotional materials suggest they are trying to revolutionize scholarly publishing. The journal accepts articles from all disciplines. It does not have an editor in the traditional sense; rather, it has an editorial team consisting of section editors with diverse disciplinary backgrounds, university affiliations, and geographic locations. When the journal receives a submission, a section editor assesses the content and determines who would be appropriate to review it, then invites the relevant expert to provide a review. The journal's description as it appears on the website is as follows:

> *Sage Open* is an open access publication from Sage. It publishes peer-reviewed, original research and review articles in an open access format. Articles may span the full spectrum of the social and behavioral sciences and the humanities.
>
> *Sage Open* seeks to be the world's premier open access outlet for academic research. As such, unlike traditional journals, *Sage Open* does not limit content due to page budgets or thematic significance. Rather, *Sage Open* evaluates the scientific and research methods of each article for validity and accepts articles solely on the basis of the research. This approach allows readers greater access and gives them the power to determine the significance of each article through article-level usage metrics. Likewise, by not restricting papers to a narrow discipline, *Sage Open* facilitates the discovery of the connections between papers, whether within or between disciplines. ('Journal Description' [n.d]: paras. 1–2).

Thus, one of the serious challenges we face today is how to distinguish legitimate efforts to be innovative in scholarly publishing from those that are fraudulent in one way or another.

The label 'predatory' is the result of a desire to make this distinction a simple one. Labeling some journals, or publishers, as 'predatory' and others as not is closely tied to initiatives such as lists, or checklists, or some other mechanism to sort out the good from the bad. But as we argue in *The Predatory Paradox*, predatory publishing is not a problem that can be addressed through simple solutions such as labels or lists. In short, it is the same set of demands and changes — the increased need for rapid turnaround from submission to acceptance to publication — that have created a situation in which so-called predatory publishing has come to thrive. Herein lies the 'paradox' that is indicated in our title and is the key word that informs our approach to these complex issues in this book. We refer to the 'predatory paradox' to capture all the nuance and complexity of the current situation in which predatory publishing practices have been able to emerge and flourish. Although many organizations and individuals have attempted to keep Beall's project alive, even after the 2017 demise of his list, it has proven extremely difficult, if not impossible, to succeed at the list approach to solving this problem. In fact, our research suggests it is virtually impossible to distinguish in simple terms between publishers or journals that are 'predatory' and those that are not.

Predatory Publishing Is Not the Only Way to Cheat the System

The rules in the game of scholarly publishing have continually changed and evolved over the centuries. Through this evolution process, many other entities have developed as part of the game. These include peer review, citation metrics, rating systems for journals, rating systems for authors, indexing systems, knowledge-sharing networks, new technologies for publishing and distributing knowledge, and new business models to support scholarly publishing. Among these entities that sustain scholarly publishing, the one that enjoys the most prominence and perhaps the longest history is double-blind peer review. Historians offer different perspectives on the origins of this institution. It was long believed, as asserted in a 1971 article by Harriet Zuckerman and Robert K. Merton, that the origins of peer review could be traced to the origins of modern science itself (Zuckerman and Merton 1971). Specifically, Zuckerman and Merton traced the origins of something resembling peer review to Henry Oldenburg, who served in a capacity that today we would call editor of the *Royal Transactions*, often touted as the first scientific journal.

More recently, however, it has been suggested that the earliest use of referees to evaluate reports of scientific research did not occur until the nineteenth century, and the term 'peer review' was not adopted until the late twentieth century (Baldwin 2019). Of course, the mechanisms and processes through which peer review is conducted have changed dramatically since the practice was first used in a form we would recognize in the nineteenth century, around the same time that journals were emerging as the primary venue for communicating scientific findings.

Despite this uncertainty about when exactly peer review began, most scholars trained in the modern academy have been taught to recognize this mechanism as the gold standard for assessing the legitimacy and credibility of scientific findings published as journal articles. We might say peer review is one of the most important and well-established elements in the game of scientific knowledge production. And it is quite remarkable that, two centuries later, we are still relying on this seemingly simple practice of vetting scientific findings by sending them to a small number of individuals who are considered experts and asking them to evaluate the findings in a double-blind process, meaning the reviewers do not know the author's identity and vice-versa. And for the most part, these reviews are conducted on a voluntary basis, without any compensation, and without any specific training — it is a task that academic professionals are expected to perform in addition to their regular paid jobs, even though many publishers make a profit from the work.

Nonetheless, as is the case in any game, some players cheat, and this cheating occurs in many forms. In the case of peer review, many 'predatory' journals are accused of cheating by claiming their articles are peer reviewed without actually sending manuscripts out for review. Of course, this can be hard for readers of a journal to detect because in traditional double-blind peer review, it is only the editor and author who see the reviews. But another form of cheating in peer review is one that has been occurring with some frequency even at well-established journals that are believed to have legitimate peer-review processes in place. This form of cheating is called 'fake peer review'. This form of cheating can be conducted in different ways; one of the most common is when journals allow authors to recommend reviewers when they submit their manuscripts. Instead of recommending legitimate reviewers, an author can cheat the system by providing a variety of email addresses that appear to be tied to real experts in the field but are actually owned by the author him or herself. Then when the individual is selected as a reviewer, the author writes their own review, which is entirely positive, and submits it from the fake email account. It might seem unbelievable that an author could get away with this fraudulent behavior, but it is quite common. In fact, in 2017, the publisher Springer Nature retracted 107 articles because of fake peer review (Gao and Zhou 2017). As this example illustrates, the system can be manipulated and players can succeed at cheating, even when we are dealing with the seemingly trustworthy publishing entities; in this case, cheaters were successful at one of the most prestigious scientific journals in existence. This phenomenon appears to have become more common in recent years, with fifteen percent of retractions reported by Retraction Watch since 2012 attributed to fake peer review (Kaplan 2015).

Another means of cheating the system is that special issues can be exploited to publish articles without adequate vetting. Again, this form of cheating is reportedly occurring even at well-established journals. For example, a scam such as this occurred recently at a journal published by Springer Nature, *Journal of Nanoparticle Research*. In this case, the journal editors had received a special-issue proposal from a team of people posing as 'eminent scientists' (Pinna and others 2020). The proposal was apparently well written enough to be accepted as a special issue, and for that issue, the editorial process was entirely turned over to the guest editors. It was only after some articles were accepted and published that the editorial staff at the journal started questioning whether peer review had actually occurred, based on the low quality of the articles. As it turned out, the guest editors had not sent any of the submissions to peer reviewers and had instead accepted articles and moved them quickly through to publication, without any vetting process ('Multiple #3 – Issue 31' 2021). The editors published their account of what happened in December 2020, referring to the journal as 'victim of an organized rogue editor network' (Pinna and others 2020). In this account, the editors go to great lengths in describing the process through which they received and vetted this special issue proposal, ultimately determining it was just the kind of timely topic on which they had been seeking special issues. Thus, they turned over editorial control of that issue to the guest editors. It was not until several months later that they noticed this issue was receiving an unusually large number of submissions — which they initially thought to be a good sign — but when they looked more closely, in their words, 'we rapidly noted that most of the manuscripts were of a low quality and/or did not fit with the topic of the special issue' (p. 375).

They go on to report that they 'acted immediately, but it was already too late because 19 manuscripts among the 80 submissions had already been accepted and/or published' (p. 375). They then conducted an internal investigation and discovered the whole effort had been a complex hoax in which the scam artists had created fake email addresses that looked like they were from real university accounts, all with the goal of creating a special issue that allowed a significant number of articles to get published in a highly prestigious scientific journal without undergoing peer review. The editors provide the following account for their failure to notice this when the special issue was first submitted: 'Have we been careless? Probably, but who would have thought scientists would go to that extent, i.e., to organize a whole rogue network and propose a sound and interesting special issue in a scientific journal, just to get a few articles published?' (Pinna and others 2020: 375). They conclude their statement by connecting this particular scam special issue to a larger set of problems in scientific research: the fact that instances of scientific misconduct like this one are becoming more frequent because of the exponential growth in the number of scientific articles published, which is, in turn, an effect of growing pressure on researchers to publish ever-increasing quantities of research, creating a situation in which it is hard for anyone to find time to stop and vet the quality of published work.

As these examples illustrate, every game has rules and systems in place that can be manipulated by those who wish to do so for personal gain or other reasons. Scholarly publishing is no different, and predatory publishing is best understood as one of the many ways in which the system can be manipulated. We are also seeing endless new varieties of ways in which legitimate publishing models can be exploited as those who intend to do so find new ways to mimic these processes for their own personal and financial gain. For example, in 'hijacked journals', cybercriminals literally 'hijack' a prestigious academic journal, taking its name, claiming to be editors, starting a false website, and then sending spam emails to authors encouraging them to submit and pay an author's fee (Asadi and others 2017; Shari and others 2018).

But, again, it is not as simple as it seems. The motivations and desires of those who have manipulated the system are not as simple as the term *predatory* might imply. It might suggest that this is a system where we can clearly identify who is the predator and who is the prey. It might imply that we have a limited number of fraudulent publishing companies in shady offices in remote locations, and they are sending out solicitation emails to naïve, unsuspecting authors who are so desperate to get their scholarship published in peer-reviewed outlets that they gladly pay a publication fee in exchange for a rapid peer-review turnaround, quick acceptance, and quick publication. But it is not that simple or straightforward. Firstly, a growing number of legitimate, well-trusted journals are charging author fees to publish articles open access. For some journals, this is the publishing model in place for every article they publish. For others, open access publishing is offered as an option for those authors who are willing and able to pay a publication fee. In both models, there is no getting around the fact that authors are, in a sense, customers, and thus, it makes sense for journals to solicit submissions from them. In fact, because commercial scholarly publishing is a business, and the number of journals in existence is continuing to increase, journals are in competition for authors, so it is not at all unreasonable that some would send out solicitation emails inviting the best authors to submit their work to a specific journal.

Secondly, many highly legitimate, well-trusted journals are offering rapid turnaround times for peer review of submitted manuscripts and publication of accepted articles. In the wake of COVID-19, scientific journals have sped up the submission, review, and publication processes to try to get new findings distributed globally as quickly as possible. As a result of this growing desire for fast distribution and easy access to the latest scientific information, new channels and media are arising and taking on greater prominence during the pandemic. For example, early in the pandemic, the flurry of excitement around research on malaria drugs, including hydroxychloroquine and chloroquine, as possible treatments for COVID-19, was initially dismissed as 'fake news' (Lecrubier 2020). But the idea gained a groundswell of support and interest on 16 March 2020, when Professor Didier Raoult, of the IHU Méditerranée Infection in Marseille, posted a YouTube video of a presentation on a study he had personally conducted that suggested that chloroquine was a successful treatment for twenty-four patients in his hospital (Raoult 2016). The YouTube video to date has received 1,460,735 views. By contrast, an open access peer-reviewed study that reported results of an in-vitro study that contrasted the antiviral properties of hydroxychloroquine to those of chloroquine was published on 9 March 2020, and currently has received only 87,728 downloads (Yao and others 2020). Although the latter study would be considered more rigorous by scientific standards — and has withstood the scrutiny of peer review — its findings are more modest in their contribution to the promise of a cure and thus less attention-grabbing than those of the French physician who reported the drug was successful on twenty-four patients in his hospital. Along these lines, we are also seeing a growing reliance on preprints, which are publications that allow scientific findings to be published rapidly before they are peer reviewed (Kupferschmidt 2020). As we keep a critical eye on the publishing trends that are emerging, we cannot ignore these pressures for faster distribution and better access to the latest scientific knowledge, even if it means distributing findings before undergoing peer review. Some of the same practices that are easy to label 'predatory' are practices that publishers are intentionally adopting to respond and adapt to these pressures. Just like any other business, the publishing industry must be able to respond to and adapt to such pressures if they are going to stay relevant in the current climate. This is the argument of Albert N. Greco (2020) in *The Business of Scholarly Publishing*. Specifically, he says, 'Scholarly publishing is not a declining industry; it is an industry in transition from one that was 100% print, a hybrid one that offers content in both print and digital formats, and a complete 100% OA digital model' (p. 7).

In short, some of the very same practices that can lead a publisher or journal to be suspected as 'predatory' — such as rapid turnaround times and speedier pace of publication — are also desperately needed innovations in scientific publishing, which has long been known for its slow pace and long turnaround times. Paradoxically, these are some of the reasons why we have trusted the scientific knowledge production processes that have evolved over the centuries. It is simply not in our nature as academics to have faith in knowledge that is quickly produced, vetted, and shared with wider public audiences. But as times change, processes need to change as well. The COVID-19 pandemic was certainly not the first situation that made us aware of the need to distribute scientific data and findings more quickly to a vast global audience, but it heightened our awareness and will likely have long-term implications for how we communicate science (Koerber 2021).

Diversity, Equity, and Inclusion in Scholarly Communication

Many of the new publishing initiatives place a rhetorical emphasis on openness and inclusion, with the idea that the principles of open access and open science, if they are widely adopted, will revolutionize scientific knowledge production, making it more available to global stakeholders and ensuring that we achieve a science that is inclusive as possible. Although diversity, equity, and inclusion in the academy are often characterized as a numbers game, those who advocate for greater diversity and inclusion in scholarly publishing go beyond numbers, reminding us we need to get more diverse stakeholders to join the scholarly conversation because this will make scientific knowledge better. For example, we have a whole history in science and medicine of either ignoring or devaluing the female body — seeing it as inherently defective, ignoring and/or disbelieving women's narration of their own bodily experiences and symptoms (Koerber 2018). This is because, for many centuries, the only people who could be knowledge producers were white men, primarily in the 'Western' world. Everyone else has automatically been subsumed into the category of 'research subject'. This is not only a social justice problem; it is a knowledge quality problem. We cannot make good scientific knowledge if only one kind of person is sitting at the table where expert knowledge is produced.

Along these lines, one recent initiative is the Coalition for Diversity & Inclusion in Scholarly Communications (C4DISC). This coalition of thirteen organizations states its mission is 'to work with organizations and individuals to build equity, inclusion, diversity, and accessibility in scholarly communications' ('Mission, Vision, and Values' [n.d.]: 1). Membership in the coalition entails a commitment to the organization's joint principles, which emphasize improving the quality of scholarly communication by ensuring broader inclusion of those voices and perspectives that have traditionally been marginalized for a variety of reasons. As expressed in the organization's Statement of Joint Principles, 'The future of scholarly communications will be positively impacted by attracting and retaining a pool of highly talented and creative professionals from diverse and/or historically excluded backgrounds who possess a wide range of skill sets and viewpoints' ('Joint Statement of Principles' [n.d.]: para. 1).

In many ways, open science and open access are intended to help us move forward in this regard — to create more opportunities for scholars in middle- or low-income nations, where universities have fewer financial resources, to have access to the journals and publications that they need to be successful in their own research. Open access, from this perspective, addresses part of the problem: It gives scholars access to published research. However, it does not solve all the problems because open access often requires authors to pay an article processing charge. These can be cost prohibitive even for some authors in higher-income countries if they do not have grant funding or institutional funding available to cover the costs. It can be completely impossible for scholars in low- or middle-income nations (although some of the larger publishers waive or reduce the fee if an author cannot afford to pay it). Thus, we are starting to see some other economic models as well. For example, PLOS has established something called the 'Global Equity Model'. Their website explains the model as follows:

> We believe scientific knowledge is strengthened by diverse perspectives, and that it accelerates progress faster when it's shared openly. Our Global Equity model removes financial barriers for researchers to participate in Open Access and Open Science by offering affordable, equitable partnership opportunities for their institutions in every region of the world. ('PLOS Global Equity Model' [n.d.]: para. 1)

Along these lines, some experts have questioned whether the economic shift that typically occurs with open access publishing — basically, shifting the economic model so that authors pay for publishing costs instead of readers or consumers — really addresses the problem. From the perspective of one economist, for example, 'economics are skeptical of claims that a change in who pays can give rise to large changes in welfare and efficiency when the underlying costs (including those imposed by providers with market power) are unchanged' (Gans 2017: 13).

These discussions about diversity, equity, and inclusion in scholarly publishing are another reason why one of this book's most important messages is that predatory publishing is not as simple as the term implies. It is not possible to clearly identify who is the predator and who is the prey. Many have argued, for instance, that it is the large commercial publishers who are the actual predators, in that they are charging exorbitant subscription prices that make their journals increasingly unaffordable to libraries, even in the US, but especially in non-peripheral nations where libraries and universities have far more limited resources. Furthermore, our research revealed that some authors knowingly submit to so-called 'predatory' journals for a variety of reasons — sometimes because they are just desperate to get a publication, or they are employed at a university where quantity of publications is emphasized over quality. Other interviewees indicated they published in 'predatory' journals as a form of defiance and resistance to the perceived monopoly of the mainstream publishers.

Chapter Contents

The book is organized around various themes that have emerged through our extensive research, which has included not only interviews but content analysis, textual analysis, legal analysis, and more. Each chapter summarizes relevant research and offers interactive activities that can be used in the classroom.[4] Reflecting our team's desire to enact open science principles as fully as possible, some of our chapters link to published datasets that allow readers to access the full text of interview transcripts, de-identified to protect the identity of interview participants, and other forms of data that support the analyses in these chapters.[5] It is our hope that readers will find these datasets useful for their own research and teaching purposes and that the availability of these datasets will enhance the credibility and depth of the analyses that the chapters report.

---

4   An important feature of the book is that it is a coauthored book, not an edited collection, reflecting the fact that the research reported in the book has been supported by a National Science Foundation grant awarded to the team in 2019. However, to give credit to the individuals whose independent research endeavors were conducted as part of this larger project, we have named a first author for each chapter. We hope that this approach enables readers to read the book in its entirety, if they so choose, but also allows individual chapters to be used as stand-alone contributions to readers' research and teaching. Along these lines, in accessing some of the published datasets, readers will notice that coding of the forty-eight interview transcripts was completed in multiple phases, with individual authors taking ownership of independent coding initiatives in accordance with their research goals.

5   See Predatory Paradox Dataverse in the Texas Data Repository.

In **Chapter 1, 'Ethical, Legal, and Policy Issues in the Knowledge Creation Paradigm: The Case of OMICS International, Open Access, and "Predatory" Publishing'**, Lyombe Eko explores the ethical, policy, and legal issues brought to the forefront by the so-called predatory publishing and predatory conferences industry, using as a case study the legal actions taken by the United States government agency, the Federal Trade Commission (FTC) against OMICS Group, Inc., and its affiliates in federal court. After providing an overview and legal analysis of the *FTC v. OMICS* Group case, the author invites readers to consider how this litigation might forever transform ethical, legal, and economic dimensions of scholarly publishing. Viewing predatory publishing from an economic perspective, in particular, raises important questions about who profits from predatory publishing and predatory conferences. This presents an opportunity to consider the different motivations at play in this complex game of 'pay to play' or 'pay to publish trash', as the Indian government calls it.

In **Chapter 2, 'Open Science, Open Data'**, Kerk F. Kee takes a broader look at 'openness' as it has been used in conversations about scientific research and publishing. 'Openness' is often touted as an antidote for all the problems that exist in scholarly publishing. The rationale is that if we can achieve greater transparency in publishing practices, there will be no more impetus for predatory publishers to go on. More specifically, the reasoning goes, predatory publishing has been able to thrive because so much of academic publishing occurs in a black box, behind closed doors. We have trusted double-blind peer review for many centuries as the gold standard that ensures the quality of scientific knowledge. But most of the time, in the way peer review traditionally operates, the readers of a scientific article simply must trust in blind faith that reviews are taking place. This practice allows predatory publishing to thrive because it creates the possibility that a journal can advertise itself as a peer-reviewed journal but then publish articles without putting them through the peer-review process. 'Open data' and 'open science' are touted as antidotes because they require researchers to share their actual data so that readers can judge the quality of the science for themselves. 'Open peer review' is another variation on this — this entails publishing the reviewer reports along with the article so, again, readers can see for themselves that peer review did occur. Chapter 2 explores how our interview participants articulated claims such as these, but also, how some interviewees push back against such claims, pointing out the limitations of openness as a solution to the predatory publishing problem.

In **Chapter 3, 'Research Quality'**, Jesse C. Starkey addresses the deceptively simple notion of quality in scholarly research. This was an important subject addressed by participants in our interview study, and a variety of definitions emerged through these interviews. Some interviewees emphasized the quality or 'rigor' of the research methods, referring primarily to technical aspects of the research, whereas others emphasized the quality of the writing, as indicated, for example, through the transparency of reporting the methods used or results discovered. Additionally, many participants focused on the morals and values of ethical research as an indicator of quality, suggesting a multifaceted approach to conceptualizing quality might be necessary. Participants were also quite adept at pointing out where quality was lacking — or where there were challenges to ensuring and protecting quality in the knowledge production process. For example, the peer-review process was simultaneously lauded as the hallmark of scientific knowledge production and criticized as falling short in ensuring the quality of published content. This chapter offers a deep dive into the various components of scholarly knowledge production, the ways stakeholders conceptualize quality in those areas, and the challenges they face in protecting the integrity of scientific knowledge as it moves through the stages of graduate student training, conducting research, vetting the research, and finally publishing it in an increasingly perilous system.

In **Chapter 4, 'Scientific Hoaxes and the Predatory Paradox: Past, Present, and Future'**, Amy Koerber examines scientific hoax articles with a focus on the weaknesses and flaws that such hoaxes can expose in the larger information ecosystem of scholarly publishing. The chapter thus reveals that scientific hoaxes further complicate any neat distinction between journals that are predatory and those that are not. Hoaxes have, in some cases, exposed specific journals as predatory. But in other cases, they have had effects beyond those that the author anticipated, exposing major weaknesses or fraudulent practices not only at journals or publishers suspected to be predatory but also at the most prestigious and well-respected journals. More importantly, publishing hoaxes have unintentionally exposed weaknesses in the mechanisms that we have long relied on to ensure research quality. For example, hoaxes have exposed flaws in even the best journals' peer-review systems, and when hoax articles continue to get cited in subsequent literature — sometimes even after retraction — they lead us to question our habit of relying on citation counts as a measure of research quality. Partly in response to hoaxes, industries have emerged around the desire to pin down the legitimacy of a particular author or publication in an environment that makes it increasingly easy for fakes to be mistaken as the real thing. For example, we now have ORCID identifiers to help us establish the identity of authors and Digital Object Identifiers (DOI) to help us pinpoint the location and verify the identity of published texts. These identifiers are becoming commonplace in academic lingo, but it is easy to overlook the fact that each of these markers emerged as a commercial development with its own complexities, nuances, and shortcomings. As we argue, these innovations reflect our desire to pin down something that is certain and real in a landscape where it is increasingly easy for fakes to circulate as the real thing.

In **Chapter 5, 'Avoiding the Pitfalls of Predatory Publishing'**, Karin Ardon-Dryer explores the important question of how emerging scholars become enculturated into the world of scholarly publishing. It has perhaps always been the case that more established scholars are faced with the task of training the new generation, but at the same time, this new generation is facing challenges never even imagined by their senior colleagues. This is one of the 'paradoxes' inherent in the predatory paradox that is the book's central focus. But we argue in this chapter that this situation is intensified today, with so many new publishing trends emerging and the pace of scholarly research increasing so rapidly. There has simply been no other era in which so many changes have occurred so quickly. Our goal in this chapter is to report what our interview research taught us about what it takes to be an effective mentor of junior scholars in this rapidly changing environment and, hopefully, provide both senior and junior scholars with a toolset that serves as a starting place for this challenging endeavor.

In **Chapter 6, 'What's Being Taught about Predatory Publishing?'**, R. Glenn Cummins surveys the content of university-based curricula. For decades, federal funders in the US have required training or instruction in research ethics to address growing concerns about the responsible conduct of research. Universities have responded to this requirement in a variety of ways, including in-person workshops, classes, or training as well as through online modules. However, systematic review of university training has revealed that efforts to satisfy funder requirements (a) most often rely on modules provided by a sole outside provider (i.e., CITI), and (b) focus on topics such as authorship or plagiarism while ignoring the growing threat to the dissemination of scientific knowledge that is posed by predatory publishers. To identify gaps in extant institutional training on predatory publishing, it is crucial to establish what current resources are available to authors and are most commonly used within scholarly research environments. This chapter provides a comprehensive assessment of the publicly available training materials provided by US universities on the topic of predatory publishing. The chapter also documents the nature and content of training resources, the modality of training materials, and the intended audience for the identified resources.

In **Chapter 7, 'Predatory Paradoxes: What Comes Next?'** Amy Koerber and Jesse C. Starkey conclude the book by summarizing the many complexities that surround the term *predatory*. The authors offer insights and case studies based on our interviews with forty-eight individuals who are stakeholders of various sorts in the game of scholarly publishing — ranging from real-life stories of authors who have fallen 'prey' to predatory publishing practices to people involved in the publishing industry who feel their publications have been wrongly accused of being 'predatory' in some capacity. They examine the misunderstandings and misperceptions that many people have about predatory publishing, and they provide readers with accurate and complete information to combat these misunderstandings and misperceptions. They advocate a view of predatory publishing that emphasizes gray areas and individual responsibility, rather than lists or hard-and-fast distinctions between journals or publishers that are predatory and those that are not. In this final chapter, we hope to leave readers with a set of tools and knowledge that prepares them to succeed in the game of scholarly publishing, and to similarly equip those who come after them.

References

Anderson, Rick. 2018. *Scholarly Communication: What Everyone Needs to Know®* (New York: Oxford University Press). https://doi.org/10.1093/wentk/9780190639440.001.0001

——. 2019. *Issue Brief 3: Deceptive Publishing*, https://doi.org/10.13021/osi2019.2419

'Annual Report'. 2020. *Multidisciplinary Digital Publishing Institute (MDPI)*. https://res.mdpi.com/data/2020_web.pdf

Asadi, Amin., Rahbar, Nader., Asadi, Meisam., Asadi, Fahime., and Paji, Kokab Khalili. 2017. 'Online-Based Approaches to Identify Real Journals and Publishers from Hijacked Ones', *Science & Engineering Ethics*, 23: 305–08, https://doi.org/10.1007/s11948-015-9747-9

Avery, Oswald T., Macleod, Colin M., and McCarty, Maclyn. 1944. 'Studies on the Chemical Nature of the Substance Inducing Transformation of Pneumococcal Types: Induction of Transformation by a Desoxyribonucleic Acid Fraction Isolated from Pneumococcus Type III', *The Journal of Experimental Medicine*, 79.2: 137–58, https://doi.org/10.1084/JEM.79.2.137

Baldwin, Melinda. 2019. 'Peer Review', *Encyclopedia of the History of Science*, https://doi.org/10.34758/7s4y-5f50

Beall, Jeffrey. 2012. 'Predatory Publishers Are Corrupting Open Access', *Nature*, 489.7415: 179, https://doi.org/10.1038/489179a

——. 2013. 'Predatory Publishing Is Just One of the Consequences of Gold Open Access', *Learned Publishing*, 26.2: 79–84, https://doi.org/10.1087/20130203

——. 2015. 'Is Frontiers a Potential Predatory Publisher? [Tweet]', *Twitter*, https://twitter.com/Jeffrey_Beall/status/659351830132998144?cxt=HHwWgICmkeC_vqYSAAAA

——. 2017. 'What I Learned from Predatory Publishers', *Biochemia Medica*, 27.2: 273–78, https://doi.org/10.11613/BM.2017.029

Biagioli, Mario, and Lippman, Alexandra (eds). 2020. *Gaming the Metrics: Misconduct and Manipulation in Academic Research*. (Cambridge, MA: MIT Press). https://doi.org/10.7551/mitpress/11087.001.0001

Bisaccio, Mike. 2020. *Announcement Regarding Brand-Wide Language Changes, Effective Immediately*, https://blog.cabells.com/2020/06/08/announcement/

Bloudoff-Indelicato, Mollie. 2015. 'Backlash after Frontiers Journals Added to List of Questionable Publishers', *Nature*, 526.7575: 613, https://doi.org/10.1038/526613f

Crawford, Walt. 2014. 'Journals, "Journals" and Wannabes: Investigating the List', *Cites & Insights*, 14.7: 1–24, http://citesandinsights.info/civ14i7on.pdf

Crosetto, Paolo. 2021. *Is MDPI a Predatory Publisher?* https://paolocrosetto.wordpress.com/2021/04/12/is-mdpi-a-predatory-publisher/

Fischer, Joern. 2020. 'Why Not to Publish in "Sustainability" (and You're Welcome to Share This Post)', *Ideas for Sustainability*, https://ideas4sustainability.wordpress.com/2020/10/30/why-not-to-publish-in-sustainability-and-youre-welcome-to-share-this-post/

'Fostering Integrity in Research: Consensus Study Report'. 2017. *National Academies of Sciences, Engineering, and Medicine* (Washington, DC: The National Academies Press). https://doi.org/10.17226/21896

Gans, Joshua G. 2017. *Scholarly Publishing and Its Discontents* (Toronto, Canada: Core Economic Research). https://www.joshuagans.com/scholarlypublishing

Gao, Jian., and Zhou, Tao. 2017. 'Stamp Out Fake Peer Review', *Nature*, 546: 33, https://doi.org/10.1038/546033a

Greco, Albert N. 2020. *The Business of Scholarly Publishing: Managing in Turbulent Times* (Oxford: Oxford University Press). https://doi.org/10.1093/oso/9780190626235.003.0006

Grudniewicz, Agnes., Moher, David., Cobey, Kelly D., Bryson, Gregory L., Cukier, Samantha and others. 2019. 'Predatory Journals: No Definition, No Defence', *Nature*, 576.7786: 210–12, https://doi.org/10.1038/d41586-019-03759-y

'Joint Statement of Principles'. [n.d.]. *Coalition for Diversity & Inclusion in Scholarly Communications*, https://c4disc.org/joint-statement-of-principles/

'Journal Description'. [n.d.]. *Sage Open*, https://journals.sagepub.com/description/SGO

Kaplan, Sarah. 2015. 'Major Publisher Retracts 64 Scientific Papers in Fake Peer Review Outbreak', *The Washington Post*, https://www.washingtonpost.com/news/morning-mix/wp/2015/08/18/outbreak-of-fake-peer-reviews-widens-as-major-publisher-retracts-64-scientific-papers/

Koerber, Amy. 2018. *From Hysteria to Hormones: A Rhetorical History* (University Park, PA: Penn State University Press). https://doi.org/10.5325/j.ctv14gp859

——. 2021. 'Is It Fake News or Is It Open Science? Science Communication in the COVID-19 Pandemic', *Journal of Business and Technical Communication*, 35.1: 22–27, https://doi.org/10.1177/1050651920958506

Kupferschmidt, Kai. 2020. 'Preprints Bring "firehose" of Outbreak Data', *Science*, 367.6481: 963–64, https://doi.org/10.1126/science.367.6481.963

Lecrubier, Aude. 2020. 'COVID-19: Could Hydroxychloroquine Really Be an Answer?', *Medscape*, https://www.medscape.com/viewarticle/927033

Linacre, Simon. 2022. *The Predator Effect: Understanding the Past, Present and Future of Deceptive Academic Journals* (Ann Arbor, MI: Against the Grain (Media), LLC). https://doi.org/10.3998/MPUB.12739277

Miller, Carolyn R. 1994. 'Opportunity, Opportunism, and Progress: Kairos in the Rhetoric of Technology', *Argumentation*, 8.1: 81–96, https://doi.org/10.1007/BF00710705

'Mission, Vision, and Values'. [n.d.]. *Coalition for Diversity & Inclusion in Scholarly Communications*, https://c4disc.org/main/mission-vision-and-values/

'Multiple #3 – Issue 31'. 2021. *The Brief by Clarke & Esposito*, https://www.ce-strategy.com/the-brief/multiple/

Petrou, Christos. 2020. 'Guest Post – MDPI's Remarkable Growth', *The Scholarly Kitchen*, https://scholarlykitchen.sspnet.org/2020/08/10/guest-post-mdpis-remarkable-growth/

Pinna, Nicola., Clavel, Guylhaine, and Roco, Mihail. 2020. 'The Journal of Nanoparticle Research Victim of an Organized Rogue Editor Network!', *Journal of Nanoparticle Research*, 22.376, https://doi.org/10.1007/s11051-020-05094-0

'PLOS Global Equity Model'. [n.d.]. *PLOS*, https://plos.org/resources/global-equity-model/

'Predatory Publishing: Discussion Document'. 2019. *COPE Council*, https://doi.org/10.24318/cope.2019.3.6

Raoult, D. 2020. 'Coronavirus : Diagnostiquons et Traitons ! Premiers Résultats [Video]', *YouTube*, https://www.youtube.com/watch?v=n4J8kydOvbc

Roberts, Jason. 2017. 'The Scourge of Illegitimate Journals: Becoming Better Informed in a Post-Beall Era', *The Official Publication of the International Society of Managing and Technical Editors*, 10.2: 13–15, http://dx.doi.org/10.18243/eon/2017.10.2.6

Shari, Mona Andoohgin., Jazi, Mohammad Davarpanah., Borchardt, Glenn and Dadkhah, Mehdi. 2018. 'Detecting Hijacked Journals by Using Classification Algorithms', *Science and Engineering Ethics*, 24.2: 655–68, https://doi.org/10.1007/s11948-017-9914-2

Smith, Wendy K., and Lewis, Marianne W. 2011. 'Toward a Theory of Paradox: A Dynamic Equilibrium Model of Organizing', *Academy of Management Review*, 36.2: 381–403, https://doi.org/10.5465/amr.2009.0223

'Springer Nature Continues to Drive OA with Launch of Brand New OA Journal Series'. 2020. *Springer Nature Group*, https://group.springernature.com/fr/group/media/press-releases/springer-nature-discover-journal/18109908

Teixeira da Silva, Jaime A. 2020. 'The Ethical and Academic Implications of the Jeffrey Beall (www.scholarlyoa.com) Blog Shutdown', *Science & Engineering Ethics*, 26: 3465–67, https://doi.org/10.1007/s11948-017-9905-3

Teixeira da Silva, Jaime A., Dobránszki, Judit., Tsigaris, Panagiotis and Al-Khatib, Aceil. 2019. 'Predatory and Exploitative Behaviour in Academic Publishing: An Assessment', *The Journal of Academic Librarianship*, 45.6: 1–8, https://doi.org/10.1016/j.acalib.2019.102071

Watson, J. D., and Crick, F.H.C. 1953. 'Molecular Structure of Nucleic Acids: A Structure for Deoxyribose Nucleic Acid', *Nature*, 171: 737–38, https://doi.org/10.1038/171737a0

Xia, Jingfeng. 2021. *Predatory Publishing, Predatory Publishing* (London: Routledge). https://doi.org/10.4324/9781003029335

Yao, Xueting., Ye, Fei., Zhang, Miao., Cui, Cheng., Huang, Baoying and others. 2020. 'In Vitro Antiviral Activity and Projection of Optimized Dosing Design of Hydroxychloroquine for the Treatment of Severe Acute Respiratory Syndrome Coronavirus 2 (SARS-CoV-2)', *Clinical Infectious Diseases*, 71.15: 732–39, https://doi.org/10.1093/cid/ciaa237

Zuckerman, Harriet, and K. Merton, Robert. 1971. 'Patterns of Evaluation in Science: Institutionalisation, Structure and Functions of the Referee System', *Minerva*, 9.1: 66–100, https://doi.org/10.1007/BF01553188

1. Ethical, Legal, and Policy Issues in the Knowledge Creation Paradigm
The Case of OMICS International, Open Access, and 'Predatory' Publishing

The paradigm of valid scientific and academic research is grounded in 1) ethically conducted research. These are scholarly investigations that follow governmental and institutionally-mandated rules on research with human subjects, conflict of interest, falsification, and fabrication of data, manipulation of research materials; 2) presentation of this research in reputable, ethically sound, peer-reviewed professional conferences that do not employ misleading and deceptive techniques to lure researchers to present in these conferences, or fraudulently associate them with profit-making ventures without their knowledge and consent and 3) ultimately publication of the research in ethically produced, peer-reviewed, scholarly journals in physical space or cyberspace. Ethical scholarly journals follow institutional and industry ethical guidelines on authorship, plagiarism, conflicts of interest, data reproducibility, intellectual property, and so on. The assumption of this professional self-regulation paradigm is that if all researchers, publishers, and other stakeholders in the knowledge creation enterprise follow tried-and-true ethical principles, scholarly research and results will have validity in the eyes of the profession, and of society as a whole. This will ultimately lead to the greatest good for all stakeholders in the scientific research and knowledge-creation enterprise (funders, regulators, academia, scholars, researchers, research institutes, libraries, databases, and so on).

Researchers and scholarly publishers ply their trade within the framework of professionally created codes of ethics. These are essentially 'epistemic constraints', to borrow Figdor's expression (2010: 153), that ensure the ethical and responsible conduct of science in the context of professional self-regulation. The paradigm of scholarly research, publication, and curation was grounded on the *laissez-faire* principles of the free flow of ideas, goods and services, and the free and uninhibited flow of discourse, academic freedom, and permissionless innovation. These legal and ethical standards, values, norms, and routines enabled scholarly research and publication to become self-regulating 'fields' of knowledge production, processing, curation, archiving, and retrieval (Bourdieu 1977). The research and publication industry is similar to a medieval craft or artisans' guild like the printers' guild, where groups of skilled artisans set and maintained the standards of goods produced, jealously guarded the integrity and reputation of their craft from those who would bring it into disrepute, punished those who fell below professional and ethical standards, and rewarded those who excelled and performed over and above expectations ('Guild' 2023).

The scholarly research and publication paradigm has evolved into a closed, hyper-competitive and highly profitable industry that is generously supported by government, research institutions, and various industries engaged in scientific and technological research for pecuniary reasons. However, it has also become a billion-dollar, transnational, oligopolistic knowledge-capitalism industry, whose stock-in-trade is digitized knowledge that is stored in subscription-based databases. This industry has set itself up as the de facto gateway to, and broker of, knowledge. It charges excessive amounts of money for subscriptions and access to scholarly journals, books, and other forms of knowledge, and it has set up barriers to exclude competition. It has become a pay-for-access, subscription, and site-licensing fee system of knowledge production, curation, and archiving dominated by a handful of university presses, foundations, and especially a few oligopolistic global corporations. Alberts and others (2014) summarized the problematic situation of elite, legacy Science, Technology and Medicine (STM) research and publishing in the age of diminishing funding and hyper-competition in academia as follows:

As competition for jobs and promotions increases, the inflated value given to publishing in a small number of so-called 'high impact' journals has put pressure on authors to rush into print, cut corners, exaggerate their findings, and overstate the significance of their work. (p. 5774)

They further lamented the fact that the situation was being made worse by the editors and reviewers of elite scientific journals who act as overzealous gatekeepers. These gatekeepers create more and more stringent conditions for access to the coveted spaces of their journals: 'publishing scientific reports, especially in the most prestigious journals, has become increasingly difficult, as competition increases, and reviewers and editors demand more and more from each paper' (p. 5774). The reality is that well-funded, elite STM publishing, 'was getting bigger and bigger, more and more exclusive, and harder for regular researchers and faculty members to feature in' (Eko and Koerber 2020: 62).

New information and communication technologies that emerged from the 1950s onwards profoundly and irreversibly changed the traditional, subscription-based, pay-for-access model of scholarly journal publishing, including computers, network technologies, digitization, CD-ROMs, databases — where huge amounts of information could be digitized, curated, and archived for easy retrieval in electronic form — telecommunications networks, and especially the advent of the internet and the World Wide Web. The internet was to become the ultimate online space on which multiple technologies and the media converged and made it possible for scholarly research and publication to be produced digitally, published, curated, and archived. These technologies also facilitated the digitization and transfer of analogue versions of journals from physical information storage spaces (libraries and archives) to the dematerialized world of cyberspace for easy access and retrieval by persons in all parts of the world (Eko and Koerber 2020). All that was needed was an internet connection. The invention of innovative search engines made searching and retrieval of material from databases as easy as typing a few key words. Additionally, United States federal government policy orientations created an enabling environment and an impetus for the rise of a market-based approach to the internet and information and communication technologies. In 1997, the Clinton-Gore administration offered the world a vision and framework for the expansion and regulation of global electronic commerce on the fledgling internet. This was a *laissez-faire*, capitalist, free-market, free-flow-of-information framework under which governments were to assume a minimalist regulatory posture towards the internet (Clinton and Gore 1997). In 2004, Google, which had launched an innovative, highly successful model of linguistic capitalism — the world's largest algorithmic-based internet search engine — announced that it had launched 'The Google Books Library Project'. This was an innovative project that had the potential to radically transform how human beings created, stored, retrieved, and utilized the mighty rivers of information and knowledge that had been accumulated since ancient humans began to paint on the walls of their caves. The Google Books project involved 'space-shifting', the digitization and transfer of whole books, including bound scholarly journals, from the real, physical geographic spaces of libraries and archives to databases and servers in cyberspace, where internet search results would display snippets from these books to readers as part of Google's commercial search or linguistic capitalism business model (Eko and others 2012).

These developments gave archives and library collections a new lease on life. Newspapers, magazine, and journal publishers licensed their archives of collective works (periodicals) to electronic databases like Lexis-Nexis, which digitized these articles and stored them in paywalled interactive databases where they were searchable, retrievable, downloadable, printable, and readable in a number of digital formats as single entities removed from the original collective periodical volumes in which they had been published. Digital databases essentially became another lucrative revenue stream for both commercial and university journal publishers (Eko and others 2012). Though the Supreme Court of the United States ruled that transferring the work of freelance newspaper reporters that was first published in physical space as part of collective works (newspapers and magazine editions) to databases and online platforms without compensating them violated their copyright (Schroeder and others 2021), that decision did not apply to contributors to scholarly journals, which operate under a different business model, and authors had no monetizable copyright claims to the scholarly articles they wrote. Some European jurisdictions recognize the intangible moral rights of authors, but these are not necessarily economic or monetizable rights.

These technological developments led to a paradigm shift in scholarly publishing — the gradual emergence of open access publishing, the model whereby scholarly publishers make their journals and books 'open' and accessible to all readers free of charge, often in exchange for processing charges paid by the author or research funder (Björk and Solomon 2012). Globalization and the interconnection of nations, peoples, educational systems, and different cultural geographies of research, knowledge creation, scholarly publication, intellectual property, and curation have resulted in a diffusion of the 'open access' model of academic research and publishing from its locus of origin in the United States to the rest of the world, where it was reinvented and applied to diverse cultural contexts without regard to the ethical, legal and cultural underpinnings of scholarly research and publishing.

Aim of This Chapter

The aim of this chapter is to explore the ethical, legal, and economic issues involved in scholarly journal publishing in the context of knowledge creation, including the transfer and monetization of academic publishing from real space (physical journals, libraries, physical archives) to the digitized, dematerialized, algorithmic-based sphere of cyberspace (the internet, databases and cloud-based curation and archival platforms). It explores the ethics of scholarly publishing from a historical, moral-philosophical, and legal perspective. It uses, as a case study, the so-called OMICS Group affair, the federal case in which the United States Federal Trade Commission (FTC) charged an international, 'predatory' academic conference organizer and journal publisher, OMICS Group, with violating federal law by engaging in misleading, deceptive and unfair business practices in the domain of scholarly conference organization and journal publishing. This case demonstrates the transfer of academic journal publishing from the realm of industry self-regulation, where professional codes of ethics recommend acceptable professional conduct, to the domain of law, which sets forth rules and regulations that command legally acceptable behavior. Violators of professional publication ethics often face no criminal or civil penalties because professions do not have enforcing powers under the law. By way of contrast, violators of federal law face criminal and civil penalties. FTC litigation against OMICS Group and landmark court rulings in the case demonstrate that the US Federal Government and federal courts consider the excesses of the publication and monetization practices of predatory publishers to be violations of laws governing business competition in the American *laissez-faire*, capitalist marketplace. This chapter explores the open access phenomenon and its ethically problematic derivative within the conceptual frameworks of deterritorialization and rule utilitarianism. The chapter describes and explains the deterritorialization (transfer) of scholarly publishing from physical space to the dematerialized realms of cyberspace, and explores the ethical challenges spawned by mercantilist journal publishers who do not care for the niceties of the paradigm of the ethical and responsible conduct of research and publishing.

Theoretical Perspective: Rule Utilitarianism

When peer reviewers, editors, and publishers make judgments about the rightness and wrongness of research actions, motives, and ends, they move into the domain of ethics or moral philosophy. In democratic societies, academic journals publish within systems of academic freedom that are guaranteed by law and are buttressed by professional publishing codes of ethics. A fundamental principle of ethical or moral reasoning is that actions must always be guided by rules or moral precepts that are designed to promote the aggregate good or the general well-being. Philosophers call this kind of ethical reasoning 'utilitarianism'. Berkeley (1712) advanced the rule utilitarian approach, which focuses on the implications and impact of rules or codes of ethics. Under this theory, all actions must be judged in terms of their conformity to rules that, if obeyed, would lead to the 'greatest good' (p. 8). Therefore, actions are judged to be morally right or wrong depending on their effects on society or on others. That is to say, acts are evaluated as morally wrong if they violate codes of ethics that are designed to result in some aggregate professional or social good. The main tenet of rule utilitarianism was memorably stated by Jeremy Bentham, who suggested that following rules would lead to 'the greatest happiness for the greatest number' (Crimmins 2021: 4). Rule utilitarianism is applicable to academic journal publishing because academic publishing duties and responsibilities are synthesized and encapsulated into codes of ethics. Professional codes of ethics or codes of conduct include the Core Practices of the Committee on Publishing Ethics (COPE). These codes of ethics are what Merrill calls 'accountability mechanisms' that ensure that peer reviewers, publishers, journalists and media systems are accountable to their professions, and to society for their messages (De Beer and Merrill 2003: 29).

The premise of this chapter is that predatory journals violate the norms of ethical and responsible conduct of research and journal publishing, thereby leading to negative consequences for scholarly publication. The legal and policy analysis that forms the basis for this chapter focuses on the actions of the United States Department of Health and Human Services (DHHS), the National Institutes of Health (NIH), and especially, the case *Federal Trade Commission v. OMICS Group, Inc.*, a landmark case in which the Federal Government of the United States sued a so-called 'predatory' conference organizer and journal publisher for engaging in anti-competitive, deceptive, and misleading practices that allegedly violated federal law. This case was unprecedented because it was the first time the federal government had sued a so-called 'predatory' publisher for engaging in practices that the government considered illegal.

Origin of Open Access Publishing

The open access phenomenon emerged in the United States in the 1990s as a result of the confluence of multiple dynamic forces, such as changing governmental and institutional research and funding priorities, as well as the emergence of information and communication technologies and databases (Tennant and others 2016). These innovative digital technologies enabled the digitization of published material. They also created the dematerialized world of cyberspace, and multiple databases and platforms that facilitated the publication, curation, and relatively easy retrieval of information and knowledge. Scholarly publication is a paradigm, or way of reviewing and publishing that is part of the knowledge production and curation system, and each country has its values, worldviews, routines, and practices that are taken for granted. At the end of World War II, the United States was the indisputable center of higher education and scientific research. The scholarly publishing industry took advantage of the post-war economic boom and used different business and marketing strategies to create demand for scholarly publications in STM, as well as the humanities and the social sciences (Greco 2016). Alberts and others (2014) suggest that generous research funding by the NIH, the National Science Foundation (NSF), and numerous other federal agencies, foundations, advocacy groups, and academic institutions, led to a 'remarkable outpouring of innovative research from American laboratories' (p. 5773). This hypercompetitive scientific research and scholarly publication system was dominated by large, prestigious university presses, institutional and oligopolistic scholarly publishers. The lucrative, and expensive (for libraries and users) subscription-based, pay-to-access system essentially made these dominant scholarly players the gatekeepers of knowledge. Alberts and colleagues suggest that things began to change when research funding stalled in the post-Cold War era due to reductions in federal and institutional funding.

In response to the closed, elitist, subscriptions and site-licensing fee model of the scholarly journal industry, and its throttling effect on the dissemination of knowledge and information, in 2000, a number of high-profile American researchers including a Nobel prize winner, Harold Varmus, sought 'to catalyze a revolution in scientific publishing' by proposing a 'paradigm shift' (Kuhn 1970) in scholarly journal publication and economics — an 'open access' publication model (Brown and others 2003). They stated that the 'essential rationale of the pay-for-access model has disappeared, now that electronic publication and Internet distribution have become routine. Instead, this business model is what stands in the way of all the benefits of open access' (Brown and others 2003: 2). These scholars argued for launching an 'open access model', a free-market, journal economics approach that would be different from the traditional pay-to-access business model of scholarly publication. The open access publication model they were proposing was premised on the idea that everything published would be open and available to all researchers:

> Open access would eliminate [corporate and university press] monopolies over essential published results, diminishing profit margins and creating a more efficient market for scientific publishing — a market in which publishers would compete to provide the best value to authors

(high quality, selectivity, prestige, a large and appreciative readership) at the best price. (Brown and others 2003: 2)

The open access model, and especially its proposed APC component would be so successful that it would revolutionize scholarly journal publishing. The idea behind the open access publication model was that scientific research and publication go hand in hand. As such, open access publishing would be funded by research funders as part of research grant budgets. As a result, everything published:

> [...] will immediately be freely available to anyone, anywhere, to download, print, distribute, read, and use without charge or other restrictions, as long as proper attribution of authorship is maintained. Our open-access journals will retain all of the qualities we value in scientific journals — high standards of quality and integrity, rigorous and fair peer-review, expert editorial oversight, high production standards, a distinctive identity, and independence. (Brown and others 2003: 1)

Open access was an attempt to shield academic research, knowledge creation and scholarly publication from the vicissitudes and shifting sands of research funding, changes in funding priorities, and funding cuts by governmental and non-governmental institutional funders. As formulated by its initiators, the open access publication model was seen as the answer to the oligopolistic, pay-for-access, subscription and site-licensing fee system of knowledge curation and archiving dominated by a handful of university presses, foundations, and especially a few oligopolistic global corporations (Johnson and others 2018).

According to Björk and Solomon (2012), the innovative open access model quickly ran into opposition from the legacy scholarly journal publishers who were the gatekeepers of the subscription-based, pay-to-access model. In an article entitled 'Open Access v. Subscription Journals: A comparison of impact', they framed the adversarial relationship between the new open access model and the traditional, subscription-based, pay-for-access mercantile model of scholarly publishing, arguing that history has shown the concerns and objections of the legacy academic publishers were overblown attempts to protect their oligopolies. The first open access journals were created in the late 1990s by individual scientists and researchers who desired to break away from the stranglehold of the legacy publishers. However,

> These journals were not considered by most academics a serious alternative to subscription publishing. There were doubts about both the sustainability of the journals and the quality of the peer review. These journals were usually not indexed in the Web of Science, and initially they lacked the prestige that academics need from publishing. (Björk and Solomon 2012: 2)

Legacy publishers and publishers' organizations were decidedly against open access. They claimed that 'the proliferation of OA would set in motion changes in the publishing system which would seriously undermine the current peer review system and hence the quality of scientific publishing' (Björk and Solomon 2012: 2). Nevertheless, these early open access journals had succeeded in breaking the stranglehold of the legacy publishers on scholarly journal publication. Some of these open access journals occupied niches in the emerging electronic publication landscape and thrived in these niches. This led to what Björk and Solomon (2012) call a 'second wave' of open access journals that consisted of 'established subscription journals, mainly owned by societies'. These publishers decided 'to make the electronic version of their journal(s) freely accessible' (p. 2). Open access, as conceptualized by Harold Varmus and his colleagues, began to take shape and diffuse from real space to virtual space, and to different cultural geographies of scholarly publishing and intellectual property. Björk and Solomon (2012) assert that:

> The third wave of OA journals was started by two new publishers, BioMedCentral and Public Library of Science (PLoS). They pioneered the use of article processing charges (APCs) as the central means of financing professional publishing of OA journals. Since 2000 the importance of the APC business model for funding OA publishing has grown rapidly. BioMedCentral was purchased in 2008 by Springer. (p. 2)

Most large commercial publishers now have lucrative, open access journals and open access book publishing divisions funded by article and book processing fees ranging from $2000 to $3000 per article (Björk and Solomon 2012), and sometimes much higher (Else 2020). In 2022, the global publishing conglomerate, Springer Nature, 'celebrated' publication of its one millionth gold open access article. The multi-national oligopolistic scholarly publishers have joined the open access movement, which they had bitterly opposed on the grounds that it undermined academic peer review, and made it an important component of knowledge capitalism. Indeed, in August 2023, *The Chronicle of Higher Education* published an article written by two publishing industry professionals who lamented what open access publishing has become — a sphere of corporate domination. The title was as apt as it was troubling: 'The Corporate Capture of Open Access Publishing' (Kember and Brand, 2023).

The open access phenomenon has revolutionized scholarly publishing and gone mainstream. By 2021, it had spawned the Directory of Open Access Journals (DOAJ), a community-curated, online, global registry of more than 17,500 peer-reviewed, open access journals covering science, technology, medicine, the social sciences, arts, and humanities. These journals make all their content available free of any charge, and without delay or user-registration requirements to all readers ('About DOAJ' [n.d.]). Other notable developments include the Open Access Publishing in European Networks (OAPEN), a collaborative that seeks to develop and implement open access in the Humanities and Social Sciences; Open Access Books | InTech, which publishes open access books and journals in the Sciences, Technology and Medicine; and the Directory of Open Access Books (DOAB), an open access book publishing service which provides a searchable index of peer-reviewed open access monographs and edited volumes, with links to full text editions of books hosted on publishers' websites or online repositories (Cordón-García and others 2013).

Despite its success, open access is not without its problems. Money has become the greatest obstacle to scholarly publishing. Outside the well-funded research universities, the burden of paying for scholarly publication under the open access model soon fell on scholars and authors desperate to publish to advance their careers, rather than on governmental and institutional funders as proponents of the model had anticipated. If anything, open access has widened the knowledge and publication gap between the haves and the have nots in the global academic enterprise and exacerbated the problem of intellectual diversity and productivity between researchers in the Global North and the Global South. These and other factors led to the emergence of multiple models of open access, the most pernicious of which is so-called predatory publishing, which takes advantage of researchers who do not have access to the legacy publication avenues or the funds to become part of the pay-to-publish open access paradigm.

Paradigm Shift in Scholarly Publishing: Open Access and the Rise of 'Predatory Journals'

The open access paradigm quickly diffused to all parts of the world, attracting in its wake for-profit 'predatory', purely mercantile, journals and 'scientific conferences' of dubious quality that do not care for the niceties of research or publication ethics and academic peer review, which are the very foundation of the open access model that had emerged in the United States. The internet and its associated social networking sites made open access a global phenomenon. While early open access journals were legitimate and mostly ethical attempts to bypass the stranglehold of the capitalist knowledge publishing industry, predatory publishers were not so. They were purely mercantilist ventures who deceptively and misleadingly took advantage of globalization — the interconnection of nations, cultures and peoples that was made possible by the internet and its innovative platforms in cyberspace — to bypass the barriers to market entry that had been erected by the traditional, legacy gatekeepers of scholarly academic publishing, and make a quick profit. They paid no heed to the niceties of the ethical and responsible conduct of research and publishing.

The phenomenon of predatory journals emerged during the first decade of the twenty-first century in response to a number of market- and technology-driven revolutionary changes that took place in the field of scholarly publishing at the end of the Cold War, the period when the internet was being transformed from a network of computers that was part of the command-and-control system of the United States Department of Defense, to a global assemblage of platforms of electronic commerce, cultural exchange, international, inter-personal, and social communication (Eko 2001). Predatory scholarly publishing emerged in the interstices between the transition of scholarly publishing from physical space (the traditional scholarly publishing model of printing and distributing scientific journals to institutional subscribers and other paying customers), to the innovative information and communication technology platforms in cyberspace. Indeed, a major factor that led to the emergence of predatory publishing was the ease of online publishing and the easy electronic transfer of money from jurisdiction to jurisdiction. This is crucial because predatory publishing is a money-making phenomenon that took advantage of the internal contradictions, shortcomings, and ferment in the field of scholarly journal publication. Predatory publishers emerged in the field of scholarly publication at a time of 'radical discontinuities', to borrow the expression of Corfield (2007), that had led to a ferment in the field of scholarly publication. These discontinuities included 1) systemic flaws, contradictions, hyper-competitiveness, change of funding priorities and disequilibrium in the academic research paradigm and scholarly publishing industry; 2) the development of information and communication technologies and the resultant digitization and transfer of journal publication and curation from the physical spaces of libraries and archives to the internet and cyberspace; and 3) the emergence of open access publishing with its lucrative article publication charge business model (Brown and others 2003; Eko and Koerber 2020).

The Legal and Ethical Challenges Posed by Predatory Publishing

Predatory journals are in fact 'parodies' of real scholarly journals. As noted in the previous chapter, the term 'predatory publishers', was coined in 2012 by Jeffrey Beall, who had started his list of suspect journals and publishers in 2008 (Beall 2012). Predatory journals are considered a bane to the field because they do not care for the niceties of tried-and-true professional publication standards. They ride roughshod over scholarly publication ethics in order to make a quick buck. The term 'predatory journal' or 'predatory publisher' has become a contemptuous, denunciative, and exclusionary epithet that members of the commercial and academic scholarly publishing industry have accepted as the appropriate nomenclature for the new category of unorthodox, commercial publishers that began to enter the scholarly publishing market in the early 2000s (Eko and Koerber 2020). Some researchers, acting out of good faith, knowingly review for predatory journals, hoping to increase the number of journals they review for, often with the mistaken expectation that this 'service' to the questionable fringe of scientific publishing would improve the quality of these predatory journals to the point where they would eventually become alternatives to the elite journals (Van Noorden 2020).

Grudniewicz (2019) advanced the following 'consensus' definition of predatory journals and publishers:

> Predatory journals and publishers are entities that prioritize self-interest at the expense of scholarship and are characterized by false or misleading information, deviation from best editorial and publication practices, a lack of transparency, and/or the use of aggressive and indiscriminate solicitation practices. (p. 211)

Predatory publishing arose out of the shortcomings of the scholarly research and publication paradigm. Within a few years of the emergence of the open access publishing paradigm, a new kind of entrepreneurial, free market, 'open access' online publisher emerged and started to take advantage of the hypercompetitive publication environment of scholarly research and publication. They mimicked open access publishing and capitalized on the lucrative APC model. They offered a quicker and shorter path to the El Dorado of scholarly publication for a fee — without paying heed to the professional and ethical standards or safeguards of traditional scholarly publishing. Their deceptive and misleading practices posed all kinds of legal and ethical challenges to the knowledge creation, publication, curation, and archiving model. It is estimated that there are more than 9,000 verified predatory journals generating some $75 million in revenues annually (Johnson and others 2018). Furthermore, some predatory publishers have been known to deliberately confuse article submitters. They do this by hijacking some legitimate journals and creating fraudulent websites that mimic the legitimate journal in order to attract submissions and fraudulently collect article publication charges (Johnson and others 2018). The danger that predatory publishers pose to the scholarly or academic publishing industry is existential because they undermine the fundamental philosophy and ethics of the academic peer review process. Johnson and others (2018) present an interesting summary of the quality control purpose of peer review that is being undermined by predatory journals. They state that the fundamental purpose of peer review is 'to ensure that only good science or scholarship gets published, and that work that does not meet acceptable standards does not enter the journal literature' (Johnson and others 2018: 49). Scholarly publication has certain frameworks or 'contextual matrixes', to borrow the expression of Pierre Legrand (2003) that shape and structure its modus operandi. By skipping the scientific publication paradigm, predatory journals have introduced discordant realities into the scholarly publication process. These issues have become salient in the light of public warnings issued by the United States DHHS, a cease-and-desist order from the NIH, and legal action undertaken by the FTC against international, so-called 'predatory publisher' and 'predatory scientific conference organizer', OMICS Group. That landmark case and its $50.1 million judgment against OMICS Group moves scholarly journal publishing from the realm of ethics — self-regulating, ethically responsible, scientific knowledge production, public presentation in conferences, and ethical publication — to the realm of law, which commands specific legal behavior under intellectual property and consumer protection law.

Predatory Publishing and its Drug Company Funders

One of the most controversial aspects of the predatory publishing phenomenon is its relationship with the global medical and pharmaceutical research industries that are derisively called 'Big Pharma'. The reality is that despite their reputation for unethical, deceptive, and misleading publication practices, some predatory publishers have financial backers with deep pockets, who have a stake in publicizing their research activities by all means possible. Many medical and pharmaceutical research funders have sponsored so-called predatory conferences, presented their research in them, and published in their journals. Researchers at global pharmaceutical corporations, including AstraZeneca, Bristol-Myers Squibb, Gilead Sciences, Pfizer, and Merck submit papers to predatory journals, and fund or participate in predatory scientific conferences. These global medical and pharmaceutical research corporations have funded and participated in the 'predatory' scientific conferences and allowed their researchers to present the results of their research in these conferences and publish them in their journals. For example, OMICS Group of Hyderabad, India, and its subsidiaries, iMedPub, Conference Series, have been a beneficiary of the sponsorship of the global medical and pharmaceutical corporations (Deprez and Chen 2017). When the major global medical and pharmaceutical corporations fund and support so-called 'predatory conferences' and allow their scientists to publish their research in predatory journals, they do so out of self-interest. These conferences become outlets for pharmaceutical and other types of research that would take a longer time to go through the regular peer-review process. This makes it clear that there is a disconnect between tried-and-true ethical research, professional conferences, and publication values, on the one hand, and the unethical practices of profit-seeking predatory conferences, on the other hand. The symbiotic relationship between these global corporations and predatory conference organizers and publishers — and they are often one and the same entity — raises issues of research validity. This unethical and irresponsible publication of research clearly goes against the values of rule utilitarianism. It does not promote the greatest good for the greatest number.

From Professional Self-Regulation to Regulated Self-Regulation: The OMICS Group Affair

The final component of this chapter focuses on the actions undertaken by the United States government in response to the excesses of the predatory publishers. The unethical and illegal actions of OMICS Group and its affiliates, iMedPub and Conference Series, brought the ire of the US federal government onto the India-based company. Johnson and others (2018) described the modus operandi of predatory journals, whose business model is to prey on unsuspecting researchers and professors who, driven by the 'publish or perish' ethos of American higher education that is fast becoming the global norm, are always on the lookout for publication outlets for their research. Predatory journals capitalize on this situation and offer themselves as options. They 'often promote themselves to potential authors through bulk, sometimes spam emails, frequently have fictitious editorial boards and in many cases use the Gold Open Access [article publication charge] model to get money upfront before an author can detect whether their article has been subjected to any peer review whatsoever' (Johnson and others: 82). The unethical practices of the so-called OMICS affair became salient regulatory policy issues when several national organizations and the

US federal government acted. Those actions included public warnings issued by DHHS, a cease-and-desist order by the NIH, and legal action undertaken by the FTC against OMICS Group and its affiliates. In effect, after OMICS Group ignored the cease-and-desist orders of the NIH, which had accused the international conference organizer and publisher of intellectual property violations, that agency referred the matter to the FTC, the independent federal government agency charged with policing deceptive, misleading, and unfair competition under the FTC Act of 1924. In 2016, the FTC sued OMICS Group in a federal court in Nevada. That was because the OMICS Group Inc. was registered in Nevada, though it had its principal place of business at HITEC City, Hyderabad, India.

The unprecedented case, 'FTC v. OMICS Group', is a legal dispute that involved NIH and FTC against academic publisher and conference organizer OMICS Group, Inc. and its affiliates, which publish hundreds of purportedly open access online academic journals and organize fee-paying international conferences. It all began in 2013 when DHHS, a major funder of research, sent a warning letter to OMICS Group, stating that 'We are aware of multiple instances where the [OMICS] website uses the name of the NIH, its Institutes, PubMed Central, or the names of NIH employees in an erroneous and/or misleading manner' (Kaiser 2013: 4). When two NIH officers became the victims of the deceptive and misleading practices of OMICS, the NIH accused OMICS of 'trademark infringement', and issued a cease-and-desist letter to the academic publisher, ordering it to 'cease and desist from employing our name or the name of any of our agencies, institutes, or employees on your website for other than true factual statements' (Kaiser 2013: 6). The NIH subsequently referred the matter to the FTC, the independent federal agency empowered to prevent persons, partnerships, and corporations from using unfair, deceptive, and misleading practices, acts, or methods of competition in the marketplace, for enforcement. In 2016, the FTC charged OMICS Group, Inc., with violating American federal law. The FTC complaint charged OMICS Group with 'deceiving academics and researchers about the nature of its publications and hiding publication fees ranging from hundreds to thousands of dollars' (FTC 2016: para. 1). The FTC also alleged that by making false claims and failing to disclose steep publishing fees to its journal article authors, OMICS Group violated Title 15 of the United States Code, section 45, which gives the FTC the power to prevent such acts ('FTC v. OMICS' 2016). The FTC's 'Complaint for Permanent Injunction and Other Equitable Relief' ('FTC v. OMICS' 2016) was filed against OMICS, two affiliated companies, iMedPub LLC, Conference Series LLC, and Srinubabu Gedela, an Indian National, who is the president and director of OMICS, iMedPub, and Conference Series. Gedela is also the owner of the fictitious business named OMICS Publishing Group. The complaint was filed at the United States District Court for the District of Nevada. It specifically accused OMICS Group and Gedela of violating academic publication ethics and federal law through falsely stating that various academic experts served as editors, members of editorial boards, or were associated with the Defendants' journals, and that the researchers' articles are:

> [...] subject to industry-standard peer review before publishing. Defendants also represent that their journals have high 'impact factors' (meaning they are cited frequently, using a metric calculated by Thomson Reuters) and are listed in PubMed Central, a well-known and prestigious database maintained by the United States National Library of Medicine (NLM) at the National Institutes of Health (NIH). ('FTC v. OMICS' 2016: 4)

The FTC's complaint also alleged that:

> [...] the defendants regularly deceive consumers while promoting academic conferences they organize. The defendants allegedly include the names of prominent researchers as participants and presenters at the conferences, which charge registration fees that can cost more than $1,000, when in fact many of those researchers often did not agree to participate in the events. (FTC 2016: para. 7)

In response, OMICS Group, iMedPub LLC, Conference Series LLC, and Srinubabu Gedela, maintained that their publication and conference organization practices were legal and that the lawsuit was being driven by oligopolistic multinational corporate interests who have a stake in the old, subscription-access scholarly journal publication paradigm. They said the big corporate publishers wanted to keep them out of the open access scholarly publishing market. Indeed, Gedela resisted any attempt to classify his journals as 'predatory'. When Jeffrey Beall classified OMICS Group as a predatory publisher and listed its 700-plus journals as such in his Beall's List of Predatory Publishers, Gedela threatened to file a $1 billion defamation lawsuit against Beall (New 2013). That threat, and alleged pressure from Beall's employer, the University of Colorado at Denver, caused the librarian to suspend his scholarly journal classification list for fear of legal liability for the list. The institution later denied that it had put pressure on Beall to shut down his List of Predatory Publishers in the face of threats of legal action by Gedela and OMICS Group, Inc. (Deprez and Chen 2017). The FTC and researchers who complained against OMICS Group had this threat in mind. These researchers had collaborated with the FTC in adducing evidence to support the FTC's complaint against OMICS. Indeed, the irony of the FTC's legal action against OMICS Group is that it turned the tables. The party that had threatened to resort to the very expensive remedies of the law against Beall soon found itself the defendant in a very expensive landmark case that was a metaphorical shot across the bows of the global predatory publishing industry.

The issue before the United States District Court for the District of Nevada, Las Vegas, was whether OMICS Group, iMedPub, Conference Series, and Gedela had engaged in unfair, false, deceptive, and misleading practices, acts, or methods of competition in the marketplace that violated the Federal Trade Commission Act. On 29 September 2017, the court granted the FTC's request for a preliminary injunction, requiring the Defendants to preserve records, provide financial accounting to the FTC, and refrain from engaging in deceptive practices. The parties were asked to submit their respective motions for summary judgment on the FTC's unfair and deceptive practices claim. The court subsequently issued a judgment and final order that:

> [...] prohibits the defendants from making misrepresentations regarding their academic journals and conferences, including that specific persons are editors of their journals or have agreed to participate in their conferences, that their journals engage in peer review, that their journals are included in any academic journal indexing service, or the extent to which their journals are cited. It also requires that the defendants clearly and conspicuously disclose all costs associated with submitting or publishing articles in their journals. The order also requires the defendants to obtain express written consent from any person the defendants represent to be associated with their academic journals or scientific conferences. ('Fed. Trade Comm'n v. Omics Grp. Inc.' 2019: 8)

The court then levied a $50.1 million judgment against OMICS Group, its affiliated companies, iMedPub LLC, Conference Series LLC, and Gedela. This amount was all of OMICS' earnings over the six-year period when the federal government commenced litigation against the company. The court ordered OMICS to refrain from engaging in misleading and deceptive practices, and from making similar misrepresentations in the future ('FTC vs. OMICS Group' 2019).

OMICS Inc v. FTC: Review by the United States Court of Appeals for the 9th Circuit

OMICS Group, iMedPub, Conference Series, and Gedela appealed the decision and fine to the United States Court of Appeals for the 9th Circuit in California. They claimed that the federal district court in Nevada erred in imposing the $50.1 million fine based on the government's petition for a permanent injunction and other equitable relief rather than a full jury trial. They added that the $50.1 million fine was not equitable. The first issue before the appellate court was whether OMICS Group, iMedPub, Conference Series, and Gedela violated Section 5(a) of the FTC Act, 15 U.S.C. § 45(a). The second issue was whether the District Court erred in holding Gedela personally liable for the unfair and deceptive practices of OMICS Group and its affiliated corporations. The final issue was whether the $50.1 million monetary relief (fine) was equitable. The court of appeals answered in the affirmative on all three issues. With respect to violation of the Federal Trade Commission Act, the court ruled that the record contained ample evidence of Defendants' deception regarding its journals' peer review practices, publishing fees, impact factors, and editorial board membership. OMICS also made false representations regarding the attendees and organizers of its academic conferences when marketing these events: 'OMICS's misrepresentations were material and their net impression was likely to, and did in fact, deceive ordinary consumers' ('FTC v. OMICS Group' 2020: 2). The court of appeals affirmed the district court's grant of summary judgment to the FTC, and against OMICS Group, concluding that the defendants violated Section 5(a) of the FTC Act. With respect to Gedela's personal liability, the appeals court ruled that:

[...] the district court properly concluded that Gedela is personally liable for OMICS's violations because he had authority over OMICS and either had knowledge of the companies' misrepresentations or was recklessly indifferent to their truth or falsity [...] as relates to Defendant's conference activities [...] Although the individual conferences were discrete events, they were part of a single scheme of deceptive business practices carried out by Defendants [...] we hold that the FTC reasonably approximated OMICS's unjust gains with respect to the entirety of its deceptive business practices. ('FTC v. OMICS Group' 2020: 4).

The court ruled that the FTC could deposit the $50.1 million in a fund to be used for equitable relief, including consumer (scholar/author) redress (reimbursement) as well as expenses related to the administration of the redress fund. It ordered that any money not used for equitable relief (reimbursement of authors and conference attendees) was to be forfeited to the US Treasury ('FTC v. OMICS Group' 2020). The question is whether OMICS will comply with the court judgment given that it found the FTC lawsuit and court decision unjust. Furthermore, OMICS is headquartered in India, where it is viewed favorably by the government to the point where it is given tax breaks and favorable treatment (Deprez and Chen 2017). It is unclear whether the FTC will be able to convince Indian courts to accept the American court decision and allow the United States government to enforce it in India. That is a diplomatic and political matter for India and the United States to resolve. One major critique of this court decision, beside the fact that it was not the outcome of a trial by jury, is that OMICS Group, and especially its affiliate, Conferences Services, were sponsored by global medical research and pharmaceutical conglomerates which saw these OMICS conferences and some OMICS journals as appropriate outlets for their research, in a highly competitive research and publication environment (Deprez and Chen 2017).

Lessons Learned from the OMICS Group Case

The 'FTC v. OMICS' case was the first case against a so-called 'predatory publisher' in the United States. The landmark case moved scholarly journal publishing from the realm of professional ethics — self-regulation of ethically responsible research, knowledge production, presentation in professional conferences, and ethical publication — to the realm of law, which commands specific legal behavior on pain of criminal penalties or civil sanctions or both. During the case, for the first time, the FTC injected the pejorative epithets, 'predatory conferences', 'predatory publication', and 'predatory journal' into mainstream American and international legal vocabulary. When the FTC first charged OMICS Group with violating federal law in 2016, it simply stated that it had charged 'Academic Journal Publisher OMICS Group' with deceiving researchers and failing to disclose steep publication fees. By the time the case was finally decided in 2019 by the United States Court of Appeals for the 9th Circuit, the FTC reported that the court had ruled against 'predatory Academic publisher OMICS'. The government and the courts had essentially adopted the epithet that had previously been coined by Jeffrey Beall to describe the emerging mercantilist 'open access' academic publishers, whose modus operandi was at variance with the proper conduct of research, organization of professional conferences, and research publication. Those terms are now legal appellations, not just pejorative epithets. Media reports of the OMICS case used the epithet to characterize the company. However, it is worth noting that in its reports of the case, *The New York Times* used the term 'predatory' in quotes (Kolata 2019).

Furthermore, the government used evidence of wrongdoing on the part of OMICS Group to prosecute the predatory publisher and its affiliates for violating federal law. The most devastating pieces of evidence used against OMICS were the publication, by OMICS Group journals, of utterly meaningless 'hoax' research papers that scholars had deliberately written and submitted to OMICS journals to prove that the company's journals did not follow the elementary principles of scholarly editing, peer review, and publication. They claimed that the only thing OMICS was interested in was the article publication fees charged for online publication of these bogus articles. These scholars essentially engaged in entrapment to provide the government evidence to prosecute OMICS. They knowingly played along with the deceptive, misleading, and unethical activities of OMICS in order to gather evidence to bolster the FTC's case against the predatory publisher ('FTC vs. OMICS Group' 2019).

Predatory publishing is a global issue. The United States government is willing to protect its institutional scientific research 'trademarks' by taking legal action against international predatory publishers who have a presence in the United States. For research and publication ethics to be globalized, codes of ethics must become globally institutionalized paradigms that are characterized by universal values that transcend narrow national research and publication traditions and frameworks.

In scholarly publishing, the rule utilitarian approach focuses on the impact of rules or codes of ethics on publication practices. The OMICS case demonstrates that if predatory publishers fail to abide by the recommendations of the professional codes of ethics of the industry, they often cross the line into the realm of illegal activity, which triggers a government response — enforcement of commandments, rules, and regulations designed to stamp out illegal, deceptive, and misleading behavior in the marketplace, for the greater good.

Conclusion

The paradigm of valid scientific and academic research is grounded in ethically conducted research and publication. Globalization and the interconnection of nations, peoples, educational systems, and different cultural geographies of research and academic publication have resulted in a worldwide ethical ferment with incalculable consequences for the ethical research and academic publication paradigm. This ferment was exacerbated by open access, which was clearly an attempt to shield academic research, knowledge creation, and scholarly publication from the vicissitudes and shifting sands of research funding, changes in funding priorities, and funding cuts by governmental and non-governmental institutional funders. As formulated by its initiators, open access was seen as the answer to the oligopolistic, pay-for-access, subscription and site-licensing fee system of knowledge curation and archiving dominated by a handful of university presses, foundations, and especially a few global corporations (Johnson and others 2018). One of the unintended consequences of open access was the emergence of for-profit predatory publishers who took advantage of the scholarly pressure to publish and trampled the conventions of ethical scholarly publication under foot in a headlong rush to make money. Their excesses resulted in governmental legal action and court rulings like the one in FTC v. OMICS Group Inc. that created an emerging regime of regulated self-regulation. This chapter has explored the dichotomy between professional codes of ethics that make recommendations, and enforceable federal law — rules and regulations that amount to commandments — within the framework of the moral philosophical perspective of rule utilitarianism. This perspective holds that all actions must be judged in terms of their conformity to rules that, if obeyed, would lead to the 'greatest good' for professions and for society as a whole (Berkeley 1712: 8).

The OMICS case is unprecedented because it injects the government into the dynamic field of scholarly publishing, treats it as a 'product' and researchers as 'consumers' who must be protected from the deceptive and misleading marketing practices of predatory publishers and conference organizers. The case also involves the US federal government in aspects of the research, conference, and publication paradigm, and makes it an arbiter of peer-review systems, journal indexing, and journal metrics, impact factors, and citation metrics. These are issues that ought to be left to individual scholars because they may raise questions about freedom of academic expression. Predatory publishing demonstrates the shortcomings of the research and open access publication paradigm that is dominated by billion-dollar oligopolistic scholarly publishers. For research and publication ethics to be globalized, codes of ethics have to become globally institutionalized paradigms that are characterized by universal values that transcend narrow national research and publication traditions, cultures, and frameworks.

Epilogue

The Challenges of Artificial Intelligence to Ethical Scholarly Publishing

Since digital information and communication technologies have transformed science communication, scientific research, knowledge creation, scholarly and academic publication, curation, and retrieval into a dynamic, ever-changing enterprise, the gatekeepers of the industry pay attention to emerging technologies that threaten to disrupt the tried-and-true paradigm. Scholarly and academic publishing now finds itself at another technological, moral and philosophical crossroads. In November 2022, a seismic event with major disruptive potential for scholarly and academic publishing was announced. A Silicon Valley-based information technology company, OpenAI, announced that it had built and released ChatGPT (short for Chat Generative Pre-trained Transformer), the prototype of a revolutionary artificial intelligence (AI) tool for general public use. ChatGPT is a chatbot, a 'computer program [set of algorithms] that uses artificial intelligence (AI) and natural language processing (NLP) to understand customer questions and automate responses to them, simulating human conversation' ('What is a chatbot?' 2023: para. 1). According to IBM Corporation, a pioneer of computer and database technologies, AI is defined in terms of what it is designed to accomplish: 'Artificial intelligence leverages computers and machines to mimic the problem-solving and decision-making capabilities of the human mind' ('What is artificial intelligence (AI)?' 2023: para. 1). This computer mimicry of human intelligence essentially tries to embed human attributes and characteristics into machines. The limits and consequences of this mimicry are contested by segments of the technological elite, academics, and politicians (Van Der Laan 2016), and, as a result, the launching of ChatGPT received a lot of media coverage around the world.

News — and media hype — about the dangers and capabilities of ChatGPT spread like wildfire. Within days, millions of people had logged on to the OpenAI website. A segment of users around the world hailed ChatGPT and its even more powerful successor, GPT-4, as a boon to society, while another segment decried it as a bane to humanity at worst. Sensing that ChatGPT posed an existential threat to its business models, Google promptly announced that it was releasing its own version of AI, a chatbot called Bard ('Meet Bard' 2023). On 29 March 2023, the nonprofit Future of Life Institute organized an open letter entitled, 'Pause Giant AI Experiments: An Open Letter' signed by more than 30,000 high tech, artificial intelligence, computer industry, and academic elites from around the world, including Elon Musk, CEO of SpaceX, Tesla, and Twitter (Anderson 2023; 'Pause Giant AI' 2023). Musk happens to be one of the co-founders of OpenAI. The open letter called for an industry-wide or government moratorium on research on 'AI systems more powerful than GPT-4' ('Pause Giant AI' 2023, para. 1). The letter presented the reasons for the moratorium in apocalyptic terms:

> AI systems with human-competitive intelligence can pose profound risks to society and humanity [...] AI labs locked in an out-of-control race to develop and deploy ever more powerful digital minds that no one – not even their creators – can understand, predict, or reliably control [...] *Should* we let machines flood our information channels with propaganda and untruth? *Should* we automate away all the jobs, including the fulfilling ones? *Should* we develop nonhuman minds that might eventually outnumber, outsmart, obsolete and replace us? *Should* we risk loss of control of our civilization? ('Pause Giant AI' 2023: paras. 1–2)

The call for an industry or government moratorium on the 'dangerous race to ever-larger unpredictable black-box models with emergent capabilities' ('Pause Giant AI' 2023: para. 4) was based on the belief that AI, like all new or emerging technologies, 'shapes and defines reality itself [...that] there is now no reality outside of [AI] technology', to use the expression of Van der Laan (2016: 20). The online letter was a call for responsible governance of and moralization about AI, a technology that has the potential to be used for good or ill, for ethical, unethical, or amoral purposes. It was a call for regulation of AI (Anderson 2023). This was the second open letter organized by the Future of Life Institute. The first open letter it coordinated had been published in 2015. It was signed by renowned British physicist, Stephen Hawking, and Elon Musk (Van der Laan).

In response to the call for an AI pause in the wake of the launching of ChatGPT, a group of ethicists challenged the signatories of the open letter for ignoring the ills of AI in contemporary society: 'hypothetical risks are the focus of a dangerous ideology called longtermism that ignores the actual harms resulting from the deployment of AI systems today' (Gebru and others 2023: para. 3). AI research and deployment is clearly not a futuristic problem. Just as the emergence of digital technologies, databases, the internet, social media platforms, and open access posed challenges to, and profoundly altered, the traditional paradigm of ethically conducted scientific research and publication, artificial intelligence has the potential to further disrupt and profoundly alter these realms of scholarly activity. Developments in AI raise multiple legal and ethical issues for scientific research, scholarly, and academic publishing. Will AI replace human peer reviewers and automate the scholarly journal publishing paradigm? Will AI be a boon for paper mills? Will AI enable the infringement of intellectual property? How will AI systems be governed in the field of scholarly and academic publishing? Will traditional and predatory publishers use Open AI's ChatGPT or Google's Bard to write encyclopedic 'meta research' compendiums on given subjects? Chatbots like ChatGPT, GPT4, and Bard are notorious for their uneven accuracy. In order to increase the ability of chatbots to generate accurate information, they have to be trained on real databases. How will these activities be regulated? AI also has the potential to give predatory publishing and paper mills a new lease on life. For example, in the 'FTC v. OMICS' case, researchers generated ethically questionable 'anti-research' or hoax articles and used these bogus articles as bait to entrap predatory publishers. Publication of these hoax articles became prima facie evidence used against OMICS in federal court. Will researchers partner with the government and use AI to generate such ethically questionable hoax articles for purposes of selectively prosecuting predatory publishers?

AI has the potential for positive use in scholarly and academic publishing. Thus, in their open letter calling for a moratorium on certain types of high-risk AI, the signatories of the tech and academic intelligentsia called for the development of 'provenance and watermarking systems to help distinguish real from synthetic and to track model leaks' ('Pause Giant AI' 2023: para. 7). AI watermarking systems will be highly relevant in scholarly and academic research and publishing because they will address issues regarding, intellectual property, disinformation, paper mills, hoaxes and other types of articles generated by human and artificial intelligence systems. In order to keep abreast of rapidly evolving AI technology, the codes of ethics of the scholarly and academic publishing industry, and of publication databases, need to be revised to include provisions on the uses of AI. Ultimately, what the 'AI pause letter' signatories were calling for is a context-specific regulated self-regulation of AI. Such a system will stand the scholarly publishing industry in good stead.

Key Takeaways

- Open access publishing emerged in the United States in early 1990s because of governmental and institutional funding priorities and the aim of allowing for a more equitable flow of knowledge in an increasingly connected world.

- The primary component of the most prevalent new open access model was article processing charges, where the costs of publishing and archiving academic articles would move from a pay-to-read model to a pay-to-publish model, allowing all published articles to be available to all readers, free of cost.

- Initially, the traditional publishers opposed open access, arguing the pay-to-publish model would undermine the credibility of scientific knowledge production and the traditional peer review system. Now, nearly all large commercial publishers have open access and open book publishing divisions that are funded by article processing charges, which have grown increasingly expensive.

- In response to the continually increasing numbers of open access journals, databases and indexes aimed at developing and legitimizing credible open access journals and publications were created.

- By placing the burden of paying to publish their work on individual scholars and researchers, a divide was created between scholars in affluent countries and institutions and those with less monetary or institutional resources to cover the increasingly expensive article processing charges.

- The term 'predatory journal' or 'predatory publisher' has become common nomenclature to categorize publications that seek to capitalize on the open access trend of pay-to-publish but do not follow the tried-and-true professional publication standards.

- Predatory journals routinely use deceptive tactics to lure authors into submitting their articles. Some commonly used deceptions are creating journal websites and names that mimic well-known journals, listing editorial board members that actually have no association with the publication, and hiding fee expectations until after a manuscript is submitted.

- The *FTC v. OMICS* case was the first case against a so-called 'predatory publisher' in the United States, effectively moving scholarly journal publishing from the realm of professional ethics to the realm of law.
- The emergence of AI technologies will impact scholarly publishing in numerous ways, both positive and negative.

Discussion Questions

1. Examine the origins of the open access movement. What are the key developments that led to disruption of the traditional subscription-access academic publishing model?
2. Someone has to pay for publishing and archiving the global knowledge base, and both the subscription model and the article processing charge model have created barriers. What are some alternatives?
3. What are the key factors that allowed predatory journals to enter into the open access environment?
4. What are some ways that the different worldviews and research practice norms may have contributed to the rise of predatory publishing?
5. Why does the predatory journal practice of not conducting peer review threaten the credibility of the body of scientific knowledge?
6. How has the sponsorship of predatory publishing companies (like OMICS group) by Big Pharma contributed to the ethical dilemmas related to academic publishing?
7. What are some possible ramifications for institutions and individuals when a journal they have submitted their work to is charged with violating both ethical codes and federal law?
8. The Indian government still supports OMICS as a legitimate business, gives them tax breaks, and has even subsidized land for OMICS to build a new headquarters. This is a clear

indication that, according to the government of India, the OMICS Group has not violated any norms related to academic publishing. How might this be a challenge when considering a code of ethics that could be applicable to the global body of academic knowledge production?

9. What are some of the potential issues that could arise from the thousands of medical and pharmaceutical research presentations and articles that were published or presented through OMICS publications or conferences and are now part of the global body of scientific research, freely available to anyone with internet access?

10. Before OMICS was formally charged with misleading authors about their services and fees, a researcher who submitted their work could claim ignorance about the credibility of the publisher. Now that the case has been decided, and the results widely covered in mainstream news media and academic-specific outlets, could authors still realistically claim ignorance if an OMICS-related publication is found on their CV? Should university administrators take action against their faculty who submit to OMICS journals? What are potential ramifications for this in terms of academic freedom?

11. Given the fact that one of the key pieces of evidence against OMICS was obtained through questionable ethical practices (entrapment), should there be a chance for OMICS to appeal or question the second ruling by the appeals court? Explain the reasons for your answer.

12. Is AI a boon (blessing) or a bane (curse) to scholarly publishing?

Activities

Activity One: Collecting the Fine

Imagine a scenario where the FTC was able to collect the $50.1 million fine from OMICS. As per the court ruling, the bulk of the fine is supposed to go to authors and conference presenters who were deceived by OMICS. However, it is likely that some individuals and organizations (such as personnel from the Big Pharma organizations that sponsored OMICS conferences) knew that OMICS was deceiving authors and profiting from that deception.

As a group or individually, answer/discuss the following questions:

1. Should the author reimbursement be divided equally among all authors around the world who submitted to OMICS journals and conferences?
2. Or should there be an attempt at establishing the truth (or otherwise) of claims of ignorance related to OMICS's predatory practices?

Activity Two: Ethics in a Global Society

The last sentence of the chapter states:

> For research and publication ethics to be globalized, codes of ethics have to become globally institutionalized paradigms that are characterized by pluralistic and universal values that transcend narrow national research and publication traditions and frameworks.

The Committee on Publication Ethics (COPE), the Directory of Open Access Journals (DOAJ), the Open Access Scholarly Publishing Association (OASPA), and the World Association of Medical Editors (WAME) are scholarly organizations that have collaborated to identify principles of transparency and best practice for scholarly publications' ('Principles of Transparency' 2019: 1). Using the principles of transparency published by these organizations, consider whether:

1. OMICS violated their principles, and
2. Do these standards allow for epistemic and cultural diversity in the global body of knowledge production?

Finally, as evidenced in Chapter 6 of this book, there is no shortage of information and training available related to scholarly publishing ethics, yet researcher still either fall prey or deliberately submit their work to journals that do not adhere to ethical publication practices.

What are some ways your institution/college/department attempt to instill or enforce ethical research practices in faculty and graduate students?

References

'About DOAJ'. [n.d.]. *DOAJ*, https://doaj.org/about/

Alberts, Bruce., W. Kirschner, Marc., Tilghman, Shirley and Varmus, Harold. 2014. 'Rescuing US Biomedical Research from Its Systemic Flaws', *Proceedings of the National Academy of Sciences of the United States of America*, 111.16: 5773–77, https://doi.org/10.1073/PNAS.1404402111

Anderson, Margo. 2023. '"AI Pause" Open Letter Stokes Fear and Controversy: IEEE signatories say they worry about ultrasmart, amoral systems without guidance', *IEEE Spectrum*, https://spectrum.ieee.org/ai-pause-letter-stokes-fear

Beall, Jeffrey. 2012. 'Predatory Publishers and Opportunities for Scholarly Societies', in *American Educational Research Association* (Washington, D. C.), 1–5, http://eprints.rclis.org/18044/

Berkeley, George. 1712. *Passive Obedience: Or, the Christian Doctrine of Not Resisting the Supreme Power, Proved and Vindicated*, 2nd edn (London: Oxford Text Archive)

Björk, Bo Christer, and David Solomon. 2012. 'Open Access versus Subscription Journals: A Comparison of Scientific Impact', *BMC Medicine*, 10.73: 1–10, https://bmcmedicine.biomedcentral.com/articles/10.1186/1741-7015-10-73

Bourdieu, Pierre. 1977. *Outline of a Theory of Practice*, translated by Richard Nice (Cambridge: Cambridge University Press). https://doi.org/10.1017/cbo9780511812507

Brown, Patrick O., Eisen, Michael B. and Varmus Harold E. 2003. 'Why PLoS Became a Publisher', *PLOS Biology*, 1.1: 1–2, https://doi.org/10.1371/JOURNAL.PBIO.0000036

Clinton, William and Gore, Albert. 1997. 'A Framework for Global Electronic Commerce' (Washington, D.C.: United States Printing Office), https://clintonwhitehouse4.archives.gov/WH/New/Commerce/

Cordón-García, José-Antonio., Alonso-Arévalo, Julio., Gómez-Díaz, Raquel and Linder, Daniel. 2013. *Social Reading: Platforms, Applications, Clouds and Tags*, 1st edn (Witney, Oxford, UK: Chandos Publishing)

Corfield, Penelope J. 2007. *Time and the Shape of History* (New Haven, CT: Yale University Press). https://doi.org/10.12987/YALE/9780300115581.001.0001

Crimmins, James E. 2021. 'Jeremy Bentham', *Stanford Encyclopedia of Philosophy*, https://plato.stanford.edu/entries/bentham/

De Beer, Arnold S., and Merrill John C. 2003. *Global Journalism: Topical Issues and Media Systems*, 4th edn (Boston, MA: Allyn & Bacon)

Deprez, Esmé E., and Chen, Caroline. 2017. 'Medical Journals Have a Fake News Problem', *Bloomberg*, https://www.bloomberg.com/news/features/2017-08-29/medical-journals-have-a-fake-news-problem

Eko, Lyombe. 2001. 'Many Spiders, One Worldwide Web: Towards a Typology of Internet Regulation', *Communication Law and Policy*, 6.3: 445–84, https://doi.org/10.1207/S15326926CLP0603_02

Eko, Lyombe, and Koerber, Amy. 2020. 'Profiting from the Paradigm Shift in Scholarly Journal Publishing: The Case of Predatory Publishers', *The Southwest Respiratory and Critical Care Chronicles*, 8.35: 61–64, https://doi.org/10.12746/SWRCCC.V8I35.715

Eko, Lyombe, A. Kumar, and Q. Yao. 2012. 'To Google or Not to Google: The Google Digital Books Initiative and the Exceptionalist Intellectual Property Law Regimes of the United States and France', *Journal of Internet Law*, 15: 12–21

Else, Holly. 2020. *Nature Journals Reveal Terms of Landmark Open-Access Option, Nature*, https://doi.org/10.1038/D41586-020-03324-Y

'Fed. Trade Comm'n v. Omics Grp. Inc.' 2019. (*Brief of the Federal Trade Commission*). https://www.ftc.gov/legal-library/browse/cases-proceedings/152-3113-omics-group-inc

Federal Trade Commission (FTC). 2016. *FTC Charges Academic Journal Publisher OMICS Group Deceived Researchers*, https://www.ftc.gov/news-events/news/press-releases/2016/08/ftc-charges-academic-journal-publisher-omics-group-deceived-researchers

Figdor, Carrie. 2010. 'Is Objective News Possible?', in Christopher Meyers (ed.), *Journalism Ethics: A Philosophical Approach* (Oxford, England: Oxford University Press): 153–64, https://doi.org/10.1093/ACPROF:OSO/9780195370805.003.0010

'FTC v. OMICS'. 2016, https://www.ftc.gov/system/files/documents/cases/160826omicscmpt.pdf

'FTC v. OMICS Group'. 2020. (*United States Court of Appeals for the Ninth Circuit*). https://www.ftc.gov/system/files/ftc_gov/pdf/CA9-Omics-Opinion.pdf

'FTC vs. OMICS Group'. 2019, https://www.ftc.gov/system/files/documents/cases/de_121_-_omics_order_granting_summary_judgment.pdf

Gebru, Timnit., Bender, Emily., Millan-Major, Angelina and Mitchell, Margaret. 2023. 'Statement from the listed authors of Stochastic Parrots on the "AI pause" letter', *Distributed AI Research Institute* (*DAIR*). https://www.dair-institute.org/blog/letter-statement-March2023

Greco, Albert N. 2016. 'The Impact of Disruptive and Sustaining Digital Technologies on Scholarly Journals', *Journal of Scholarly Publishing*, 48.1: 17–39, https://doi.org/10.3138/jsp.48.1.17

Grudniewicz, Agnes., Moher, David., Cobey, Kelly D., Bryson, Gregory L., Cukier, Samantha and others. 2019. 'Predatory Journals: No Definition, No Defence', *Nature*, 576.7786: 210–12, https://doi.org/10.1038/d41586-019-03759-y

'Guild'. 2023. ed. by The Editors of Encyclopedia Britannica. *Encyclopedia Britannica*, https://www.britannica.com/topic/guild-trade-association

Johnson, Rob., Watkinson, Anthony and Mabe, Michael. 2018. *'The STM Report: An Overview of Scientific and Scholarly Publishing'*, https://www.stm-assoc.org/2018_10_04_STM_Report_2018.pdf

Kaiser, Jocelyn. 2013. 'U.S. Government Accuses Open Access Publisher of Trademark Infringement', *Science*, https://www.science.org/content/article/us-government-accuses-open-access-publisher-trademark-infringement

Kember, Sarah, and Brand, Amy. 2023. *'The Corporate Capture of Open Access Publishing'*, https://www.chronicle.com/article/the-corporate-capture-of-open-access-publishing

Kolata, Gina. 2019. 'The Price for "Predatory" Publishing? $50 Million', *The New York Times*, https://www.nytimes.com/2019/04/03/science/predatory-journals-ftc-omics.html

Kuhn, Thomas S. 1970. *The Structure of Scientific Revolutions*, 2nd edn (Chicago: The University of Chicago Press)

Legrand, Pierre. 2003. 'The Same and The Different', in *Comparative Legal Studies: Traditions and Transitions*, ed. by Pierre Legrand and Roderick Munday, 240–311, https://doi.org/10.1017/CBO9780511522260

'Meet Bard'. 2023. *Google, Inc.* https://bard.google.com/?utm_source=sem&utm_medium=paid-media&utm_campaign=q3enUS_sem6

Nathanson, Stephen. [n.d.] 'Act and Rule Utilitarianism', *Internet Encyclopedia of Philosophy*, https://iep.utm.edu/util-a-r/

New, Jake. 2013. 'Publisher Threatens to Sue Blogger for $1-Billion', *The Chronicle of Higher Education*, https://www.chronicle.com/article/publisher-threatens-to-sue-blogger-for-1-billion/

'Pause Giant AI Experiments: An Open Letter'. 2023. *Future of life Institute*, https://futureoflife.org/open-letter/pause-giant-ai-experiments/

'Principles of Transparency and Best Practice in Scholarly Publishing'. 2019. *COPE, DOAJ, OASPA, and WAME*, https://doi.org/10.24318/cope.2019.1.12

Schroeder, Eric P., Underwood Jr, Brian M. and Bedo, Nicholas A. 2021. 'When Copyright First Met the Digital World: A Retrospective and Discussion of New York Times v. Tasini, 533 U.S. 483 (2001)'. *American Bar Association*, https://www.americanbar.org/groups/communications_law/publications/communications_lawyer/2021-summer/when-copyright-first-met-digital-world-retrospective-and-discussion-new-york-times-v-tasini-533-us-483-2001/

Tennant, Jonathan P., Waldner, François., Jacques, Damien C., Masuzzo, Paola., Collister, Lauren B. and others. 2016. 'The Academic, Economic and Societal Impacts of Open Access: An Evidence-Based Review', *F1000Research*, 5.632: 1–57, https://doi.org/10.12688/F1000RESEARCH.8460.3

Van der Laan, J.M. 2016. *Narratives of Technology*. (New York: Palgrave Macmillan), https://doi.org/10.1057/978-1-137-43706-8

Van Noorden, Richard. 2020. 'Hundreds of Scientists Have Peer-Reviewed for Predatory Journals', *Nature*: 1–4, https://doi.org/10.1038/d41586-020-00709-x

'What is artificial intelligence?'. 2023. *IBM*, https://www.ibm.com/topics/artificial-intelligence

'What is a chatbot?'. 2023. *IBM* https://www.ibm.com/topics/chatbots#:~:text=A%20chatbot%20is%20a%20computer,to%20them%2C%20simulating%20human%20conversation.

2. Open Science, Open Data
The 'Open' Movement in Scholarly Publishing

Predatory journals are now a global challenge in academic journal publishing. For example, Xia and colleagues (2015) documented that junior researchers from Asia and Africa are among those who have fallen prey to predatory journals. Furthermore, Omobowale and others (2014) revealed that the Nigerian government's requirement for researchers to publish in international journals (i.e., Western and English journals) and the emphasis on quantity of publications (not quality) created the condition for Nigerian researchers to seek publication opportunities in predatory journals. Also, in Turkey, Demir (2018) reported that academic incentives for quantity of publications and researchers' fear of job loss, among other reasons, are what drive some Turkish researchers to submit their work to predatory journals. Perhaps another reason why some Turkish researchers pursue predatory journals is because, as Tutuncu and others (2022) reported, Turkish national journals tend to have an insider bias (about 30% of their publications), making researchers without coauthors in the core networks of journal editors at a disadvantage. Additionally, Shehata and Elgllab (2018) found that the reason some Arab researchers published in predatory journals was because of the ease and speed of publishing their work, compared to traditional academic journals. Moreover, Wallace and Perri (2018) concluded that, based on a sample of 1,284 articles that were included in the Research Papers in Economics archive and published in journals included in Beall's list, in the field of economics, some of the researchers in about ninety countries had published articles in journals that Beall's list characterized as predatory. Iran, the United States, Nigeria, Turkey, and Malaysia were listed as among the top five countries.[1] Overall, there are many cases of non-Western researchers in peripheral[2] nations (Wallerstein 1991) publishing their research in predatory journals.

Although the research on predatory publishing experiences often emphasizes non-Western researchers, the reference to the US above reveals that predatory journals are also a challenge among researchers in central nations. Interestingly, some Western researchers from central nations submit their work to predatory journals to inflate their CVs with the motivation to get hired, tenured, and/or promoted. For example, Pond and colleagues (2019) documented that among the forty applicants for a faculty position (i.e., tenure-track Assistant Professor position that requires a PhD) in a pharmacy department in the US, nine (or 22.5% of) applicants had published half or more of their publications in journals identified on Beall's List. In another study, Pyne (2017) reported that the majority of faculty researchers at a small business school in Canada had published their work in predatory journals.

As the literature (e.g., Wallace and Perri 2018; Xia and others 2015) shows, researchers from at least ninety countries, including those from Western cultures such as the US, have submitted their work to journals labeled as predatory. Moreover, the situation is even more challenging because many researchers in the world have also reviewed manuscripts for predatory journals, even while being fully aware that these journals were labeled as predatory (Van Noorden 2020). While some predatory journals do have peer-review processes, their practice is questionable in that they often do not invite reviewers who are the most qualified to review the manuscripts and they allow a very short turnaround window for willing reviewers, which in turn generate minimal revision suggestions for authors to address, compromising the traditional rigor of journal peer review, as discussed in Chapter 1. Also, additional challenges exist in peripheral nations, in that non-Western researchers

---

1 As we have acknowledged elsewhere in this book, Beall's list was far from perfect. However, as some of the literature discussed in this chapter makes clear, some researchers have used it as an authoritative source of identifying predatory journals.
2 In this chapter we use Wallerstein's (1991) terms 'center' and 'periphery', from his world systems theory, to express the ways in which nations participate in the world economy, based on their level of development. Other scholars have applied these terms similarly when discussing the global politics of scholarly publishing (e.g., Koerber and others 2020; Lillis and Curry 2010).

in these nations are pressured to publish their work in international journals without access to the cultural capital that Western researchers have (Koerber and Graham 2017).

How is the 'open' movement in scholarly publishing relevant to this growing problem? In the previous chapter, we explored the complex relationship that exists between open access and predatory publishing. In this chapter, we continue this exploration, and extend it to include open science. As examined in the previous chapter, open access publishing emerged in the 1990s, taking advantage of digital publication modes to overcome the economic barriers that were preventing many people and institutions across the globe from having access to subscription-only journals. Open science shares the word 'open' and relates in some ways to open access, but with a focus on access to the data behind the research, not just the published research itself. Specifically, open science has been defined as 'the process of making the content and process of producing evidence and claims transparent and accessible to others' (Munafò and others 2017: 5). This definition emphasizes transparency and accessibility as two principles of sharing research content and process that, together, lead to authors making scientific claims with evidence. Moreover, open science has also been defined as science that is practiced with transparency and integrity, and with an emphasis on collaboration and inclusion (Freiling and others 2021).

Even though the terms open science and open access are sometimes used interchangeably, they are two distinct movements. Open access refers to moving the articles beyond paywalls and publishing books and articles in a public fashion so that the research findings can be accessible openly, benefiting researchers as well as the public. In traditional non-open access publishing, the costs of academic publishing are to be borne by the readers and/or their institutions. In open access publishing, the costs by publishers are shifted to the researchers and/or their research funders, or shared among research institutions and other actors. While making the articles and the research findings openly available to the research community and the public has some clear benefits, open access does not address public access to the data behind the findings, thus making it a distinct practice from the core principles advocated by the open science movement.

As we demonstrate in this chapter, 'openness' has a complex relationship with predatory publishing. Although it is often touted as a solution to various problems in scholarly publishing, 'openness' can also create new problems, especially when we consider this complex situation from a global perspective. The chapter begins with an introduction to the basic concepts of open science, including the rationale espoused by its advocates as well as the key principles that readers across the disciplines need to understand about open science. Next, we present a subset of our interview data in which participants offer valuable first-hand insights into the complex relationships that exist among open access, open science, and predatory journals.[3]

A Closer Look at Open Science Principles

Why are the principles of transparency, accessibility, integrity, collaboration, and inclusion important? Are these principles not already upheld in scientific research? Although some would argue that science has been 'open', in principle, since the seventeenth century ('Open Science for the 21st Century' 2020), the recent emphasis on open science is often traced to psychology, as a response to what is now known as the 'replication crisis' (Dienlin and others 2021; Fox and others 2021; Pratt and others 2020). More specifically, in experimental psychology, critics have noticed recently that several landmark studies could not be replicated with similar results by other researchers after the studies had been published (O'Boyle and others 2017; Simmons and others 2011). These incidents called into question the integrity of the published studies, the quality of the research findings, and hence the overall credibility of the scientific enterprise. Given these concerns, advocates for open science began calling for reproducibility, replicability, and generalizability of published research (Dienlin and others 2021) as well

---

[3] Coding to support this chapter's analysis was conducted in an early phase of the project, at a time when the transcripts had not yet been de-identified. Thus, we have not provided a published dataset specific to this chapter. However, readers may access the published dataset for chapter 7, available at https://doi.org/10.18738/T8/3RZARP. This published dataset (see "NVivo file paradox theory 12.26.22.nvp") includes the full text of interview transcripts, de-identified to protect participants' anonymity, although the coding evident in this file was conducted at a later phase of the project.

as transparency and accountability by the researchers (Chauvette and others 2019). These conversations around open science have drawn attention to the research practices that non-transparent and non-accountable researchers have engaged in to compromise reproducibility, replicability, and generalizability of their work.

In a survey to study the prevalence of questionable research practices, Bakker and others (2021: 722) operationalized the practices that may have led to the 'replication crisis' as the following:

1. Collecting more data for a study after first inspecting whether the results are statistically significant.
2. Filling in missing data points without reporting that those data were imputed, e.g., through multiple imputation, mean substitution, etc.
3. Excluding data points, such as outliers, after first checking the impact on statistical significance.
4. Not reporting studies or key variables that failed to reach statistical significance (e.g., $p \leq .05$).
5. Reporting a set of results as the complete set of analyses when other analyses were also conducted but these are not reported.
6. Reporting an unexpected finding or a result from exploratory analysis as having been predicted from the start.
7. Adopting another type of statistical analysis after the analysis initially chosen failed to reach statistical significance. For instance, using OLS instead of logit.
8. Adding or dropping covariates in order to reach statistical significance (e.g., $p \leq .05$) on a key variable.
9. Rounding off a p-value to meet a pre-specified threshold (e.g., reporting $p = .054$ as $p = .05$).[4]

They concluded in the study that many researchers reported having engaged in one or more of these practices, and those who were surveyed

---

4   As reported in Bakker and others (2021), Table 1: https://doi.org/10.1093/JOC/JQAB031

also believe that while these practices are generally rejected in the scientific community, the practices are prevalent.

Although the recent call for open science is usually traced to psychology, it has echoed across the disciplines. For example, in the field of communication, Dienlin and others (2021) proposed seven recommendations as open science practices that could reduce and/or prevent questionable research practices. Firstly, they suggested publishing research materials, data, and code openly to share with the research community. Secondly, they proposed preregistering studies before the actual research is conducted and submitting registered reports after research completion. Thirdly, they recommended conducting replications of previous studies. Fourthly, they advocated for collaboration with other researchers to increase transparency and early detection of errors. Fifthly, they encourage fostering open science skills as a 'de facto approach' (p. 9) so researchers become familiar and proficient with these practices. Sixthly, they argued for implementing guidelines to demonstrate to the greater research community how to achieve transparency and openness. Finally, they believe in the importance of journal editors incentivizing open science practices to increase the uptake of open science by researchers. Dienlen and others concluded their recommendations with the argument that 'The most important reason to adopt open science practices, however, is epistemic' (p. 20). In other words, they believe that these practices should be the key methods to create knowledge, the main components of the philosophy of knowledge, and the theory of what constitutes scientific knowledge. In the next section, we discuss three of the open science practices from Dienlen and colleagues' discussion that we see as particularly relevant to the issue of predatory publishing: preregistration, open data sharing, and open peer review.

According to open science advocates, open science practices need to be carried out during various points in the research process. For example, preregistration should take place before data collection, whereas open data sharing and open peer review could take place during peer review and after publication. We elaborate on these three practices with more details below.

Preregistration

Among the seven recommendations by Dienlin and others (2021), the practice of preregistration especially needs explanation, as this practice is not always immediately clear to some researchers. Preregistration refers to the official documentation and registry of the hypotheses to be tested, the design of the study, and the plan for data analysis before the data is collected and analyzed (Nosek and others 2018). Preregistration also involves having the documented research plan submitted as a manuscript for peer review, with an introduction to the topic, methodological steps, predetermined sample size from power analyses, as well as any previous results from a pilot study (Dienlin and others 2021).

Once the study is preregistered with a journal, the reviewers and editor can compare the final manuscript with the preregistered study plan to determine if the researchers engaged in any questionable research practices, such as those explicated by Bakker and others (2021). Nosek and others (2015) also explain that preregistration can (a) help others to discover research (published and unpublished) when it is entered into a public registry, and (b) verify the difference between confirmatory and exploratory research, also known as 'hypothesis-testing versus hypothesis-generating research' (p. 3). At the heart of preregistration is the rationale of having a gatekeeping mechanism to prevent questionable research practices that escape the peer-review process, leading to more replication crises after publications.

Furthermore, through the practice of preregistration, studies with sound methodology which turn out to have null results should not be rejected simply because they do not reach statistical significance. Supporters of open science principles in general, and preregistration specifically, argue that registering a study with a journal and conducting methodologically sound research will help address the replication crisis by forcing journals and editors to look at the quality of the science, rather than the statistical significance of the results (Fraser and others 2018). To that end, many believe that open science practices such as preregistration can help address the issue of predatory publishing by reducing the chances that authors will feel pressured to submit to sub-par journals as a way to put research without statistical significance into circulation.

Open Data Sharing

The second practice is that of open data sharing (Morey and others 2015). By openly sharing research data along with a manuscript submitted to a journal, the researchers allow future readers to re-examine the reported findings using the associated dataset, thus further increasing the transparency of the data analysis leading to the findings. Pusic (2014) contends that data sharing can facilitate the re-analysis of open data that could allow new conclusions and interpretations not initially included in the original manuscript. Similarly, Chauvette and others (2019) add that data sharing can help future readers build upon original data, offer critiques of the reported data analysis, validate research findings, and test new and emerging theories. In other words, collaboration with and inclusion of future readers in the research process are made possible through open data sharing.

Furthermore, Morey and others (2015) take open data sharing to the next level by suggesting that researchers can share their research data with the reviewers during the review process. This level of openness allows reviewers the opportunity to interrogate the research and verify the findings during the peer-review process to assess the integrity, rigor, and quality of the submitted research manuscript. In other words, as early as the peer-review process, the practice of data sharing can serve as another gatekeeping mechanism to filter out research findings with questionable practices. McGrath and Nilsonne (2018) maintain that open data sharing can serve three main purposes: enabling critical scrutiny (by both the reviewers and future readers), facilitating cumulative science (by allowing future readers to add to the original dataset for analyses of an even bigger dataset), and allowing re-use of data (by making the data available permanently). While the connection between open data and predatory publishing may not be as clear cut as the other components of open science explored in this chapter, it can be argued that making data sets open protects against various forms of research fraud by allowing readers to directly assess the quality of the research, without relying exclusively on the opinions of blind peer reviewers to ensure research quality.

Open Peer Review

The practice of peer review before an article is published dates back to 1665 (Longley Arthur and Hearn 2021). The traditional form of peer review is double blind (meaning both the authors and the reviewers are anonymous to each other) for two reasons. Firstly, if the reviewers do not know the authors, the reviewers can provide the most rigorous reviews based solely on the content of the manuscript, without being biased by any prior knowledge of the reputation of the authors and/or relationships with the authors. Secondly, the identity of the reviewers will be unknown to the authors, allowing the reviewers to provide the most honest reviews, without concerns about any possible backlash. Therefore, double-blind peer review was designed to be a rigorous method of assessing the legitimacy of ideas being presented in a research manuscript and providing suggestions for improvement to the manuscript before it is formally printed and disseminated to the broader research community (Moed and others 1985). As Pratt and others (2020) argued, 'Journals are central gatekeepers to the field and, of course, have the responsibility to keep poorly conducted research from being published' (p. 12).

However, double-blind peer review as a practice has also received criticisms, such as questions about the selection of reviewers, including their credibility and accountability. The blind nature of traditional peer review can be a problem when some reviewers provide weak, unfair, harsh, and/or careless reviews because they know that their identities will not be known to anyone other than the editor (Ferguson and others 2014). Furthermore, traditional peer review operates much like a 'black box' that occurs behind closed doors. Readers have trusted double-blind peer review for many centuries as the gold standard that ensures the quality of scientific knowledge. However, most of the time, in the way peer review traditionally operates, the readers of a scientific article must simply trust on blind faith that reviews are taking place. In response, some advocates for open science principles also propose the practice of open peer review.

For example, open review has been referred to as 'a major pillar of Open Science' (Ross-Hellauer 2017: 1). As its name suggests, open review refers to practicing openness and transparency during the peer review process. Nosek and Bar-Anan (2012) explain that the goal of open review is to make the evaluation and assessment of research transparent and public rather than closed and private. According to Fox and others (2021), what constitutes open peer review varies from one advocate to another in the open science movement, but in general there are four layers: open identities, open reports, open prereview, and open final-version commenting.

Firstly, the practice of open identities allows authors and reviewers to be openly known to each other. Moreover, peer reviews are published together with the articles reviewed, thus ensuring fairness and collegiality. Secondly, the practice of open reports entails recognizing good reviewers, helping them earn recognition for their fair and collegial critique, and potentially even garner citations. The practice of open reports could provide the missing incentives for reviewers to provide more thorough reviews. Thirdly, open prereview leverages the 'wisdom of the crowd' through a Yelp-like platform to allow any reader to review a manuscript before publication. The cumulative score given to a manuscript can be openly displayed to the public on the crowd-sourcing platform. Fourthly, open final-version commenting allows the public, including researchers, readers, citizen scientists, and others to comment on published manuscripts. Given its open nature, the authors of the articles are expected to respond to the comments and engage with the public in open communication about science even long after the manuscript is published. All the layers of open peer review could be powerful tools to help combat predatory publishing, especially since one of the primary issues surrounding predatory journals is a *lack* of peer review of any sort.

Through removing the review process from the 'black box' of blind or double-blind reviews, open peer reviews could potentially help combat predatory publishing in two main ways. Firstly, researchers who are considering submitting to a specific journal could examine some of their published articles and the accompanying reviews to confirm whether sufficiently rigorous reviews were being conducted. Secondly, and perhaps more importantly, opening the review process may remove some of the fear and anxiety junior researchers feel when they consider submitting their work to an academic journal. As discussed in Chapter 3, one reason researchers may turn to predatory journals is because they are afraid of the review process. It could be argued that if the process and results of peer review were more transparent, some of that fear would be removed, and authors might be less likely to turn to predatory journals out of fear of being harshly judged by their peers during the review process.

Given these arguments, open science principles are often touted as an antidote to the questionable research practices and the 'replication crisis' advocates seek to address. However, as explored in the next section, our interview participants' insights into the concept of openness in scholarly publishing also suggest some of the limitations that we may face in implementing open research practices.

Open Science, Open Access, and Predatory Publishing: A Complex Relationship

With these various meanings of 'openness' in scholarly publishing as a backdrop, in this section we explore how some of our interview participants understand open access, open science, and how these concepts relate to predatory publishing in their experiences. The stories our participants tell about falling victim to predatory journals, along with their lack of awareness of open science, misunderstanding of open science, and confusion about the relationship between open science and open access, further illustrate the complexity of this situation.

Stories of Falling Prey to Predatory Journals: The Complexity of 'Open'

As discussed earlier in this chapter, scientific openness in the open science movement mainly referred to the open sharing of research data, supporting analytic code, and materials such as, for example, survey items, stimulus materials, and experiment programs. It does not include publishing articles via an open access route. In fact, the Center for Open Science featured a blog post in 2020 arguing that open science and open access are in conflict with each other: Open access incentivizes publishing as much content as possible, regardless of quality, because the publisher stands to gain financially through article processing charges (Mellor and others 2020). Open science, by contrast, aims to increase the quality of published research by making the data behind a publication fully accessible to readers. In an argument that may seem counter-intuitive, the authors then present preprints as a possible solution:

> With preprinting, publishing is a relatively trivial act. Authors need only meet modest moderation criteria for their preferred preprint service. When most anything can be published, publication recedes as the key incentive. What takes its place? Evaluation. Journals have historically confounded publication with evaluation. If the paper meets the evaluation criteria, then it is published. Therefore, publication is the act that signals credibility for authors' work and evaluation — peer review — is an impediment to achieving that reward.
>
> Preprinting separates publication from evaluation. Publication itself no longer signals credibility. If publication doesn't signal credibility, then peer review is no longer a barrier for authors to overcome to get the reward of publication. Peer review becomes a service authors need to achieve credibility. (Mellor and others 2020: 5–6)

As this example makes clear, the concept of openness in scholarly publishing is more complex than it might first appear. However, some of the major aspirations for openness in the academic community are clear: to address the 'replication crisis' and a myriad of related problems that are perceived in scholarly publishing today.

In our interviews with stakeholders in scholarly publishing, openness was sometimes mentioned as an antidote to predatory publishing. For example, some interviewees observed that predatory publishing has been able to thrive because much of academic publishing occurs in a black box, behind closed doors, during the blind peer-review process. These practices allow predatory publishing to thrive because they make it possible for a journal to broadly advertise itself as a quality research outlet that practices double-blind peer review but then to publish articles without actually putting them through the peer-review process. Open access also has a complicated relationship with predatory publishing. Over the years, some have argued that predatory publishing exists because of open access publishing (Beall 2012), and as a result, to some extent, open access journals have been demonized and wrongly understood as predatory just because they charge authors a publication fee (Beall 2013).

Through the perspectives of our interviewees, we gained some valuable insights into these complex relationships between open science, open access, and predatory publishing and how these relationships play out in the daily realities of stakeholders in scholarly publishing. As revealed through the insights of several participants, the unethical and unprofessional methods, deceptive means and objectives of predatory journals have been prejudicial to the integrity of academic journal publishing. For example, when asked if he had personal experiences with predatory journals, a participant in Southeast Asia revealed,

> I had, actually. I was the coauthor. My colleague put my name [on the paper...] Suddenly I saw my name is there [in name of the predatory journal]. And when I asked my colleague – Why you sent it? – And she paid [the APC...] I said – Why you're doing this? You should ask me first step. (P39)[5]

The participant actually was aware of predatory journals. However, he became a victim due to the choice of his coauthor. In other words, predatory journals can pose a challenge even to those who are aware of the phenomenon. A communication researcher from South America recounted a particularly compelling example:

> I have one sad story [...] It was four years ago [...a colleague] she was an assistant professor [...] And she had this very good article that somehow, she thought she had submitted it to the International Journal of Communication, IJOC [...] She didn't tell anyone. We only learn after the fact. Again, junior professor, inexperienced. She [said], 'I have my article. I received a special call [...] It's going to be [...]' And the name of the predatory journal, I don't remember exactly the name. But it was very similar to the IJOC [...] So she submitted her article and the article was published next month [...Then] they asked her to pay processing fees, because it was open access and whatnot [...] At the time I was her tutor. So she said, 'Hey, I received this thing, but it's open access. So I understand being open access, processing fees.' And I said, 'Yeah, I know. It's expensive. So what's the name of the journal?' 'It's the IJOC.' And I said, 'IJOC is open access [but] it doesn't charge [...] So that's when she showed me the journal and I said, 'This is not the IJOC' [...] So of course, a big shock to her [...] she lost the manuscript. Because then she asks the journal to [retract] the article, and of course they didn't

---

5 Our Texas Data Repository Dataverse includes a table showing participant demographic information. See https://doi.org/10.18738/T8/QUBMLI ("Participant Occupation and Regional Demographics Table"). All quotations from interviews are reported without correction of grammatical errors or other irregularities. Some quotes were abbreviated using [...] to achieve clarity of the original message.

do that [...] because it looks prestigious to have someone from a decent school publish in there. And she [didn't] know where to turn to. (P47)

This story demonstrates that predatory journals can confuse seemingly informed researchers, even in academic departments where colleagues have a greater understanding of predatory journals. It signals to us not to underestimate the scope of the ethical problems posed by the deceptive practices of predatory journals. It also demonstrates that in the event an author refuses to pay, the predatory journal still gains a paper to make their journal look more 'gray' and/or legitimate.

Falling prey to predatory journals was also reported by STEM researchers we interviewed. For example, an environmental chemistry researcher in East Asia commented on his experience as a master's student: 'I submitted [my paper...] The following morning, I [got] an email saying my paper has been accepted. No review, comments, nothing and I was now asked to pay [...] at that time it was US$150' (P10). This was his very first journal submission, so he did not question the quick acceptance notice and the request for payment. He continued, 'The funny thing is the paper I had coauthored with some senior researchers, and they never said anything, they just gave me the $150 and I paid.' Surprisingly, the quick acceptance and payment request did not raise questions with his senior collaborators, and they complied with making the payment.

The same participant went on to narrate an experience during his PhD training: 'My supervisor [...] had a list of journals that he recommended for us to publish. So when I submitted, I waited [...] for a month, then came the reviewer comments from [...] three different reviewers commenting on the work.' What the participant received was a surprise to him, as he said, 'This is totally different to what I had experienced [...] I started doing more research with what was really going on [...] Then I saw the journal that I had published was mentioned on Beall's list.' The participant concluded his story, 'I didn't know that it was predatory journal until I tried to publish my first work as a PhD candidate. That's when I realized — Oh, I submitted my first paper [to] a predatory journal!' This story demonstrates how junior researchers, especially graduate students, are prone to falling prey to predatory journals. They do not have knowledge and experience to recognize that receiving no reviews is unusual, even when coauthoring with senior researchers.

These experiences demonstrate some of the ways in which predatory journals can undermine the ethics and integrity of the academic journal publishing enterprise.

As these stories make clear, researchers do fall prey to predatory journals. So how can these incidents be explained? Our data tell us three reasons, which collectively suggest the confusion and conflation between open science and open access. Firstly, we observed that there is a lack of awareness of open science in the research community. For example, a participant in East Asia admitted, 'I don't have a very clear definitions about what the open science movement's about' (P46). Another participant in Southeast Asia also stated, 'I'm actually not very familiar with it' (P41). A noticeable portion of our interview participants directly stated that they did not know or know much about open science. This finding from our data resonates with Bakker and others (2021), when they reported that many researchers in their study expressed being unfamiliar with what constitutes open science practices.

Furthermore, a librarian in South Asia observed that there is a lack of awareness of open science outside of the Western world: '[E]xcept a few countries in Europe and US, this issue of open science has not been very well discussed [...] In [my country], there is few discussion, but we never able to have any kind of forum which promote open science' (P17). Also, a participant in North America, who is the editor of a highly reputable journal, suggested that open science may not be relevant to non-STEM disciplines, such as social sciences and humanities: 'I think it's [open science] more on the hard sciences' (P33). We understand that open science advocates are working to raise awareness and establish relevance. It may simply be a matter of time before the research community becomes aware of open science and recognizes its relevance. Yet, even for those that had heard of it, confusion about open science is common.

Secondly, among those who have heard of the open science movement, we observed confusion about the distinction between open science and open access. Although open science and open access are distinct by definition, we observed that the two movements are often collapsed in the way participants talked about them. For example, a participant in Western Europe explained, 'So open science would include [...] preregistrations, publishing materials openly, but also publishing the papers with unrestricted access' (P38). Unrestricted or open access publishing is discussed because participants want their peers to be able to read and cite their work easily. For example, a publishing professional in North America observed, 'I think most people who talk about open access also extend it to other kinds of open science, including data, as a research output' (P25). A journal editor in Western Europe commented, 'The ultimate goal would be open science, and open access is [...an] important part of open science, where open science means, really, open communication, including communicating your results' (P36). In these examples, we observed that participants naturally conflate open science and open access. But open access does not address the replication crisis, which is a key motivation behind open science.

Thirdly, participants also discussed their confusion surrounding open science. For example, a participant in North America shared, '[S]omeone in my field [...] championing open science [...] used the term preregistering [...] left me really baffled' (P37). This excerpt suggests that key terms in open science, such as preregistering, can be confusing for the target audience. He continued, '[...] these are just not things in my vernacular.' This finding resonates with Bakker and others (2021), as they reported that 'when discussing preregistration, as many as 26% (71/268) indicate that they or their colleagues were unfamiliar with the concept' (p. 730).

While open science advocates may argue for the need to further educate the target audience, our research suggests this may be an uphill battle. This is because many readers may already have a different understanding of key words such as 'preregister'. As one participant revealed, 'To me preregistering means like registering for a conference' (P37). Certain terminologies within open science may impede its diffusion given how certain key words such 'preregister' are not commonly used as intended by open science advocates, and this lack of understanding presents a ripe opportunity for predatory journals to exploit researchers by similarly offering opportunities to preregister manuscripts. Moreover, this participant hints at some perceived overlaps and confusion about the relationship between open science and open access, which are some of the main concerns raised in this chapter.

On a related note, when we asked participants about the open science movement, which includes a push for more preprint publications, much of the discussion surrounding these repositories of unreviewed scholarly manuscripts centered on the challenges preprints may introduce to the scholarly knowledge production world, rather than its benefits. A challenge one participant voiced was that preprints were being used by authors as a way to avoid lengthy peer review processes (P22). Another perspective was the difficulty faced by indexing services about how to track publications as they are posted on preprint servers, given DOIs, submitted to journals, peer reviewed, and then potentially published in a journal after rounds of revision (P22). However, the bulk of participants who viewed preprints as a potential challenge to the knowledge production process were concerned with the notion that 'people don't differentiate between peer-reviewed publications and what appears on preprint service, you know?' (P23). Due to general audiences potentially not understanding the importance of peer review, there was a fear that reliance on science in preprints 'could lead to bad decisions being made' (P11), such as in the early days of the COVID-19 pandemic, when virus origin theories, posted on preprint servers, made their way into mainstream media outlets (P20). However, an interesting nuance to the discussion surrounding preprints was the speculation that preprints might be a solution to predatory journals,

> [...] because you can get your data out there and you can cite that in your grant requests or whatever else you need. It's transparent but it's not peer-reviewed and it's enduring unlike a predatory journal that might disappear tomorrow. At least you know the preprint server will be enduring. (P28)

This idea was expounded by another participant who noted that 'You can't say on the one hand that preprints are great, and the other hand say that everything in the predatory journals is trash' (P15) because from their perspective, if peer review was held as the gold standard for ensuring quality, what was the actual difference between predatory journals and preprint servers? From this perspective, preprints exemplify the paradox facing academic researchers in the modern publishing environment — do they serve the purpose of disseminating scientific knowledge in a timely manner, or do they threaten the credibility of scientific research by removing the gatekeeping function of peer review?

Conclusion

This chapter first discussed what constitutes open science and the origin of the open science movement as a response to the 'replication crisis' in psychology. Secondly, we explained three important open science practices, namely preregistration, open data sharing, and open peer review. Thirdly, we provided evidence to show that it may be easy for Western researchers to minimize the threat of predatory journals in the global context, but that threat is real. Specifically, we presented evidence of the prevalence of predatory journals in both the Western and peripheral nations through a literature review, as well as evidence from our interviews of how the push for open science can accidentally help predatory journals to thrive when many researchers around the world conflate open science and open access. When considered in this global context, rather than exclusively from a Western perspective, the limitations of seeing open science as an antidote to predatory publishing become clearer. For those scholars who do not have access to the infrastructure that makes data sharing possible, or who do not have adequate knowledge of open access, open science, and the relationships between them, open science does not necessarily serve as the remedy to predatory publishing that some Western scholars proclaim it to be. Through the stories of our participants, we see that the threat posed by predatory journals has real-world impact on scholars across the globe and that open science may not always be the foolproof antidote.

What are the implications for open science? Firstly, even if open science advocates can articulate how it is different from open access, many of the systemic conditions that led to the predatory journal problems remain. For example, our research (as reported here and emphasized in other chapters of this volume) revealed a lack of awareness, pressure to publish, and most importantly, global disparities related to these factors. Thus, open science advocates would be wise to consider how the open science movement can thrive and succeed under the same set of conditions that has made open access an easy victim of predatory journals. They must be acutely mindful of these global structures that have given rise to predatory journals. One possible means of safeguarding open science is to follow the suggestions set forth by the International Science Council in 2020. In their working paper, they lay out an argument for open science that positions practices of openness as necessary for the public good, while simultaneously addressing challenges related to equitable access to information, especially in terms of national and institutional abilities to pay for their researchers to access global information repositories that are housed behind paywalls ('Open Science for the 21st Century' 2020).

Secondly, the notion of openness advocated by the open access movement has been used and abused as a deceptive tool by predatory journals. Furthermore, some participants in our study also talked about open science and open access as related or synonymous. Given this confusion, open science advocates should be actively concerned about the possibility of open science becoming victimized by predatory journals in due time, if nothing intentional is done to preemptively safeguard the open science movement. One possible solution could be an open science training program adaptable to the socio-cultural-political complexity of central and peripheral nations. However, as shown in Chapter 6 of this volume, there are numerous freely accessible information repositories aimed at increasing knowledge related to scholarly publishing ethics, open access, and open science — yet they are largely underutilized. Alternatively, if open science policies are adopted at the national or institutional levels, the cultural shift toward and knowledge of open science practices may gain more momentum than if left up to individual researchers or disciplines.

Thirdly, the literature review suggests that some researchers knowingly publish in predatory journals in order to inflate their CV. Given this phenomenon, we argue that this culture of deception may have always been there. Predatory journals simply provide another venue for it to manifest. If the latter is the case, the open science practices of preregistration, open data sharing, etc., will only address the symptoms, but not the root cause of the replication crisis. However, for authors who are guided by ethical principles, open science practices will assist in distinguishing between publications that were produced following accepted scientific processes and those that were not. Furthermore, as more journals move toward adopting open science principles and requiring authors to submit their data for review alongside their manuscripts, it may become more difficult for deceptive practices to make their way into the scientific record.

Fourthly, we ('we' in the broadest sense to reflect those of us in the academy) need to stop assuming a media-literate body of researchers. Given the proliferation of predatory journals, and the lack of awareness of such journals documented in our interviews, there will be greater numbers of graduate students who do not understand quality versus suspect research, and who do not know how to adequately vet information they find. How is open science addressing this emerging trend? While students who work with prominent researchers receive informal mentoring that would protect them from predatory journals, such mentoring/education is too often assumed and/or implicit. Our fear is that when we encourage informal guidance, we assume it is happening. The gravity of this concern necessitates that we encourage more formal discussion of this topic in an explicit fashion for graduate students through coursework, education of junior faculty through mentorships, annual reviews, and the like. Mentors, along with an overall institutional culture that encourages and supports ethical and open research practices can help address this issue, as is shown in Chapter 5 of this volume.

Fifthly, and related to our last point above, open science advocates should note that the time it takes for most researchers to publish in traditional journals creates graduation and career barriers for junior researchers, especially those in the peripheral nations. If open science is to add additional layers to the publication process in a fashion that would further complicate the publication timeline, we worry the movement will not receive much support, especially among the next generation of researchers, who will likely experience such practices as barriers to their participation in the research community. Open science advocates would be wise to ask: Who are we pushing out by upholding certain open science standards, especially those among the next generation of researchers? Along these lines, we discovered during the course of this project exactly how time consuming it can be to implement open science principles. When we decided to make our qualitative dataset available in the Texas Data Repository, we first had to comb through all forty-eight transcripts to remove any information that could potentially lead a participant to be identified. This was not a simple matter of using a search and replace command, but rather, required line-by-line reading of each transcript to remove any text that could possibly have this result.

Our team was able to complete this task because we had grant support to pay a research assistant to do the work, but if we had been operating with fewer resources, it would not have been possible to complete this work, and thus, we would not have been able to implement open science principles for this project.

Our last concern is that reviewers, editors, or readers might begin using open science practices such as preregistration and open data sharing as heuristics for high quality. In other words, the culture surrounding open science may begin to suggest that for research to be considered high quality, it must be open, and that data must be made available for public scrutiny. If so, what are the implications for research data that cannot be made available, due to the socio-political-cultural complexity of certain peripheral nations? To what degree would such a practice create a wider gap between the Western (central-nation) and non-Western (peripheral-nation) researchers?

On this note, we would like to end the chapter with a quote from Markowitz and others (2021), 'The absence of open science does not guarantee bad science, nor its mere presence guarantee good science' (p. 758). Although sharing materials can be considered a necessary condition for high quality, it is not a sufficient one. This quote is important as we consider what the 'quality' of scientific research is: the topic of the next chapter.

Key Takeaways

- The recent emphasis on open science has been a response to the 'replication' crisis, first examined in psychology, when critics noted that several seminal studies in experimental psychology could not be replicated.
- The key components of open science are reproducibility, replicability, and generalizability of published research.
- Three open science practices that can help combat predatory publishing are preregistration, open data sharing, and open peer review.
- The practice of preregistration refers to the official documentation and registry of the hypotheses for testing, the design of the study, and the plan for data analysis before the data is collected and analyzed.
- Open data sharing is the practice of sharing research data along with a manuscript submitted to a journal, thus allowing future readers to re-examine the data, increasing the transparency of the study, and encouraging replication.
- Open peer review refers to practicing openness and transparency during the peer-review process, which could take place in four layers: open identities, open reports, open prereview, and open final-version commenting (Fox and others 2021).
- Despite being separate movements, there is misunderstanding and confusion between the principles of open science and open access.

Discussion Questions

1. Why are the principles of transparency, accessibility, integrity, collaboration, and inclusion important?

2. Are these principles not already upheld in scientific research?

3. What might be factors that compel researchers not to be transparent or accountable about the methods and results of their work? (NB: some of the ideas that may come up in discussions could be linked to Chapter 3 of this volume and the themes that emerge as 'challenges to quality'.)

4. What might be some barriers to researchers adopting preregistration as a regular practice in their work?

5. What are some potential challenges of open data sharing that may make some researchers feel the practice is not applicable to their work? (NB: We're specifically thinking about qualitative researchers and their datasets — through our experience with making our data set open, we discovered a range of challenges qualitative researchers face, as opposed to quantitative researchers and their associated types of data.)

Activities

Activity One: Preregistration Exercise

1. Have the class search for journals in their field that have options for preregistration. Compile the list and share with faculty and graduate students to encourage participation in study preregistration.

2. Have students seek out faculty (they could simply ask their advisors or mentors in the department) and interview/survey them about preregistration and whether they have used it or would consider using it. If the class finds that most faculty in their program/department/college do not use (or have never heard of) preregistration, the class could present the topic at a faculty brownbag or another similar venue (and they can share their list of journals that offer preregistration in their field).

Activity Two: Open Data Sharing in Qualitative Research

This activity is intended to help junior researchers examine the complexities of implementing open data sharing with qualitative research. This could be a good activity for a qualitative methodology or data analysis class. Our team gave a presentation on the challenges of making a qualitative data set open. You may view the slides online.[6] Alternatively, have the class use a qualitative data set they are familiar with, and base the following discussion questions on their dataset:

- Why should we care about open science in the context of qualitative research?
- How do we implement open science principles in qualitative research?
- What challenges will we face in implementing open science for qualitative research?

---

6   https://doi.org/10.11647/OBP.0364#resources

2. Open Science, Open Data

- Discuss the benefits and complications of open data and qualitative research (the resource linked above lists some of them and includes citations).
- Below is an image of the attributes we collected from participants, and a snippet of interview transcript that had some identifying information that had to be removed to protect the identity of the participant.
- Using the images below as a starting place, have the class discuss the challenges of ensuring participant confidentiality, specifically in terms of the 'complications' offered by the resource slides linked in the activity introduction.

Case Classifications		
Name	Created on	
Person	4/14/2020 9:07 AM	
Name		Type
Name		Text
Sex		Text
Age Group		Text
Occupation		Text
Country of Birth		Text
job title		Text
current employer		Text
area of specialization		Text
years in current position		Text
highest academic degree		Text
institution awarding highest degree		Text
ethnicity		Text
country of current residence		Text

Fig. 2.1 STEPP Research Team, *Case Classifications Example* (2020). © STEPP Research Team

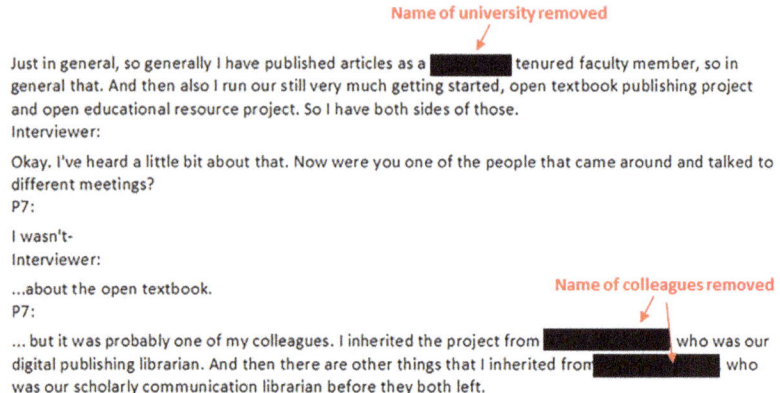

Fig. 2.2 STEPP Research Team, *Transcript Deidentification Example* (2020). © STEPP Research Team

Activity Three: Worst-Case Scenario: Predatory Journals Hijacking Open Science Principles

Imagine this scenario: You are a researcher looking for a journal to publish your latest manuscript. You find a perfect one — and they are asking for the dataset to be submitted as well, as an indicator of adherence to principles of open science. You agree and submit the manuscript along with the dataset. Months later, you see a published article that seems to be using data identical to yours... yet you have not heard anything from the journal about acceptance or revisions. You attempt to reach out to the journal and receive no response. You reach out to the author of the manuscript you suspect is using your data set, asking them where they gathered their data. They reply that they purchased it from a database of raw data, supplied by the journal. You now suspect that the journal stole your data and sold it to another researcher.

- What can you do?
- Is this a potentially realistic scenario?
- What measures could authors take to ensure something like this could not happen?

References

Bakker, Bert N., Jaidka, Kokil., Dörr, Timothy., Fasching, Neil and Lelkes, Yphtach. 2021. 'Questionable and Open Research Practices: Attitudes and Perceptions among Quantitative Communication Researchers', *Journal of Communication*, 71.5: 715–38, https://doi.org/10.1093/JOC/JQAB031

Beall, Jeffrey. 2012. 'Predatory Publishers Are Corrupting Open Access', *Nature*, 489.7415: 179, https://doi.org/10.1038/489179a

——. 2013. 'The Open-Access Movement Is Not Really About Open Access', *TripleC: Communication, Capitalism & Critique*, 11.2: 589–97, https://doi.org/10.31269/TRIPLEC.V11I2.525

Chauvette, Amelia., Schick-Makaroff, Kara and Molzahn, Anita E. 2019. 'Open Data in Qualitative Research', *International Journal of Qualitative Methods*, 18: 1–6, https://doi.org/10.1177/1609406918823863

Demir, Selcuk Besir. 2018. 'Predatory Journals: Who Publishes in Them and Why?', *Journal of Informetrics*, 12.4: 1296–311, https://doi.org/10.1016/j.joi.2018.10.008

Dienlin, Tobias., Johannes, Niklas., Bowman, Nicholas David., Masur, Philipp K., Engesser, Sven and others. 2021. 'An Agenda for Open Science in Communication', *Journal of Communication*, 71.1: 1–26, https://doi.org/10.1093/joc/jqz052

Ferguson, Cat., Marcus, Adam and Oransky, Ivan. 2014. 'Publishing: The Peer-Review Scam', *Nature*, 515.7528: 480–82, https://doi.org/10.1038/515480A

Fox, Jesse., Pearce, Katy E., Massanari, Adrienne L., Riles, Julius Matthew., Szulc, Łukasz and others. 2021. 'Open Science, Closed Doors? Countering Marginalization through an Agenda for Ethical, Inclusive Research in Communication', *Journal of Communication*, 71.5: 764–84, https://doi.org/10.1093/JOC/JQAB029

Fraser, Hannah., Parker, Tim., Nakagawa, Shinichi., Barnett, Ashley and Fidler, Fiona. 2018. 'Questionable Research Practices in Ecology and Evolution', *PLOS ONE*, 13.7: e0200303, https://doi.org/10.1371/journal.pone.0200303

Freiling, Isabelle., Krause, Nicole M., Scheufele, Dietram A. and Chen, Kaiping. 2021. 'The Science of Open (Communication) Science: Toward an Evidence-Driven Understanding of Quality Criteria in Communication Research', *Journal of Communication*, 71.5: 686–714, https://doi.org/10.1093/JOC/JQAB032

Koerber, Amy and Graham, Hilary. 2017. 'Theorizing the Value of English Proficiency in Cross-Cultural Rhetorics of Health and Medicine: A Qualitative Study', *Journal of Business and Technical Communication*, 31.1: 63–93, https://doi.org/10.1177/1050651916667533

Koerber, Amy., Starkey, Jesse C., Ardon-Dryer, Karin., Cummins, R. Glenn., Eko, Lyombe and others. 2020. 'A Qualitative Content Analysis of Watchlists vs Safelists: How Do They Address the Issue of Predatory Publishing?', *Journal of Academic Librarianship*, 46.6, https://doi.org/10.1016/j.acalib.2020.102236

Lillis, Theresa and Curry, Mary Jane. 2010. *Academic Writing in a Global Context: The Politics and Practices of Publishing in English* (New York: Routledge)

Longley Arthur, Paul and Hearn, Lydia. 2021. 'Toward Open Research: A Narrative Review of the Challenges and Opportunities for Open Humanities', *Journal of Communication*, 71.5: 827–53, https://doi.org/10.1093/JOC/JQAB028

Markowitz, David M., Song, Hyunjin and Hardman Taylor, Samuel. 2021. 'Tracing the Adoption and Effects of Open Science in Communication Research', *Journal of Communication*, 71.5: 739–63, https://doi.org/10.1093/JOC/JQAB030

McGrath, Cormac and Nilsonne, Gustav. 2018. 'Data Sharing in Qualitative Research: Opportunities and Concerns', *MedEdPublish*, 7.255 (F1000 Research Ltd): 1–12, https://doi.org/10.15694/MEP.2018.0000255.1

Mellor, David T., Nosek, Brian A. and Pfeiffer, Nicole. 2020. 'Conflict between Open Access and Open Science: APCs Are a Key Part of the Problem, Preprints Are a Key Part of the Solution', *Center for Open Science Blog*, https://www.cos.io/blog/conflict-between-open-access-and-open-science-apcs-are-key-part-problem-preprints-are-key-part-solution

Moed, H. F., Burger, W. J.M., Frankfort, J. G. and Van Raan, A. F.J. 1985. 'The Use of Bibliometric Data for the Measurement of University Research Performance', *Research Policy*, 14.3: 131–49, https://doi.org/10.1016/0048-7333(85)90012-5

Morey, Richard D., Chambers, Christopher D., Etchells, Peter J., Harris, Christine R., Hoekstra, Rink, and others. 2016. 'The Peer Reviewers' Openness Initiative: Incentivizing Open Research Practices through Peer Review', *Royal Society Open Science*, 3.1: 1–7, https://doi.org/10.1098/RSOS.150547

Munafò, Marcus R., Nosek, Brian A., Bishop, Dorothy V.M., Button, Katherine S., Chambers, Christopher D. and others. 2017. 'A Manifesto for Reproducible Science', *Nature Human Behaviour*, 1: 1–9, https://doi.org/10.1038/s41562-016-0021

Nosek, Brian A., Alter, G., Banks, G. C., Borsboom, D., Bowman, S. D. and others. 2015. 'Promoting an Open Research Culture', *Science*, 348.6242: 1422–25, https://doi.org/10.1126/SCIENCE.AAB2374

Nosek, Brian A. and Bar-Anan, Yoav. 2012. 'Scientific Utopia: I. Opening Scientific Communication', *Psychological Inquiry*, 23.3: 217–43, https://doi.org/10.1080/1047840X.2012.692215

Nosek, Brian A., Ebersole, Charles R., DeHaven, Alexander C., and Mellor, David T. 2018. 'The Preregistration Revolution', *Proceedings of the National Academy of Sciences*, 115.11: 2600–06, https://doi.org/10.1073/PNAS.1708274114

O'Boyle, Ernest Hugh., Banks, George Christopher., and Gonzalez-Mulé, Erik. 2017. 'The Chrysalis Effect: How Ugly Initial Results Metamorphosize Into Beautiful Articles', *Journal of Management*, 43.2: 376–99 https://doi.org/10.1177/0149206314527133

Omobowale, Ayokunle Olumuyiwa., Akanle, Olayinka., Adeniran, Adebusuyi Isaac and Adegboyega, Kamorudeen. 2014. 'Peripheral Scholarship and the Context of Foreign Paid Publishing in Nigeria', *Current Sociology*, 62.5: 666–84, https://doi.org/10.1177/0011392113508127

'Open Science for the 21st Century: Draft ISC Working Paper'. 2020. *International Science Council*, https://council.science/publications/open-science-for-the-21st-century/

Pond, Brooks B., Stacy D. Brown, David W. Stewart, David S. Roane, and Sam Harirforoosh. 2019. 'Faculty Applicants' Attempt to Inflate CVs Using Predatory Journals', *American Journal of Pharmaceutical Education*, 83.1: 12–14, https://doi.org/10.5688/ajpe7210

Pratt, Michael G., Kaplan, Sarah and Whittington, Richard. 2020. 'Editorial Essay: The Tumult over Transparency: Decoupling Transparency from Replication in Establishing Trustworthy Qualitative Research', *Administrative Science Quarterly*, 65.1: 1–19, https://doi.org/10.1177/0001839219887663

Pusic, Martin V. 2014. 'Removing the Rose-Coloured Glasses: It's High Time We Published the Actual Data', *Medical Education*, 48.3: 334–35, https://doi.org/10.1111/MEDU.12312

Pyne, Derek. 2017. 'The Rewards of Predatory Publications at a Small Business School', *Journal of Scholarly Publishing*, 48.3: 137–60, https://doi.org/10.3138/jsp.48.3.137

Ross-Hellauer, Tony. 2017. 'What Is Open Peer Review? A Systematic Review', *F1000Research*: 1–37, https://doi.org/10.12688/f1000research.11369.1

Shehata, A.M.K. and Elgllab, M.F.M. 2018. 'Where Arab Social Science and Humanities Scholars Choose to Publish: Falling in the Predatory Journals Trap', *Learned Publishing*, 31.3: 222–29, https://doi.org/10.1002/leap.1167

Simmons, Joseph P., Nelson, Leif D. and Simonsohn, Uri. 2011. 'False-Positive Psychology: Undisclosed Flexibility in Data Collection and Analysis Allows Presenting Anything as Significant', *Psychological Science*, 22.11: 1359–66, https://doi.org/10.1177/0956797611417632

Tutuncu, Lokman., Yucedogru, Recep and Sarisoy, Idris. 2022. 'Academic Favoritism at Work: Insider Bias in Turkish National Journals', *Scientometrics*, 127: 2547–76, https://doi.org/10.1007/s11192-022-04355-0

Van Noorden, Richard. 2020. 'Hundreds of Scientists Have Peer-Reviewed for Predatory Journals', *Nature*: 1–4, https://doi.org/10.1038/d41586-020-00709-x

Wallace, Frederick H., and Perri, Timothy J. 2018. 'Economists Behaving Badly: Publications in Predatory Journals', *Scientometrics*, 115: 749–66, https://doi.org/10.1007/s11192-018-2690-1

Wallerstein, I. M. 1991. *Geopolitics and Geoculture: Essays on the Changing World-System* (Cambridge, England: Cambridge University Press)

Xia, Jingfeng., Harmon, Jennifer L., Connolly, Kevin G., Donnelly, Ryan M., Anderson, Mary R. and others. 2014. 'Who Publishes in "Predatory" Journals?', *Journal of the Association for Information Science and Technology*, 66.7: 1406–17, https://doi.org/10.1002/asi.23265

3. Research Quality
Understanding Definitions of and Challenges to Quality in the Knowledge Production Process[1]

> Quality is a characteristic of thought and statement that is recognized by a nonthinking process. Because definitions are a product of rigid, formal thinking, quality cannot be defined.
> Robert M. Pirsig, *Zen and the Art of Motorcycle Maintenance* (1974: 200)

Quality is integral to scholarly research and publishing, but we have struggled to agree on how to define it. This is due, in part, to the complexity and dynamic nature of research and publishing. For example, a graduate student may come out of a high-quality program (based on published rankings), produce low-quality research (based on a professor's or other peer assessment), improve the manuscript's quality through peer review, then publish it in a low-quality journal (based on impact factor), but then get picked up by the media and distributed to a wide audience, thus resulting in high readership and citation numbers (an indicator of quality).

By addressing this topic through empirical research and gathering insights from diverse stakeholders in the scholarly publishing world, this chapter provides an overview of perspectives on quality in all stages of scholarly knowledge production, situated in a world where we face numerous threats to the global publishing enterprise. From the training

---

1   Portions of this chapter were previously published in *Discover Education*. The original manuscript is available online at https://doi.org/10.1007/s44217-022-00007-w. The dataset (NVivo file) that accompanies the published article is also relevant to this chapter and is available at https://doi.org/10.18738/T8/LD7SSX.

of graduate students, to the production of research, to the vetting process for manuscripts, and finally into the publishing and dispersal of peer-reviewed scholarly publications, this chapter provides a glimpse into how people in the business of academic publishing — both leaders and emerging talent — view quality in terms of scholarly knowledge production and distribution, all while navigating a wide array of ethical pitfalls.

But why does understanding what constitutes quality in scholarly knowledge production even matter? One might question whether such an exploration is simply a matter of egocentric navel-gazing, an opportunity for those of us in the ivory tower to justify research simply for research's sake. It matters because institutions of higher education are the training ground for the individuals who go on to make great changes in society. So how can we safeguard those hallowed grounds so that they do not succumb to the continued assault ('In Defense of Knowledge' 2020) on knowledge and facts — especially in an environment where predatory journals are eroding the credibility of academic publishing?

Our findings echoed what scholars in diverse fields have been grappling with for decades — there is a systemic flaw in global higher education that focuses on *quantity* over *quality* (e.g., Pyne 2017; Skolnik 2000), giving rise to an environment where journals that tout fast turnaround times or guaranteed manuscript acceptance are viewed as career-savers, rather than threats to academic integrity. Yet our study adds some important nuances to the conversation — we share the combined voices of stakeholders across the publishing world, and from around the globe. This chapter presents their perspectives, coupled with previous empirical research, to attempt a holistic understanding of the difficult task of defining and understanding quality in the context of scholarly research and publication in an environment fraught with potential ethical challenges.

Predatory Journals are a Marker of Low Quality

An important backdrop to the discussion of quality in scholarly knowledge production is the growing threat of predatory publishers, journals, and conferences. The term 'predatory' and how it came to be associated with digital publications claiming to contribute to the scholarly knowledge production environment is explored in depth in other chapters of this book, so here we position predatory journals and their publishing practices as the opposite of 'good quality' open access, due to the low-quality science they publish, the editorial team (often fake), the peer review (also often fake), and culminated by their focus on profits over services. One of our study participants was particularly critical of the role predatory journals played in 'preying on people's ignorance' (P02),[2] especially outside the sphere of Euro-American[3] institutional affluence, where scholars have fewer resources and often less training about publication ethics, and work within institutional cultures that value quantity over quality.

Background

A quick scan of the literature on 'quality in higher education' shows scholars from numerous fields addressing the topic in a range of ways. Since 2020 alone, researchers have examined service quality in higher education from a marketing perspective (Alfy and Abukari 2020), the economic perspective of quality graduate education (Bairagya and Joy 2021), sustainability in higher education (Vykydal and others 2020), the business of higher education (Cavallone and others 2021), teaching quality (Giraleas 2021), and a range of other topics including labor and learning outcomes, student satisfaction, and civic engagement (Bloch and others 2021). But one area that has surprisingly been neglected in the literature of quality in higher education is quality in the knowledge production process.

One component of that process is peer review. Rigorous peer review has long been the hallmark of successful, high-quality scientific publications (Roll 2019). The review from impartial peers is supposed

---

2   Our Texas Data Repository Dataverse includes a table showing participant demographic information. See https://doi.org/10.18738/T8/QUBMLI ("Participant Occupation and Regional Demographics Table"). All quotations from interviews are reported without correction of grammatical errors or other irregularities. Some quotes were abbreviated using [...] to achieve clarity of the original message.
3   The terms 'Euro-American' and 'non-Euro-American' are used in this chapter to describe sociocultural and demographic populations in place of 'Western and Eastern' or 'Global North or South' to reflect the geographic contexts we are trying to describe.

to ensure the credibility of the scientific process, offer authors ways to improve their manuscripts, and increase the quality of publications that ultimately lead the way to scientific advancements (Roll 2019). Yet in recent decades doubt has been cast on the peer-review process, partly spurred by the rise in predatory journals (although some mainstream, well-known journals are now under fire for their peer-review quality — see Vazire 2020 for examples). Articles and blogposts in mainstream media with academic and general audiences have tackled the issues with peer review in recent years (e.g., Carroll 2018; Humphries 2021; Michael 2019; Vazire 2020) and concluded that despite its flaws and inadequacies, peer review is still the best option for vetting scholarly knowledge production. Therefore, despite attempts to revamp the peer-review process, it remains the primary way of vetting the quality of manuscripts that end up being published in scholarly journals — and thus an important element when attempting to understand quality in the knowledge production process. Lack of peer review is also a common trait of predatory journals, making their potential impact on the global body of knowledge even more damaging.

When examining quality in the production and distribution of scholarly research, much of the existing literature (Lindsey 1989; McGrail and others 2006; Zerem 2017) points to the quality of the journal as a primary indicator of scientific research quality, with special emphasis placed on impact factors and more recently, H-Index rankings. Yet the impact factor was not even designed for this purpose (McKiernan and others 2019). To further complicate the issue, some indexing and impact ranking organizations are fraudulent, requiring readers and potential authors to be more critical in their assessment of journals, rather than simply relying on statements of index inclusion or impact metrics listed on a journal or publisher's website.

Now, with the rise of predatory publishing venues (Shrestha and others 2019) targeting desperate scholars who need lines on their CV (Pond and others 2019), individuals and organizations have been trying to develop ways to vet the quality of scholarly publication outlets. More recently organizations — both for- and non-profit — have joined this endeavor. Forrester and others (2017) compared the established services typically used by librarians to find information about journals with new services aimed at directly helping authors select journals.

They found that even when using identical search terms, the different services returned vastly different results, suggesting that an inherent bias pervades many of the tools (many are owned by specific publishing companies). Yet Forrester and colleagues (2017) remained hopeful in their conclusion, noting that 'as these tools increase the transparency of journal information and their editorial processes, this could lead to an overall improvement in academic quality control' (p. 286). Koerber and others (2020) compared two approaches to classifying journals and publishers — safelists and watchlists — and found challenges with either approach, suggesting that the 'list' approach to classifying safe or predatory publishing outlets may not be the answer to the paradox of predatory publishing.

While there are a few published frameworks that try to delineate specific markers of quality in academic research (e.g., Frambach and others 2013; Tracy 2010; Welch and Piekkari 2017), succinct markers of quality remain elusive. However, when looking at quality in academia, many scholars (e.g., Biggs 2001, 2011; Bowden and Marton 2003; Brennan and Shah 2000; Lagrosen and others 2004; Suleman 2018; Teeroovengadum and others 2019) rely on the landmark works of Lee Harvey and Diana Green (1993) who argue for a multi-dimensional conceptualization of quality. Therefore, embracing epistemic diversity and acknowledging multiple definitions of quality will be our road map to understand this complex issue: 'What does quality in scholarly knowledge production mean to you?'

Challenges to Quality

> If we can show that a world without quality functions abnormally, then we have shown that Quality exists, whether it is defined or not.
> Robert M. Pirsig, *Zen and the Art of Motorcycle Maintenance* (1974: 210)

We begin our journey of understanding quality in scholarly knowledge production where Phaedrus began envisioning a world without quality in *Zen* — where the absence or low levels of quality causes a breakdown in functionality. It is often easier to say what is wrong with something, and to note the *absence of quality*, rather than defining markers of quality in concrete terms. When our participants were asked what quality in scholarly publication meant to them, they often answered as if they were sitting with Phaedrus as he began his intellectual journey. They shared examples of where quality was *missing*, and confirmed many common notions about the challenges of being researchers (knowledge producers) in higher education: the Euro-American perspective on research remains dominant, evaluation methods around the world differ drastically, the increasing pressures to publish lead to a cycle of constant rejection and pressure to sensationalize findings, peer review is not as unbiased as we want to think, and strong mentorship for graduate students and junior scholars is sometimes lacking.

Pressure to Publish

The 'publish or perish' paradigm in higher education places the academic researcher as the 'product' that needs to deliver the 'service' of producing scholarly publications, creating a system where the institution feels obligated to evaluate whether their 'product' is producing the 'service' at the most cost-effective rate, in order to benefit the institution's bottom line. From an institutional perspective, higher numbers of publications equal higher quality, but from an individual perspective, the pressure to continually 'fling [manuscripts] to a journal [...] rather than taking the time and the effort to really prove yourself wrong' (P45) has led to a degradation in the quality of scholarly knowledge production. This pressure to publish was especially salient to some PhD students, where their national systems require them to publish before their degree can be conferred (e.g., a country in Southeast Asia, P15; and a country in Africa, P03), placing publications as 'kind of the currency of the field' (P08). An interesting nuance in the statements about pressure to publish was the notion that this soaring need for scholars to find outlets for their work was being met by 'creating new journals' (P32, P35), many of them falling into the 'predatory' category. A scholar from Southeast Asia agreed with the sentiment that the pressure to publish led to the rise in predatory journals, stating, 'There is a demand for it because, [for] I and other academics here, there is a pressure to publish' (P41). In large part, this continually mounting pressure to publish has stemmed from a rise in institutional valuation of the quantity of publications, rather than the quality.

Valuing Quantity Over Quality

The complicated interaction between personal ethical values and institutional pressures was especially salient as participants discussed the trend in academia to value the number of publications racked up by an individual, rather than the impact, practical application, or other less concrete markers of quality in those publications. This concept was addressed from a range of angles, including scholars noting cultures of publishing where, during the tenure process, the types of journals a manuscript appears in does not matter (P02), or commenting that 'in some areas, unfortunately, they're mainly counting publications not thinking about quality and so you can just publish a lot and you're considered productive' (P08) and 'in many parts of the world, there is no discernible difference between the quality and the quantity' (P24).

Others spoke about the focus on quantity over quality from a human resources perspective, with one participant from North America noting 'there are really perverse incentives in academia […] quality has become […] a question of numbers […] the number of publications per academic' (P22). A European participant agreed, noting that 'if one criterion is only the number of publications, then this incentivizes to publish in such predatory journals or [be] published in the lower journals' (P38). This fracture between institutional and individual perceptions of quality in terms of the numbers of publications produced exemplifies one of the challenges of understanding quality in scholarly knowledge production.

Having to Adhere to Euro-American Publishing Standards

Given the global flow of information facilitated by technology, it was no surprise that scholars felt compelled to address the challenges associated with navigating the differences between their disciplinary expectations on national, regional, and global scales and spoke to the 'different publishing cultures across all these countries' (P10). They noted both the pressure to publish in English and in high-ranking journals, along with a desire to produce work that was meaningful and useful in their native countries. Another scholar added 'quality is associated with the Western world' noting that while they were not necessarily opposed to this global view, there were other regions that were producing high quality work too but were not being recognized because 'they don't meet the kind of processes that the Western publication industry is familiar with' (P41). This speaks to the complexity of evaluating quality in a global context when considering scholars who produce work in accordance with their local or regional environments, who may then face a different set of standards or expectations at the national or international scale, creating a scenario where the purpose or functionality of their research products changes depending on the context in which they are operating. Scholars from outside the Euro-American regions may also find themselves struggling to produce knowledge that is both beneficial and useful for their home environment and acceptable in the global sphere of knowledge production.

When they talked about global inequalities, participants emphasized resources as an important difference among disciplines and scholars from different nations or even different institutions within a specific country. One European researcher hypothesized that researchers working outside the Euro-American sphere of affluence '[...] just didn't have the resources or the knowledge of how to do things properly' (P18). This notion of inequities in resource availability between scholars working inside or outside of affluent Euro-American regions was also addressed in terms of how a supposedly global organization like the International Communication Association (ICA), the flagship organization of the Communication discipline, perpetuates biases (P34). They further suggested that international organizations can, in some cases, contribute to an environment where scholars working in resource-poor countries or institutions are expected to maintain the same quality standards as resource-rich scholars — and when they fail to do so, it perpetuates biases against non-Euro-American scholars in Euro-American journals and professional organizations.

Values related to international standards of methodology were also questioned by one participant who stated, 'international publishing means Western publishing', and then went on to give the example of Latin America, a region this participant suggested has:

> [...] their own research cultures, and they are very good in building their own databases and own publication networks [...] in Latin America, they developed a very good and working network. They

have prestigious journals with high impact factor. They cite each other, extremely, so they are good at that. We can see that their research is, we can speak about Latin American research integrity because these articles meet their standards. When you are not Latin American, it will be different for you. (P35)

Thus, despite the obvious benefits of having a global flow of information, it became clear that the new global environment for knowledge production also presents new challenges to understanding what constitutes quality across the world.

Getting Rejected

While rejection is a constant occurrence in the life of an academic, the realization by one scholar that 'there's an 80% rejection rate [...] for the good journals in the US, that means, on average, you have to submit at least four times and go through peer review four times probably just to get published' (P15) led them to wonder how that affects the knowledge production process. Another scholar suggested that constant rejection may lead to desperate scholars turning away from traditional, reputable publishers, and instead, to 'just rely on predatory journal[s]' (P03).

While rejection of manuscripts due to poor methodology, bad journal fit, or sub-par writing was accepted as a marker of quality assurance, getting rejected unfairly was a particularly salient issue for scholars working outside the Euro-American regions. The anecdotal evidence shared by our participants pointed to perceptions that the researchers' country affected their likelihood of acceptance, such as the story shared by one scholar who argued that 'when you submit your paper from Nigeria, and the same paper is submitted claiming that it is from Harvard, the referees will extremely overvalue the paper [from Harvard]' (P35). This suggests that the objectives for some journals do not necessarily coincide with how knowledge producers across the globe believe their work should be received. The perception that unfair rejections happen to scholars working outside the Euro-American region highlights the issue with conceptualizing quality from a singular standpoint and has led to centuries of erasure of epistemic diversity in scholarly knowledge production.

Needing to Sensationalize Findings

Due to some of the institutional and disciplinary pressures mentioned in the sections above, several of our participants mentioned the temptation to over-sensationalize their work as a challenge to producing quality science (P15, P38), suggesting a 'preponderance of people just wanting cool findings that you just throw at whatever high-impact journal' (P45).

Another senior scholar spoke of the importance of instilling a sense of personal responsibility in junior scholars not to succumb to 'temptations to maybe make the story a bit more streamlined [...], or to make it a bit more simple, a bit easier to understand' (P38). Another scholar added nuance to this discussion, stating that they were:

> [...] always skeptical for research that support author hypothesis. Because if everything is supported then of course it may show that you are smart enough to predict everything but also it would say that probably you picked the result that just support your hypothesis. (P31)

But the trend of only publishing research that supports hypotheses or that is statistically significant is not just an issue for authors to address — it is also relevant to the journal editors and reviewers that function as gatekeepers. Many scholars spoke of the additional pressure from journals to only publish work that supported their hypotheses, rather than understanding that 'sometimes negative results can be very important as well' (P26), and that 'I think it's really important to have some of these venues that publish the negative things as well, because a lot of times an advance comes off something negative not off something positive' (P08). One participant summed up the issue of feeling pressured to sensationalize their work and not publicize negative results as 'the most harmful thing probably for scientific progress [...] Because a null finding can be much more revealing than a finding' (P48).

Flawed Peer Review System

Despite peer review's continuing status as the gold standard for gatekeeping quality in scholarly knowledge production, it is not without its flaws and issues. Although only a couple of our participants offered a concrete definition of what a rigorous or stringent peer-review process might look like; as in the case of the fictional students in *Zen*, our participants could identify when a peer review had *not* been good, noting markers such as minimal reviewer comments (P04, P05, P10) or being asked to review manuscripts that are not within their expertise (P08). Through examining the flaws of peer review, and the challenges those flaws present in terms of quality in the knowledge production process, participants identified several major challenges to quality in the peer-review system: issues with reviewers; actions of deliberate fraud; the length of time peer review often takes; disbelief in the reality of double-blind reviews; and authors fearing the review process, rather than embracing it as part of the knowledge production process.

Issues with Reviewers

When considering the role of peer reviewers, scholars were especially sensitive to the difficulty of getting people to conduct constructive, critical reviews, leading one participant to share their fears of not wanting 'to be the peer reviewer who says no to an article that costs someone their job' (P06). Participants also noted that often reviewers are pressed for time, resulting in lower quality reviews, with comments like, 'I think a lot of times, you know, the reviews are rushed in and they're not as careful' (P08), and 'we're all overworked and there's no way we can put that much scrutiny into every empirical claim' (P12).

Another participant hypothesized that some of the systemic issues of peer review revolved around the fact that,

> [...] most of the reviewers are junior people [...] Senior [scholars] don't want to review [...] the mentality is 'I did all my reviews in the past, I've done my dues' [...] But the cost to the whole process because the junior people are good at finding faults, they're really good, they'll find a methodological flaw [...] but we need a certain maturity or time to be able to see the bigger thing. And so I think that's one of the things which is ecologically terribly missing in terms of production of good research is to get attention of senior reviewers. (P33)

Actions of Deliberate Fraud

Other participants noted that while peer review is important to vet scholarly work, 'there's a lot of evidence that the peer-review process is imperfect' (P45) and 'there's fraud in peer review too [...] but let's just assume that's all there is right now' (P14) and 'there are sometimes systemic failures to maintain a high level of peer review' (P22). In considering the potential for fraud or unethical practices in publishing, one participant shared a story of a colleague's review process where 'the editor had asked him to include a bunch of citations from that same journal' (P16), indicating there was a definitive effort on the part of the editorial staff to try to increase the impact factor of the journal through citation milling.

The concept of systemic failure was echoed by another participant who agreed peer review was the best way to ensure quality in vetting manuscripts 'when it's not used in a predatory way, you know what I mean? Like, "Oh, I hate that person"' (P16). Other participants noted instances of people having to find their own reviewers, which could lead to them selecting people who would review their work favorably, rather than with an honest and critical eye (P25, P26).

The Peer Review Process Is Too Lengthy

Length of time from submission to publication was also suggested as a challenge to the process of getting new knowledge out to a wider audience, with one participant stating that many researchers 'don't want to wait for the peer review to happen in like more than six months', and continuing that many scholars 'are looking for the journals that can publish very swiftly' (P19). At least four other participants (P13, P25, P26, P27) pointed to the speed from submission to publication as a reason for selecting journals with less stringent peer-review practices, as summarized by this comment:

> They also are concerned about the timeframe, for them it's too long, they cannot wait. They want a quick publishing and quick response, they want to publish immediately. Some of them they don't want to go through the reviewing process, so that is very, very sad. (P39)

Double-Blind Is a Myth

Others doubted the double-blind process with comments such as, 'I think double blind is a myth' (P33), or questioned the validity of publishers claiming a double-blind process: 'we hold double-blind peer review as our tried-and-true standard, but nobody really knows what that is. You don't really know because it is double blind and it's all behind the scenes' (P21).

The idea that double-blind peer reviewing is a myth was especially salient to participants working outside of the Euro-American regions who often felt their work was unfairly rejected, simply because of their country of origin or the ethnic identities associated with their names, 'I would say editors and reviewers judge based on your name, based on your country, or based on your institution, and that should not be the case [...] because that's not fair' (P26). Along similar lines, another scholar claimed that non-Euro-American scholars faced additional scrutiny of their data:

> [...] the authors in the other developing countries and sometimes the reviewers, they don't know too much about the context. So they always do want lots of details. But that is not the case for the US journal or for the submissions that are using the US data. (P46)

The notion of bias against international scholars was expanded upon by another scholar who shared experiences of being an editor for a journal and having difficulty securing reviewers for submissions from outside the Euro-American regions: 'Many scholars for example refused or declined to review articles outside their country. For example, there are a lot of American scholars who won't do article reviews from developing countries' (P31).

Authors Afraid of the Peer Review Process

Another important nuance in authors' perceptions of the review process was addressed by some of our participants who felt the review process was too critical and unfair, or who saw 'the review as punishment' (P42) or wanted 'no hassle' (P15). Often, comments about the need for ensuring manuscripts were properly vetted before publication were also followed by doubts about the equity of the system, suggesting some scholars 'publish in predatory journals because there is no very stringent peer-review system or language is not a barrier in that because even a low-quality writings are also accepted in predatory journals' (P17).

Inconsistencies in Evaluation Methods

When we move from the macro-context of the global flow of information down to a more micro-level of quality assessment at the institutional level, defining quality becomes even more problematic. Academia, by its very nature, encompasses all fields, meaning an approach that works for a certain field may not work for another, as one participant noted: 'the disciplines are so, you know, different' (P08), a point emphasized by another participant who pointed out the differing expectations of research output between disciplines, 'Like in the field of Computer Science [...] they don't value the journal publication too much. They value the conference proceeding publication' (P46).

A bigger problem identified by several scholars from various parts of the world was summarized by one European participant who noted that 'there is some assessment system, but nobody cares' (P35), and then went on to share that quality research was not valued as much as being connected to the right people in the country where they work. A scholar from South Asia noted their national system of ranking publications did not 'look at the readership' (P19). This scholar went on to say, 'They don't look at the quality of the journal. They only look at the ratings' (P19) before continuing to describe how this has lowered the production of quality research because so much focus has shifted on playing the ratings game.

At the institutional level, defining quality remains problematic due to the inconsistencies in evaluation methods between institutions and fields, such as varying methods for evaluating research production or placing higher importance on different forms of production. These inconsistencies make it difficult to assess quality in knowledge production between institutions or fields. Furthermore, the vast differences in evaluation of the knowledge production process (e.g., impact, citations, tenure and promotion) position evaluation methods more as a challenge to quality than a marker of its existence due to the necessity for researchers to consider how their work will be evaluated rather than focusing on the extension of knowledge and scientific applications.

Lack of Mentorship

There was some evidence, through the anecdotal narratives shared by our participants, that a lack of mentorship related to publishing ethics was allowing junior scholars to make mistakes in how they chose publication outlets for their scholarship, suggesting a flaw in the systematic role of mentors in preparing junior scholars to enter the academic publishing field. A North American university librarian summarized the problem of effective mentoring for junior scholars, stating:

> But I'm just flabbergasted by how many students we have, who will go through the whole process and get their PhD, and then contact me a year later or more and not know how to approach these issues of how to avoid publishing in something that's not good for them [...] Because their advisors didn't talk to them about it or it never came up. I don't know how to fix that. (P06)

There are challenges at every step of the process when we consider how scholars view themselves and their work within the system of global scholarly knowledge production. These challenges suggest that much work is still needed to understand how to bridge the gap between institutional perspectives on quality and individual actions that produce the work in question.

Defining Quality

> He singled out aspects of Quality such as unity, vividness, authority, economy, sensitivity, clarity, emphasis, flow, suspense, brilliance, precision, proportion, depth and so on; kept each of these as poorly defined as Quality itself...
> Robert M. Pirsig, *Zen and the Art of Motorcycle Maintenance* (1974: 202)

Just as Phaedrus, the alter-ego of the narrator in Pirsig's *Zen and the Art of Motorcycle Maintenance*, attempted — unsuccessfully — to draw a definition of quality out of his students, so did we with the interview participants, asking them to define 'quality' in relation to scholarly publishing in any way they saw fit. And just like the fictional students in *Zen*, our participants struggled to concisely define quality, instead turning to ways that quality can be demonstrated in the various steps of scholarly publishing, just as the students did in *Zen*. Some participants aligned quality with equally hazy concepts, such as 'science [that] has been done properly' (P18), whereas others attempted to define markers of quality in a more concrete way. Here, we can see the applicability of a multi-dimensional conceptualization of quality as our participants attempted to describe quality throughout the scholarly knowledge production process — from the training of graduate students in research ethics, to conducting the research, evaluating it, and eventually publishing and disseminating it. In the following sections, we show how participants described quality in each step of the knowledge production process.

Importance of Institutional Culture

For some of our participants, quality in terms of graduate student training is embodied at the institutional level, where the emphasis on ethical publication practices needed to come from the top down. One participant noted, 'It needs to be first in the administration because when the administration care about predatory journal I think the student will just follow and the scientists also we just follow' (P03). Another participant pointed toward the human resources graduate students have in their departments as a marker of quality: 'The first thing I always tell them is that they need to talk with people in their department, and not just their advisor, the more the merrier in a lot of ways' (P06). The point about the importance of the departmental culture was emphasized further by a junior scholar as he reflected on his faculty mentors during his graduate training: 'I got to participate kind of hands on really early in research studies and projects that allowed me to kind of sharpen my skill set and fully determine if an academic route, again is where I wanted to go' (P37).

Modeling Ethical Research Behavior

There was a unanimous sense from our participants that modeling ethical research behavior is the most powerful way to ensure graduate students emerge from their training with the intention of maintaining ethical research practices throughout their career. Senior faculty typically spoke about their role in training graduate students in terms of 'individual responsibility' (P34) and 'being guards of [graduate student training]' (P04), noting that faculty need 'to become more vigilant I suppose as educators in that regard' (P34).

Other faculty pointed toward the necessity of being open about the process of producing quality research, saying, 'I try to give them a realistic picture' (P34), and emphasizing the importance of sharing the ways their own careers and success in academia unfolded as he continued by saying, 'You don't see the trajectories. You don't see how much help they got, or maybe the compromises they had to make in their lives with regards to family, all these kinds of things' (P34). Another senior scholar agreed that openness is key, adding nuance related to the two-way flow of information needed between senior faculty and students when she stated, 'Another way is make them be open [...]. Make them feel confident that we can speak about their research project freely' (P03).

When reflecting on the type of training they received about publishing ethics during their graduate training, one participant stated, '[My advisor] did sit us down and she gave us the ethics talk, and made sure what we were doing was correct and good to publish, but besides that, there wasn't too much guidance' (P30). Yet despite that lack of mentoring related to publishing ethics, somewhere along the way the participant picked up the importance of following ethical practices, and now tries to instill those qualities in their mentees.

This notion of modeling behavior for their mentees was echoed by several other scholars with comments such as, 'The students are there. They're looking [at] those things, those behaviors, so we are teaching them. So then we need to be an example, a good example to them' (P26), and 'So it is far beyond supervising [...] It is kind of mentoring them [...] all that type of skills that you can help them to acquire' (P03). One young researcher exemplified how the culture of ethical research is handed down from mentor to mentee as he said 'I've been trained by people [...] who have the highest standards of research [...] I try to pass that on now to the students I'm teaching, and I'm advising' (P34). Conversely, one participant noted that bad ethical behaviors can also be modeled when she said, 'the student know that the supervisor don't care about what type of journal he sees' (P03), emphasizing the crucial role mentors play in protecting quality in graduate student training.

Throughout the interviews, our participants repeatedly spoke about the role of faculty mentors, increasing awareness and efficacy of research integrity, and addressing cultural differences in international academies as ways to increase the quality of graduate student training related to scholarly knowledge production. The importance and centrality of mentors who model ethical research practices embodies the conceptualizations of quality as both a process and an end result, so that when graduate students move into the job market they are prepared to carry out research in an ethical manner. (See Chapter 5 for more on this topic.)

Committing to Ethical Behavior

Committing to ethical behavior when no one was looking was discussed in a range of ways, from statements relating to values such as, 'Just behaving, being a good citizen in the scholarly world and not doing bad things with regard to your own research' (P05) and 'the moral value of honesty is essential for the scientific process to progress' (P08) to more concrete suggestions related to research practices, 'not tampering with data' (P19) and 'don't go and steal someone else's work' (P30). Participants touched on the need for ethical behavior in every part of the research process, from going through the 'IRB process' (P02), to 'respecting your subjects' (P10) to 'present your results as it is' (P02). Ultimately, committing to ethical behavior was best summed up by this participant who said, 'you have to be dedicated to the truth, period, no matter what' (P08).

Following Scientific Protocol

Following scientific protocol was the method of producing quality research that our participants mentioned most frequently. Some participants directly connected quality to following scientific protocol with statements like, 'quality research is research that follows the scientific method' (P02) and 'Following scientific good practice' (P24). While some participants broadly associated quality with scientific protocol, others delved more deeply into specific aspects that must be present to demonstrate that protocol was followed. Rigor was mentioned explicitly by numerous participants (P09, P14, P16, P31, P41, P48), along with replicable methods (P02, P08, P12, P19, P25, P31, P38, P46, P48) as ways to ensure scientific protocol was being followed, as summarized by this participant: 'I realize quality is a judgment call, but to me it is very key about [...] very clear methods, very clear controls, very clear descriptions of all your methods, ultimately in science, it's supposed to be repeated' (P08).

Dedication to Transparency

After committing to ethical behavior and following scientific protocol, a dedication to transparency was the next most common attribute of quality in scientific knowledge production addressed by our participants. Some framed transparency as 'being willing to show your work' (P04), whereas others positioned it as 'giving appropriate credit to the people who were involved' (P09) or mentioned specific mechanisms to increase transparency such as 'preprints are one step in the right direction to giving a little bit more transparency because you can see how the work evolved' (P12). An interesting nuance emerged between the qualitative and quantitative scholars in terms of inductive versus deductive reasoning and how information emerges from data differently from those perspectives, but one qualitative scholar still noted the importance of transparency even in the inductive process:

> If you can be transparent and collect as much data along the way about what you've done, how you've done it, why you've done it, who you've done it with, what your results [are]. The more open you can be about that, the more likely you are to pick up what went wrong, what went right, share it, build on it. (P21)

Know Your Field

Because reproducibility is considered essential to science, our participants were adamant that a scholar who knows their field will be better equipped to produce quality research, stating 'Academic research, especially a rigorous research journal, would ask you to have both knowledge of the past but also build new things for the future' (P31). In this sense, quality was couched as 'fitting your study in with the rest of the field' (P08) while still 'accepting the results that you are getting even though sometimes it could be that they don't agree with the literature'

(P26). There was also an insistence that 'a good quality article should be able to build on some sense of some people in the past and have their own new ideas that help us to understand the phenomenon or explain the phenomenon' (P31).

Research that Has Been Deeply Thought About

This theme emerged primarily from the researchers we interviewed, showing a dedication to embracing the internalized process of knowledge creation, where 'the researcher has to be curious on something. It's the research that the researcher would do even if they had no gain, nothing to gain from doing that' (P27) and 'Quality for me has therefore also a lot to do with a kind of passion' (34). Additionally, there was a sense that researchers needed to take the time to produce research that 'has been thought over and discussed' (P06), and that 'Ultimately I can still stand behind what I would have wrote then ten years ago' (P34) so that the research 'can create a dialogue with the existing literature' (P46) and continue to build upon the existing knowledge base.

Peer Review as a Marker of Quality in Journals

In general, when our participants were asked about how manuscripts and scholarly journals are judged for quality, they agreed it was through 'robust' (P11) or 'rigorous peer review' (P14, P22), or through a 'stringent peer review process' (P04), calling the peer-review process 'essential' (P05) to producing quality scholarly publications, and thus ensuring the quality of the journals themselves. Our participants broadly credited the watchful eyes of the editorial team and reviewers with the quality of a journal, as summarized by a researcher from South Asia:

> You should look at a journal where the editorial board looks at your paper, critically comments on your paper, puts in for reviewers, and reviewers look at your paper again, and review the comments and try to seek your answers on the questions raised, and help you to improve upon the paper. (P19)

Others were more specific in their emphasis that peer review is what elevates a journal to a place of quality with comments such as '*Science* makes a hell of a difference [...] The quality of peer review is so much greater [...] and so the *Nature* is the same. They're top journals' (P18) and 'the more prestigious the journal is, the more prestigious the reviewer [...] That means that the review process is also [...] higher quality' (P26).

One participant whose job entailed assisting new journals to get started also noted the importance of transparency in the peer-review process, and his continual work to get journals to provide 'evidence of their peer-review process and trying to get them to improve their processes there so they are more transparent as well' (P29). Another participant with editorial experience also noted that the quality of the reviewers directly affected the quality of the journal, but placed the responsibility on the editor(s) to:

> [...] choose, or at least get the attention of the right reviewers, then the right set of reviewers for different papers. And it requires an understanding of the paper, it requires the understanding of the reviewer, it requires that you command enough attention of the potential reviewer, that he or she will be investing that much time in your journal because people invest times in journals because they believe in it, they like the work and so on. So there are a lot of art elements to this. (P33)

A further nuance emerged in the discussion of rigorous peer review and journal quality when one participant noted, '*The Lancet* got in trouble for a COVID article. It has an extremely rigorous peer-review process so there are no foolproof methods of assessing quality that work 100% of the time' (P22). This notion that even well-respected journals might have questionable peer-review practices was corroborated by another participant who shared that a top-tier journal in their field 'only requires one reviewer' (P30). The participant questioned the quality of a single-reviewer process by saying, 'So you only have to please one reviewer, which at first I was very leery [...] because if you get someone who really doesn't like your work, it's done. If you get someone who likes your work, but doesn't want to put in the time to improve it, then is that really a good paper that's coming out?' (P30).

Peer Review as Quality Assessment for Individual Manuscripts

Many participants put their full faith in the peer-review process when it was undertaken rigorously and by peers with the correct expertise with comments such as, 'For me, quality research is peer reviewed and from a journal where I can look up what their peer-review policies are' (P07) and 'I wouldn't trust the peer review, the quality of the process unless the work were being judged by true peers, people with a true understanding of that material' (P5). This notion of peer reviews serving as a filter for manuscripts before they are published was summarized by a participant who stated:

> Well, I think having the peer review is a good filter because the manuscript is supposed to be reviewed by at least three people, which is the editor and two reviewers. In theory, those reviewers should not have any direct contact with the main author or the author, the coauthors, at least in the three previous years or something like this. Those reviewers are supposed to be experts on the field. I think this is a good filter. It's not the best, for sure. But at least I think if the editor did a good job selecting a good reviewer, that can be a really nice filter. (P26)

One participant with decades of experience as a leading scholar positioned the peer-review process as the ultimate way 'to assure quality and integrity in academic publishing' (P32), with another participant simply stating that 'good academic publishing would have independent, unbiased reviewers' (P38). The closest description of what a quality peer review should look like came from one participant who stated:

> So a reviewer's job is to evaluate the theoretical soundness of a paper, whether the arguments made on theoretical grounds are sound, which means they have accurate premises with references that are true, plus a logical conclusion. And whether the methodology is sound, and for that, we have methodological criteria. (P48)

One final nuance to the importance of peer review in protecting the quality of scientific knowledge was an exploration of the potential positive impacts a more open peer review process could have on the quality of reviews that are conducted, which would ultimately improve the quality of the individual manuscripts, and thus the journals, and ultimately the entire field of study:

Frontiers, for example. They have created a highly technological version of the peer review process [...] one feature that I think tremendously improves their quality [...is] the option for open review [...] you submit, you get an anonymous review, the reviewers anonymously review, but then after they submitted their first review, they have an option to make their reviews open. So then the author can directly engage with the reviewer either anonymously or openly [...] There's not just accountability on the side of the author. Of course, you have to make sure that at an early stage of this process, the reviewer is protected. So the reviewer is anonymous and can actually reject freely and then the name will not be revealed. But once it's through this stage, then the reviewer can work together with the author to then ultimately publish the paper. And I have also no problem then to put the reviewers on the paper as someone who contributed to the paper. I would say, if I'm a reviewer, I wrote sometimes twenty, thirty pages, single-space as a review and I saw many things implemented in the paper. If the authors put me in a note, in an acknowledgement [...] I think that's great. And in review processes and merit cases, you can bring this on and say, 'Look, my reviews actually helped to make the paper better. What's wrong with that? (P48)

While it would be wonderfully satisfying to end this section with some concise definition of quality in scholarly knowledge production, the reality is that quality is just as diverse, nuanced, complex, and ever-changing as the fields themselves. Thus, rather than a concise, unified definition of quality to conclude this section, we instead offer a roadmap for celebrating the epistemic diversity offered by a global system of knowledge production. Using a multi-faceted conceptualization of quality, we surmise that quality is both a process and an end goal. Thus, we can now turn a more critical lens on who is qualified to judge whether quality exists at each stage of the knowledge production cycle.

Judging Quality in Graduate Student Training

Quite simply, the faculty at an institution are the judges of graduate students, and thus tasked with ensuring quality in the students they mentor and teach. Faculty often serve in multiple roles for graduate students — as teachers in coursework, as supervisors in research and teaching capacities, and as guides or collaborators in research endeavors. In attempting to measure or assess graduate student education in terms of excellence, challenges emerge. How can one measure the quality of graduate student training based on the faculty in the department or the resources available to the student? Is it conceivable that a student with average faculty and few material resources might discover the next great scientific advance? In short, the answer is yes, which leads to the necessity of examining other dimensions of quality in terms of graduate student training and the development of ethical (and quality?) research practices.

Aside from the faculty who oversee a graduate student's education, there are also some external sources of quality checking at the graduate student level. For example, manuscripts that are submitted for peer review in academic journals can serve as another point where the work of the graduate student is assessed for quality. Meaningful critiques of submitted work can often serve as encouraging turning points in a young academic's career, whereas critical evaluations without suggestions for improvement can have the opposite effect — they may discourage young scholars from seeking rigorous peer review out of fear of being cruelly rejected. Finally, the penultimate assessment of quality would seem to be whether or not a graduate student can be employed in their job or career of choice soon after graduation — thus assigning the gatekeeping role of quality assessment to the faculty hiring search committees. When looking at quality in graduate student training with the backdrop of predatory publishing, it becomes even more complex to judge graduate student quality. If graduate students are not properly trained in how to vet academic journals, can they be held responsible for publishing their work in a predatory journal? The role of mentors, advisors, and senior faculty in ensuring graduate students understand the potential pitfalls of predatory publishing is discussed in detail in Chapter 5.

Judging Quality in Scholarly Research Production

Judging quality in the production of scholarly knowledge is a tricky process during the actual knowledge production process itself. The most salient judgement of quality typically comes *after* the research has been conducted — in the form of peer review. Yet when participants shared their perspectives of what constitutes quality in terms of the knowledge production process, they often listed attributes such as transparency, rigor, and other elements of ethical research practices that may be difficult for a peer reviewer to assess. For researchers working in collaborative teams, or in environments where there are opportunities for informal peer reviews during the research process, this issue of judging quality before submission to a journal seems to resolve itself. But what about researchers who work independently, or who are not housed in a department or institution where pre-submission reviews are possible? How can researchers in those positions ensure they are producing quality work? Possible solutions are discussed in the section below.

Judging Quality in the Vetting Process for Scholarly Publications

While there is a large consensus in both the study we conducted and the scholarly and mainstream literature that peer review is the gold standard for vetting scholarly publications and ensuring the quality of published academic manuscripts, there is almost no discussion in those same venues of who 'judges the judges' so to speak. While there are agreed-upon elements of a quality peer review (e.g., clarity, constructive criticism, attention to detail, etc.), there is really only one gatekeeper that sees the peer reviews and has the authority to determine their quality — the editor(s) of the journal (Michael 2019). Yet editors may or may not be providing guidance on their reviewers' performance — and in some cases they may not be expert enough in the content area to judge whether or not the review was accurate and fair. So what can be done to ensure the quality of the primary component responsible for quality scholarly knowledge being disseminated to the public and communities of interest? Some possible suggestions are offered in the concluding chapter of this volume.

Judging Quality in the Production and Distribution for Scholarly Publications

Judging the quality of publication and distribution of scholarly publications is a complicated mix between individual and institutional evaluations, coupled with third-party matrixes aimed at categorizing or ranking journals. At the individual level, as noted by our participants, journals are often judged by the articles they publish, as well as how they move authors through the process, and how their peer-review process is perceived. These individual perspectives are often at odds with institutional perspectives. A case in point is the participant who noted that they did not like (or respect) the top-ranked journal in their field because they rely on a single peer reviewer. Other participants also shared narratives of receiving lackluster peer reviews from top-ranked journals, indicating a rift between personal experiences and the perceptions of quality at the institutional/departmental/field levels.

In terms of institutional judgements of quality, numerous examples of field- or department- or institutional-level 'lists' of credible or preferred journals were given by participants. In addition to those instances, there are third party organizations, such as Directory of Open Access Journals (DOAJ) and the Committee on Publication Ethics (COPE) that gatekeep membership as a way of safeguarding (or encouraging) quality journals. Other indices, such as Scimago Journal & Country Rank, or Clarivate's Journal Citation Reports attempt to rank journals based on citations, acceptance rates, or other identified markers in an effort to delineate quality journals from those that are sub-par or even predatory.

An added complexity related to judging quality in the production and distribution of scholarly publications is the issue of citations, and how citation numbers are used to evaluate whether an individual is creating impactful (quality?) research. The i10-index and citation counts embedded in Google Scholar are a perfect example of this complexity. Some institutions have begun looking at citation counts when evaluating their faculty, leading to a cycle where researchers might be inclined to over-cite themselves as a way to bump up their citation counts and i10-index (a ranking that indicates how many publications an author has with more than ten citations). Additionally, given that Google Scholar does not discern between known predatory and legitimate publications, authors who are looking to game the system and get higher citation rankings may be able to self-cite and submit sub-par publications to predatory journals.

Conclusion

When discussing the quality of the production of scholarly research, participants addressed the defining characteristics of quality research, challenges in producing quality work, and mechanisms they knew about to safeguard or increase research quality in their environments. When examining these elements in the context of increasing numbers of predatory publications vying for author submissions, the individual, ethical components of ensuring quality in the knowledge production process become even more important to safeguard academia.

One of our interview participants, a young North American publishing consultant, described the ethics of quality, touching on many of the separate strands mentioned by participants above:

> To me quality is multifactorial [...] Are we ethically reporting the data? And what's the meaning, the purpose behind the data, behind the research? Is this to advance science, advance patient care? Or advance somebody's academic ego? And also quality means, I guess, does it properly answer the research question? And I think ethics falls into quality. If you follow the ethical guidelines, then [...] it's quality research, and quality research should be reported and should be made available to the public. (P49)

From these definitions of quality we can already begin to see the disparate ways quality is understood in relation to producing knowledge — from the transformation of the researcher in their pursuit of new ways of seeing and interpreting the world, to how well the researchers carried out those activities, to how well the journals or publishers carried out their stated purpose of vetting and distributing scholarly knowledge — and begin to grasp how impossible of a task it may be to come to a unified explanation of quality in terms of scholarly knowledge production. Although our participants did not put forth a definition of quality that could be operationalized, their comments did reveal four primary areas where quality can be addressed in the production of scientific knowledge: training graduate students, the actual production of the research, how the research is vetted, and finally, how it is published. Through paying close attention to quality at each of these stages of knowledge production, it may be possible to successfully navigate the pitfalls of predatory publishing and to create impactful, meaningful knowledge in all areas of research and scholarship.

Key Takeaways

- Quality is integral to scholarly publishing, but concrete definitions remain elusive.
- Predatory journals are widely considered to be a threat to scholarly publishing.
- Challenges to research quality identified by our work include the following: the constant pressure to publish; valuing the quantity of publications over their quality; the dominance of Euro-American publishing standards; having manuscripts repeatedly rejected for publication; pressure to sensationalize research findings; a flawed peer-review system; issues with the quality of peer reviewers; actions of deliberate fraud; length of the peer-review process; the myth of double-blind reviews; fear of the peer-review process; inconsistencies in institutional evaluation methods; and lack of mentorship for junior researchers.
- Definitions of research quality identified by our research include the following: a strong institutional culture; modeling ethical research behavior by senior researchers; committing to ethical behavior; following scientific protocol; a dedication to transparency; knowledge of your field; taking the time to think deeply about your research; and peer review.
- At each stage of the knowledge production process there are gatekeepers tasked with judging the quality of the research.
  - Faculty are the primary judges of quality during graduate student training.
  - Judging quality during research production is a combination of informal peer checks and balances (e.g., team collaborations) and individual adherence to ethical principles of research (e.g., transparency and rigorous data analysis).
  - Peer review is the primary way to judge quality as manuscripts move from production to publication.

- Journal rankings and citation numbers are often the primary indicator of quality after the publication of scholarly knowledge.

Discussion Questions

1. Why is it important to understand quality in all the stages of the knowledge production process?
2. Are there other challenges to quality that you can think of that are not included in this chapter?
3. Of the challenges to quality identified in this chapter, ask individual participants to list them in order of most importance to least. Then, as a group, discuss similarities and differences in the ranking and why the group felt certain challenges were most salient.
4. What are some ways to overcome the pain of having a manuscript rejected?
5. Why is peer review discussed as both a challenge to quality and a way to help define it?

Activity

Important note: Begin this activity BEFORE assigning the chapter as reading material. This activity could be included during a larger thematic discussion of research ethics or even a research methods class.

Steps:

1. Read the short quotes about quality from *Zen* in class (or post them on a discussion board for an asynchronous course). Facilitate a short verbal discussion (10–15 min) about how the group defines quality in terms of research production, then capture class thoughts for later re-examination (e.g., digital document, poster, audio/video capture). [Quotes are at the beginning of chapter sections]

2. Present class with a definition for 'predatory publishing' [see Chapter One for the definition used in this book, or use a definition of your choice from existing literature].

3. Ask the class to connect the attributes of quality they developed in Step 1 to the topic of predatory publishing they discussed in Step 2. Capture the themes they develop related to quality and how it relates to the *challenges to quality* presented by predatory publishing and the *definitions of quality* that are the markers of ethical research practices (To make the activity more concrete for lower-level students, the facilitator might want to discuss a specific journal or individual article that either contains markers of quality or which shows a clear absence of quality).

4. Read the chapter and compare how the class discussion of quality in terms of predatory publishing and research publication ethics relates to what is presented in the chapter. Some follow-up discussion questions for after the class has read the chapter could include:

   o Did the class consider the different global environments and pressures that affect researchers and scholars in different national settings?

   o For settings outside the Euro-American sphere: How does the pressure to publish in English and in Euro-American journals affect your confidence in conducting ethical research?

   o Faculty could share stories of getting their manuscripts rejected to help the students understand that it is part of the writing process and can serve as a way to improve manuscripts.

   o Discuss peer review and how, despite its flaws, it still serves as an important gatekeeping mechanism for scholarly knowledge production.

   o Introduce the importance of mentorship and encourage students to have frank discussions with their mentors and advisors about research ethics.

- Discuss the importance of institutional culture and ask students to reflect on the research behaviors they have seen from their faculty.

- Ask students to reflect on what they know about their field. The class could collaborate to develop a list of leading scholars in the field, and to research which journals are respected and credible in the field.

- Show students examples of peer review and discuss whether it was 'quality' or not. For example, the facilitator could show the class some examples of peer review they have received from one of their publications, or the class could attempt to find examples of open peer review on Publons.

References

Alfy, Shahira El and Abukari, Abdulai. 2020. 'Revisiting Perceived Service Quality in Higher Education: Uncovering Service Quality Dimensions for Postgraduate Students', *Journal of Marketing for Higher Education*, 30.1: 1–25, https://doi.org/10.1080/08841241.2019.1648360

Bairagya, Indrajit and Joy, Bino. 2022. 'What Determines the Quality of Higher Education? A Study of Commerce Graduates in Kerala (India)', *Journal of the Asia Pacific Economy*, 27.1: 1–25, https://doi.org/10.1080/13547860.2020.1870067

Biggs, John. 2001. 'The Reflective Institution: Assuring and Enhancing the Quality of Teaching and Learning', *Higher Education*, 41: 221–38, https://doi.org/10.1023/A:1004181331049

——. 2011. *Teaching for Quality Learning at University: What the Student Does* (New York: McGraw-Hill Education)

Bloch, Carter., Degn, Lise., Nygaard, Signe and Haase, Sanne. 2021. 'Does Quality Work Work? A Systematic Review of Academic Literature on Quality Initiatives in Higher Education', *Assessment & Evaluation in Higher Education*, 46.5: 701–18, https://doi.org/10.1080/02602938.2020.1813250

Bowden, J., and Marton, F. 2003. *The University of Learning: Beyond Quality and Competence* (London: Routledge)

Brennan, J., and Shah, T. 2000. *Managing Quality in Higher Education: An International Perspective on Institutional Assessment and Change* (Maidenhead, UK: Open University Press)

Carroll, Aaron E. 2018. 'Peer Review: The Worst Way to Judge Research, except for All the Others', *The New York Times*, https://www.nytimes.com/2018/11/05/upshot/peer-review-the-worst-way-to-judge-research-except-for-all-the-others.html

Cavallone, Mauro., Ciasullo, Maria Vincenza., Douglas, Jacqueline and Palumbo, Rocco. 2021. 'Framing Higher Education Quality from a Business Perspective: Setting the Conditions for Value Co-Creation', *Studies in Higher Education*, 46.6: 1099–111, https://doi.org/10.1080/03075079.2019.1672644

Forrester, Amy., Björk, Bo-Christer and Tenopir, Carol. 2017. 'New Web Services That Help Authors Choose Journals', *Learned Publishing*, 30.4: 281–87, https://doi.org/10.1002/leap.1112

Frambach, Janneke M., van der Vleuten, Cees P.M. and Durning, Steven J. 2013. 'AM Last Page: Quality Criteria in Qualitative and Quantitative Research.', *Academic Medicine*, 88.4: 552, https://journals.lww.com/academicmedicine/Citation/2013/04000/AM_Last_Page__Quality_Criteria_in_Qualitative_and.29.aspx

Giraleas, Dimitris. 2021. 'Can We Assess Teaching Quality on the Basis of Student Outcomes? A Stochastic Frontier Application', *Studies in Higher Education*, 46.7: 1325–39, https://doi.org/10.1080/03075079.2019.1679762

Harvey, Lee, and Green, Diana. 1993. 'Defining Quality', *Assessment & Evaluation in Higher Education*, 18.1: 9–34, https://doi.org/10.1080/0260293930180102

Humphries, Mark. 2021. 'The Absurdity of Peer Review. What the Pandemic Revealed about Scientific Publishing', *Elemental/Medium*, https://elemental.medium.com/the-absurdity-of-peer-review-1d58e5d9e661

'In Defense of Knowledge and Higher Education'. 2020. *American Association of University Professors*, https://www.aaup.org/report/defense-knowledge-and-higher-education

Koerber, Amy., Starkey, Jesse C., Ardon-Dryer, Karin., Cummins, R. Glenn., Eko, Lyombe and others. 2020. 'A Qualitative Content Analysis of Watchlists vs Safelists: How Do They Address the Issue of Predatory Publishing?', *Journal of Academic Librarianship*, 46.6, https://doi.org/10.1016/j.acalib.2020.102236

Lagrosen, Stefan., Seyyed-Hashemi, Roxana and Leitner, Markus. 2004. 'Examination of the Dimensions of Quality in Higher Education', *Quality Assurance in Education*, 12.2: 61–69, https://doi.org/10.1108/09684880410536431

Lindsey, Duncan. 1989. 'Using Citation Counts as a Measure of Quality in Science Measuring What's Measurable Rather than What's Valid', *Scientometrics*, 15.3–4: 189–203, https://doi.org/10.1007/BF02017198

McGrail, Matthew R., Rickard, Claire M., and Jones, Rebecca. 2006. 'Publish or Perish: A Systematic Review of Interventions to Increase Academic Publication Rates', *Higher Education Research and Development*, 25.1: 19–35, https://doi.org/10.1080/07294360500453053

McKiernan, Erin., Schimanski, Lesley., Nieves, Carol Muñoz., Matthias, Lisa., Niles, Meredith, and others. 2019. 'Use of the Journal Impact Factor in Academic Review, Promotion, and Tenure Evaluations', *PeerJ Preprints*, 8: 1–12, https://doi.org/10.7287/peerj.preprints.27638

Michael, Ann. 2019. 'Ask The Chefs: Peer Review Quality', *The Scholarly Kitchen*, https://scholarlykitchen.sspnet.org/2019/09/12/ask-the-chefs-peer-review-quality/

Pirsig, Robert M. 1974. *Zen and the Art of Motorcycle Maintenance* (New York City: Bantam Books)

Pond, Brooks B., Stacy D. Brown, David W. Stewart, David S. Roane, and Sam Harirforoosh. 2019. 'Faculty Applicants' Attempt to Inflate CVs Using Predatory Journals', *American Journal of Pharmaceutical Education*, 83.1: 12–14, https://doi.org/10.5688/ajpe7210

Pyne, Derek. 2017. 'The Rewards of Predatory Publications at a Small Business School', *Journal of Scholarly Publishing*, 48.3: 137–60, https://doi.org/10.3138/jsp.48.3.137

Roll, Shawn C. 2019. 'The Value and Process of High-Quality Peer Review in Scientific Professional Journals', *Journal of Diagnostic Medical Sonography*, 35.5: 359–62, https://doi.org/10.1177/8756479319853800

Shrestha, Jiban., Subedi, Subash., Shokati, Behzad and Chaudhary, Amit. 2018. 'Predatory Journals: A Threat to Scholarly Publishing', *Journal of Education and Research*, 8.1: 89–101, https://doi.org/10.3126/jer.v8i1.25482

Skolnik, Michael. 2000. 'Does Counting Publications Provide Any Useful Information about Academic Performance?', *Teacher Education Quarterly*, 27.2: 15–25

Suleman, Fátima. 2017. 'The Employability Skills of Higher Education Graduates: Insights into Conceptual Frameworks and Methodological Options', *Higher Education*, 76: 263–78, https://doi.org/10.1007/s10734-017-0207-0

Teeroovengadum, Viraiyan., Nunkoo, Robin., Gronroos, Christian., Kamalanabhan, T. J. and Seebaluck, Ashley Keshwar. 2019. 'Higher Education Service Quality, Student Satisfaction and Loyalty: Validating the HESQUAL Scale and Testing an Improved Structural Model', *Quality Assurance in Education*, 27.4: 427–45, https://doi.org/10.1108/QAE-01-2019-0003

Tracy, Sarah J. 2010. 'Qualitative Quality: Eight "Big-Tent" Criteria for Excellent Qualitative Research', *Qualitative Inquiry*, 16.10: 837–51, https://doi.org/10.1177/1077800410383121

Vazire, Simine. 2020. 'Peer-Reviewed Scientific Journals Don't Really Do Their Job', *Wired*, https://www.wired.com/story/peer-reviewed-scientific-journals-dont-really-do-their-job/

Vykydal, David., Folta, Martin and Nenadál, Jaroslav. 2020. 'A Study of Quality Assessment in Higher Education within the Context of Sustainable

Development: A Case Study from Czech Republic', *Sustainability*, 12.11: 4769, https://doi.org/10.3390/SU12114769

Welch, Catherine, and Piekkari, Rebecca. 2017. 'How Should We (Not) Judge the "quality" of Qualitative Research? A Re-Assessment of Current Evaluative Criteria in International Business', *Journal of World Business*, 52.5: 714–25, https://doi.org/10.1016/j.jwb.2017.05.007

Zerem, Enver. 2017. 'The Ranking of Scientists Based on Scientific Publications Assessment', *Journal of Biomedical Informatics*, 75: 107–9, https://doi.org/10.1016/j.jbi.2017.10.007

4. Scientific Hoaxes and the Predatory Paradox
Past, Present, and Future

In 2015, Johannes Bohannon, along with three coauthors, published an article titled 'Chocolate with High Cocoa Content as a Weight Loss Accelerator' in the *International Archives of Medicine* (Bohannon and others 2015).[1] The article reported results from a study that divided participants into three groups, with a different diet assigned to each group, and concluded that 'Subjects of the chocolate intervention group experienced the easiest and most successful weight loss' (p. 1). When the study was published, Bohannon and his team also produced a press release that was widely circulated and well received. Soon after the article and accompanying press release were published, the study's findings were picked up and reported by several high-profile media outlets with dramatic headlines such as 'Slim by Chocolate' and 'Why You Must Eat Chocolate Daily' (Bohannon 2015).

'Johannes Bohannon' is actually a science journalist whose real name is John Bohannon. In a personal account published later, Bohannon (2015) described the article as an intentional hoax that he and his coauthors had carried out in response to a request from a German film crew who was making a documentary on the 'junk-science diet industry'. To implement the hoax, Bohannon and his coauthors created an 'Institute of Diet and Health' that existed only as a website, and he

---

[1] The retracted article is no longer available at the publisher's website. However, it is archived at several locations. The version we cite is an archived version available through Wikipedia, https://en.wikipedia.org/wiki/File:Chocolate_with_high_Cocoa_content_as_a_weight-loss_accelerator.pdf

assumed the name 'Johannes Bohannon' as lead author of the study. Bohannon (2015) narrates the rest of the events as follows:

> Other than those fibs, the study was 100 percent authentic. My colleagues and I recruited actual human subjects in Germany. We ran an actual clinical trial, with subjects randomly assigned to different diet regimes. And the statistically significant benefits of chocolate that we reported are based on the actual data. It was, in fact, a fairly typical study for the field of diet research. Which is to say: It was terrible science. The results are meaningless, and the health claims that the media blasted out to millions of people around the world are utterly unfounded. (para. 3)

As Bohannon's account makes clear, his team's research was conducted and accurately reported in the article, so there is nothing false about the publication in that sense. However, the study enrolled only fifteen participants and, thus, the dramatic conclusions that the article reported were not statistically sound, and nowhere in the article was the sample size mentioned. Another problem was that the authors had not received Institutional Review Board approval to recruit participants and conduct their research (Schwitzer 2015). Such approval would usually be indicated in the text of the manuscript that is submitted to a journal.

These omissions reflect basic problems in the quality of the science, and they would have been detected if the article had undergone a legitimate peer-review process. The article had not undergone peer review, but rather, according to Bohannon (2015), the journal's editors accepted the version that was submitted, without requesting any revisions, and they published it as soon as they received the publication fee of 600 Euros from the authors. As Bohannon explains, he had submitted the piece to *International Archives of Medicine*, as well as nineteen other journals, all of which he believed to be, in his words, 'fake'. His belief was proven correct when the 'paper was accepted for publication by multiple journals within 24 hours' (Bohannon 2015: para. 2). By Bohannon's own account, the 'Chocolate with High Cocoa Content' hoax study was intended to expose weaknesses in our system of reporting scientific findings to expert audiences as well as the wider public:

If a study doesn't even list how many people took part in it, or makes a bold diet claim that's 'statistically significant' but doesn't say how big the effect size is, you should wonder why. But for the most part, we don't. Which is a pity, because journalists are becoming the de facto peer review system. And when we fail, the world is awash in junk science. (Bohannon 2015: para. 5)

In short, Bohannon and others' (2015) hoax tested the system, and the system failed. The journal editors who accepted and published the article, as well as the science journalists who reported uncritically on the study, looked bad as a result.

Scientific hoaxes such as Bohannon's have been studied by communication scholars for their rhetorical characteristics and effects. For example, Finneman and Thomas (2018) identify 'central characteristics of hoaxing' as 'untruths framed as truths', carried out by 'someone in a position of power over a public and influence via entertainment' (p. 353), and Reilly (2020) defines hoaxes as 'ambiguous forms of communication that channel deception, humour, and mischief in the targeting of victims and the approbation of audiences' (p. 266–67). Along similar lines, scientific hoaxes have been characterized as opportunistic rhetorical acts: 'as reactions to and perpetuations of a particular kairos — an opportunity to speak up' (Walsh 2006: 3). Secor and Walsh (2004) offer a more comprehensive definition, suggesting that a hoax is 'characterized by a constellation of rhetorical features: it involves the production of discourse, a perpetrator with intentions, an audience that is first engaged and then duped' (p. 71).

In this chapter, we take a broader view of scientific hoaxes such as Bohannon's. Specifically, through a close examination of Bohannon's 'Chocolate with High Cocoa Content' hoax in the context of other notable scientific hoaxes, we explore the various types of weakness that such hoaxes can expose in the larger information ecosystem of scholarly publishing. As we argue, Bohannon and his colleagues' 'Chocolate with High Cocoa Content' hoax is interesting not only for the rhetorical effect of exposing one specific journal as predatory, or for drawing attention to an isolated instance of poor media reporting practice, but because of the flaws that it exposes in our entire system of scholarly communication. Thus, scientific hoaxes further complicate any neat distinction between journals that are predatory and those that are not. Hoaxes have, in some cases, exposed specific journals as predatory. But in other cases, they have had effects beyond those that the author anticipated, exposing major weaknesses or fraudulent practices not only at journals or publishers suspected to be predatory but also at the most prestigious and well-respected journals. More importantly, publishing hoaxes have unintentionally exposed weaknesses in the mechanisms that we have long relied on to ensure research quality. For example, hoaxes have exposed flaws in even the best journals' peer-review systems, and when hoax articles continue to be cited in subsequent literature — sometimes even after retraction — they lead us to question our habit of relying on citation counts as a measure of research quality.

A Closer Look at the 'Chocolate with High Cocoa Content' Hoax

Bohannon and his colleagues' 'Chocolate with High Cocoa Content' article was retracted shortly after it was published, and the editors of *International Archives of Medicine* published a retraction notice dated 10 June 2015 (Editorial Office 2015). The editors' decision to retract this article ostensibly served to correct the scientific record and prevent the erroneous data reported in the published study from being circulated in subsequent literature. This manner of correcting the scientific record is an important purpose of retractions, as defined by the Committee on Publication Ethics (COPE):

> Retraction is a mechanism for correcting the literature and alerting readers to publications that contain such seriously flawed or erroneous data that their findings and conclusions cannot be relied upon. Unreliable data may result from honest error or from research misconduct. (Wager and others 2009: 202)

Although the editors' retraction of Bohannon's hoax article seems to correct the scientific record, it does not entirely align with these COPE guidelines. For example, the editors' language in the retraction notice is confusing. The retraction notice published on the journal's website states that the manuscript had been published 'accidentally' and that it 'was finally rejected and never published as such.' Furthermore, the journal editors did not fully follow the COPE guidelines, which state that 'Notices of retraction should... be linked to the retracted article wherever possible (i.e., in all electronic versions)' (Wager and others 2009: 201). It is not clear why, but in this case, the retracted article is no longer available at the journal's website. In fact, making the situation even more confusing, the Digital Object Identifier (DOI) for the original article now links to a study called 'The Comparison of Resilience and Spirituality in Addicted and Non-Addicted Women' (Ramezani and others 2015). This is extremely problematic, given that the sole purpose of a DOI is to provide a unique and persistent identifier that links to a published article, and it is the publisher's responsibility to maintain the integrity of that link ('How the 'Digital Object Identifier' Works' 2001). In short, this retraction seems to be intended as a 'mechanism for correcting the literature', as the COPE guidelines advise, but the error that needed to be corrected was not an error made by researchers; rather, it was, according to this retraction notice, an error made by the publisher.

The series of events preceding the article's retraction is also subject to dispute. According to a 28 May 2015 Retraction Watch post, the hoax article was available on the journal's website on the morning of 28 May but appears to have been retracted later that same day (Schwitzer 2015). A 28 May 2015 Facebook post (Perez 2015) from someone who appears to be one of the journal's editors also indicates the article was retracted on that same date. By contrast, the retraction notice that appears on the journal's website (Editorial Office 2015) indicates 10 June 2015 as the publication date of the notice; it is not clear why the retraction notice would be published almost two weeks after the article was retracted on 28 May. In addition to this confusion about the date of retraction, these different sources also offer varying accounts of the series of events that preceded retraction. Perez's Facebook post suggests that the article was never accepted by the journal — that it was published 'by mistake', based on a misunderstanding of a managing editor who had been copied on Bohannon's initial email submission. The Facebook post even claims that sometime after the article was accidentally published due to this miscommunication, 'the manuscript was rejected by the editorial board.' However, Bohannon offers a different narrative of events. He quotes an email acceptance notice that is also quoted by Retraction Watch. In this personal email correspondence that Bohannon had apparently shared with Retraction Watch, the journal editors praised Bohannon and his colleagues' article for its high quality and potential contributions:

> I'm contacting to let you know your manuscript 'Chocolate with High Cocoa Content as a Weight-Loss Accelerator' has been pointed by our editors as an outstanding manuscript and could be accepted directly in our premier journal *International Archives of Medicine.* (McCook 2015)[2]

Adding even more confusion, Perez's Facebook post was edited on 10 June 2015, almost two weeks after its initial 28 May publication, to add the second paragraph, which seems to be an attempt to account for the journal's problematic set of actions. This 10 June edit also contributes to a discrepancy about the length of time that the fake article was available on the journal's website. For instance, Perez's (2015) Facebook post suggests it was online for only a few days (from Thursday one week to Monday of the next week, with no specific dates given). However, Retraction Watch indicates that the article was accepted soon after Bohannon submitted it in early March and was not retracted until 28 May 2015.

It may be easy to look at this situation in retrospect and conclude that so many problems are apparent in this article that no one could ever take it seriously, and because it was retracted and is no longer available, its damage was minimal. In fact, any science journalist or academic researcher who took time to assess the *International Archives of Medicine*'s online presence would have had good reason to question the credibility of this journal. For instance, a search in PubMed Central's journal list reveals that the journal was indexed from 2008 until 2014 but is 'no longer participating' ('PMC Journal List' [n.d.]). Articles

---

2   The Retraction Watch post (McCook 2015) includes a hyperlink that appears to link to the email correspondence that is quoted here. However, at the time of publication of this chapter, the link does not work.

published in the journal are full of grammatical errors, indicating a lack of attention to copy editing, at the very least, and probably indicating an absence of peer review as well. The journal publishes a lot of articles on a wide range of topics. For example, Volume 14, published in 2014, includes fifty articles. These are indexed in PubMed Central as the entire volume, without any indication of issue numbers. Categories include Case Reports, Hypothesis, Original Research, Reviews, and Short Reports. The journal website linked from its current publisher, iMedicalPublisher.com, describes the journal as 'The new megajournal on all areas of medicine', and says the journal is 'Really international' ('International Archives of Medicine' [n.d.]). These obvious cues should be enough to raise questions about the journal's legitimacy, even aside from the glaring scientific flaws already noted in the hoax article itself. However, none of these factors, and even the fact that the article was retracted, were obvious enough to stop the article from being cited in subsequent literature. In fact, when this chapter was written, the article had been cited twenty-eight times, according to Google Scholar.[3] Although some of these citations refer to the article as an example of a publication in a predatory journal, other citations are in legitimate journal articles that genuinely cite the scientific findings reported in the article. Specifically, as shown in Table 4.1, almost one-third of these citations (eight out of twenty-eight) cite the article to support a scientific claim.

---

3   According to a Google Scholar search conducted on 11 May 2022, the article had twenty-eight citations. These citations continued to accrue during the writing of this book.

Table 4.1 Citations of Bohannon Hoax Article. © STEPP Research Team.

Citations Supporting or Refuting Bohannon's Hoax Article

Article Information	Details of Citation
(Alkalaj 2017)	Cited as an example of a scientific hoax.
(Arias-Castro 2019)	Cited as an example of a scientific hoax.
(Beall 2018)	Cited as an example of a scientific hoax.
(Camps-Bossacoma and others 2019)	**Cited to support a scientific claim.**
(da Costa 2021)	Article is cited an example of scientific fraud.
(Elkhateeb and AL Harbi 2018)	**Cited to support a scientific claim.**
(Gauthier 2016)	Cited as an example of a scientific hoax.
(Giraldo and others 2017)	**Cited to support a scientific claim.**
(Goldschmidt [n.d.])	**Cited to support a scientific claim.**
(Grass and Stark 2015)	Cited as an example of a scientific hoax.
(Kawakami 2020)	Cited as an example of a scientific hoax.
(Kyas and others 2021)	Unable to determine purpose of citation.
(Lee and others 2019)	**Cited to support a scientific claim.**
(Malinowski 2019)	Cited as an example of a scientific hoax.
(Malinowski 2020)	Cited as an example of a scientific hoax.
(Moore 2016)	Cited as an example of questionable statistical calculations.
(Mukerji 2017)	Unable to determine purpose of citation.
(Müller 2021)	Cited as an example of a scientific hoax and faulty statistical analysis.
(Peck 2021)	Cited as an example of a scientific hoax.
(Ponce 2018)	Cited as an example of a scientific hoax.
(Rahman and Citrakesumasari 2018)	**Cited to support a scientific claim.**
(Ramos and others 2017)	**Cited to support a scientific claim.**
(Rodríguez-Lagunas and others 2019)	**Cited to support a scientific claim.**
(Sauerwein 2019)	Cited as an example of a scientific hoax.
(Steel and others 2019)	Acknowledged as a hoax and is presented as an example of faulty statistics for an in-class activity in a statistics class.
(Stylianou 2022)	Unable to determine purpose of citation.
(Teixeira da Silva and Al-Khatib 2016)	Cited as an example of a scientific hoax.
(Wooven and Snider 2019)	Unable to determine purpose of citation.

None of the eight publications that cite the Bohannon hoax article to support scientific claims acknowledges that the publication was retracted, even though all these publications appeared well after the 10 June 2015 publication date of the *International Archives of Medicine*'s retraction notice. Instead, these eight publications cite the Bohannon hoax article as if it were any other legitimate peer-reviewed scientific text. For example, a 2017 review article (Ramos and others 2017) cites the Bohannon study, along with several other sources, to support the claim that appears in the following sentence: 'In addition, despite the fact that cocoa products commercially available are frequently high-caloric foodstuffs, they have been reported to have a similar [anti-obesity] effect in humans' (p. 5). The note that cites the Bohannon and others article includes a CrossRef link that links to the DOI, which now links to a different article, as noted above. This 2017 review article, interestingly, is published in the journal *Antioxidants*, which is published by MDPI. The Bohannon hoax article is also cited in another article (Rodríguez-Lagunas and others 2019) published in the MDPI journal *Molecules*. This article cites the Bohannon hoax article to support the claim that 'anti-obesity actions of cocoa have been reported' (p. 7). Oddly, the Bohannon hoax article is also cited at the end of the following sentence, which does not seem to have anything to do with the findings reported by Bohannon and his coauthors: 'Regarding the health questionnaire, the university students reported, logically, a good health status, far away from suffering chronic diseases involving neoplasm and cardiovascular diseases, the main causes of death in the Spanish population' (p. 8). These citations of the Bohannon hoax article, well after it was retracted and without any acknowledgement that it was a hoax, raise some serious concerns about the quality of content published in these two MDPI journals. It appears, at least in these two cases, that authors are citing literature without paying much attention to its quality — or maybe without even reading the texts they are citing — and peer reviewers are not catching these sloppy citation practices.

Another citation of Bohannon and others appears in a 2019 article in the *Journal of Agricultural and Food Chemistry* (Camps-Bossacoma and others 2019). This article, 'Role of Theobromine in Cocoa's Metabolic Properties in Healthy Rats', links to the Bohannon hoax article through

Google Scholar instead of CrossRef, but like the other citations, this one cites the study without any acknowledgement that it is fraudulent or that it has been retracted. Specifically, the Bohannon hoax article is cited in the following sentence: 'Cocoa effects on body weight increase have already been reported both in animal models and humans, [...] and it has been postulated that cocoa is a weight loss accelerator' (p. 3611). Unlike the other two journals, published by MDPI, this journal is published by the American Chemical Society, described on its website as follows: 'As a non-profit scientific organization with more than 140 years' experience, we are a champion for chemistry, its practitioners and our global community of members' ('About ACS' [n.d.]). This organizational affiliation may seem to grant legitimacy to the journal. Again, though, it is troubling that the Bohannon hoax study is cited uncritically, as a source within the authoritative scientific record, to support a statement about cocoa's weight-loss properties. This must lead us to question the overall legitimacy of the article and the soundness of the science that it reports.

Persistent citation of retracted articles is not uncommon. In fact, Retraction Watch keeps a list of retracted articles that have received the highest number of citations ('Top 10 Most Highly Cited Retracted Papers' [n.d.]). The top article on the list was published in 2013 in *New England Journal of Medicine* and retracted in 2018 (Estruch and others 2013). The Retraction Watch site reports that the article has 2735 citations. Next on their list is a *Lancet* article published in 1998 and retracted in 2018; Retraction Watch indicates 1509 citations of this article. A recent study exposes the serious nature of this problem by examining a high-profile retraction case that involved the work of Scott S. Reuben (Bornemann-Cimenti and others 2016). Reuben was a well-established medical researcher who studied pain medicine. In 2009, it was discovered that he had fabricated data in many of his published studies, which led journals to retract twenty-five of his published articles. Bornemann-Cimenti and others (2016) track the extent to which Reuben's articles continued to accrue citations for many years after they were retracted. Although some of the citations note that the article has been retracted, many do not (Peng and others 2022).

According to Hyland (1999), 'the attribution of propositional content to another source' (p. 341) is a fundamental rhetorical feature of academic writing. Problematic citation practices include the citation of retracted articles, before or after the article is retracted (Bolland and others 2022); citation, knowingly or unknowingly, of articles published in predatory journals (Akça and Akbulut 2021); or citing an article without having read it (Akça and Akbulut 2021; Wetterer 2006). Offering an especially concerning example, Wetterer tells the story of an outright falsehood that was perpetuated for many years among ant scientists, about the extinction of a particular ant species that allegedly occurred on the Atlantic Islands of Madeira due to the invasion of an exotic species. According to Wetterer's analysis, this myth was perpetuated and became accepted as scientific fact reported in peer-reviewed journal articles because of practices that he labels 'quotation error and citation copying' (p. 352). In short, scientists were repeating the myth that this species had been made extinct, based on a misinterpretation of an 1898 article (Stoll 1898) that ended up being widely cited as the source of this information. Wetterer speculates that Stoll's report was misinterpreted because his article was published in German, and the person who initially cited it mistranslated his findings; thus, the erroneous belief that Stoll's report was based on first-hand evidence became widely cited in subsequent literature, even though, according to Wetterer, Stoll never claimed to have access to first-hand evidence.

Thus, like many of the other phenomena explored in this book, the phenomenon of sloppy citation practices is nothing new; it is well documented in science, and the phenomenon of poor citation practices has been documented and studied well before the relatively recent development and proliferation of predatory journals. In the case of the Bohannon hoax, articles that cited it later are articles that were presumably subject to actual peer review, and they link directly to the Bohannon and others' study, which was retracted shortly after it was published, without acknowledging that it was retracted. An especially puzzling aspect of this case is that it is not clear how the authors of these articles would have located a correct version of Bohannon and others' study, given that its DOI — which is supposed to provide a unique and persistent link to a digital publication — does not even link correctly to the retracted article.

In short, the Bohannon 'Chocolate with High Cocoa Content' hoax may have been designed to expose substandard publishing practices at predatory journals, but it ultimately exposed a much larger, more complex set of problems. Everything was broken in this situation, including the various checks and balances that are expected to detect bad science and prevent it from being shared with the public. The science reported in this article was conducted, but it was conducted poorly by anyone's standards. A thorough peer review would have detected the obvious flaws in the research and would have prevented the paper from being published. A proper retraction, meaning that the retraction notice would appear along with the original article at the original DOI, and a more careful vetting of the literature by scientists after the article was published, may have prevented the retracted article from subsequent citations. However, in addition to all these scientific problems, the science journalists who reported on the findings also should have done due diligence by asking questions to relevant experts about the science behind the article.

Retractions of published articles are not uncommon, even at journals that are not predatory. In fact, the frequency of article retractions is on the rise, and even the most prestigious journals in their respective disciplines are not immune (Bornemann-Cimenti and others 2016). The extent to which the citation of a retracted article will alter the course of science depends on the nature of the evidence that is cited. If the evidence is in line with most other evidence, then the effect may not be too great, but if it is the only study that is cited to support a claim that departs from other available evidence, then this is obviously problematic. For all these reasons, retractions of published articles, whether they are published in a 'predatory' journal or not, are something that researchers and other stakeholders in scholarly publishing need to be aware of.

Bohannon's Other Hoax: The *Science* Sting

Bohannon's chocolate diet hoax followed closely after a larger sting operation he had carried out for the journal *Science* in 2013 (Vergano 2013b). In this sting operation, Bohannon acted on behalf of *Science*, producing a fake research article on lichen as a supposed cure for cancer. Unlike the cocoa diet article, which reported results of research that the authors had conducted, the lichen article's contents were entirely fabricated. Bohannon used false author names, submitting the paper to several journals and varying the author's name from one journal to the next, and he reported conclusions that were completely unfounded. He even suggested that the new drug was immediately available to patients, without conducting any clinical trials to ensure its safety. Another important distinction between the two hoax attempts is that Bohannon never moved forward with publishing the lichen cancer article. Rather, in the *Science* sting operation, whenever Bohannon received an acceptance notice from a journal, he withdrew the article and informed the editors he had discovered flaws in the research (Lowe 2013). Thus, Bohannon's fake cancer article never became part of scientific record, unlike the cocoa diet study.

This 2013 sting was a much larger operation than the 2015 cocoa diet hoax. Also, whereas the cocoa diet hoax article specifically targeted journals that Bohannon had reason to believe were predatory, the *Science* sting operation targeted open access journals much more broadly. In fact, it is clear in some of the discourse surrounding this sting operation that the operation, sponsored by *Science*, was explicitly intended to expose weaknesses in open access publishing. For example, in the article that Bohannon (2013) published after the hoax, he says the following:

> Over the past 10 months, I have submitted 304 versions of the wonder drug paper to open-access journals. More than half of the journals accepted the paper, failing to notice its fatal flaws. Beyond that headline result, the data from this sting operation reveal the contours of an emerging Wild West in academic publishing. (p. 60)

This language is noteworthy for the extent to which it vilifies open access publishing, identifying open access publishing, broadly defined, as the target for the sting operation, failing to make any distinction between those journals that are legitimate and those that are not, and failing to direct any attention to the question of the quality of a journal's peer-review procedures, aside from whether the journal adopts open access publishing practices. Bohannon then proceeds to make some inaccurate claims about open access publishing, such as the following statements:

> Most of the players are murky. The identity and location of the journals' editors, as well as the financial workings of their publishers, are often purposefully obscured. (p. 60)

The vague and all-encompassing nature of these statements is suspect, and the fact that no evidence is provided to support these claims raises serious questions about their accuracy and credibility.

As the sting operation unfolded, Bohannon's generalizations about open access publishing did not hold up. In fact, the sting operation resulted in a wide range of responses from the target journals, working against the prospect of making any widespread generalizations about the quality of open access journals. Specifically, Bohannon submitted the lichen article to 304 open access journals, making only slight changes to the versions that he submitted to each journal. Of these 304 submissions, 255 journals agreed to review the article, and 157 accepted it for publication (Lowe 2013). Among these journals, it turned out that some of the high-profile publishers that publish exclusively open access content proved themselves to be most resistant to the sting attempt. For example, two Hindawi journals rejected the spoof article, whereas two Elsevier journals accepted it (Bohannon 2013). Hindawi is a well-known open access publisher whose mission is clearly stated on their website: 'Maximizing the impact of research through openness. Because science works best when research is open' ('Open Access Publishing for the Scientific Community' [n.d.]: para. 1). Several of Hindawi's journals were at one time included on Beall's list (Berger and Cirasella 2015). However, Hindawi journals were later removed from Beall's list, with the acknowledgment that they had improved their practices since the time they were initially added to the list. Beall is quoted in an interview that occurred later as saying 'I reanalyzed [Hindawi] and determined that it did not belong on the list [...] It was always a borderline case' (Butler 2013: 434).

Only one journal that was targeted in this sting operation — *PLOS ONE* — rejected the paper outright because of ethical concerns. However, even though many open access journals came out looking better than expected, Bohannon (2013) ultimately concluded that Beall's list is a better predictor of flawed procedures than the Directory of Open Access Journals (DOAJ):

> The results show that Beall is good at spotting publishers with poor quality control: For the publishers on his list that completed the review process, 82% accepted the paper. Of course that also means that almost one in five on his list did the right thing — at least with my submission.

> A bigger surprise is that for DOAJ publishers that completed the review process, 45% accepted the bogus paper. 'I find it hard to believe,' says Bjørnshauge, the DOAJ founder. 'We have been working with the community to draft new tighter criteria for inclusion.' Beall, meanwhile, notes that in the year since this sting began, 'the number of predatory publishers and predatory journals has continued to escalate at a rapid pace.' (p. 64)

This disparity between Beall's list and DOAJ is significant in context of discussions about the 'watchlist' versus 'safelist' approach (Koerber and others 2020), in so far as it suggests that Beall's watchlist was a more accurate predictor of suspect journals than DOAJ's safelist. But it also works against the possibility of making broad generalizations about any category of journal in that neither method of categorizing journals proved to be airtight in this situation.

This series of events may explain why at the end of his commentary, in the 'Coda' section, Bohannon (2013) adopts a more generous stance toward open access:

> From the start of this sting, I have conferred with a small group of scientists who care deeply about open access. Some say that the open-access model itself is not to blame for the poor quality control revealed by Science's investigation. If I had targeted traditional, subscription-based journals, Roos told me, 'I strongly suspect you would get the same result.' But open access has multiplied that underclass of journals, and the number of papers they publish. (p. 65)

This outcome of Bohannon's *Science* sting operation, once again, exposes the problem of making any simple distinction between predatory and non-predatory publishers.

Aftermath of the Bohannon–*Science* Sting Operation: Reform, Fallout, and Backlash

It could be argued that Bohannon's *Science* sting operation had some positive impact. For instance, Bohannon notes in a published interview that both the DOAJ and the Open Access Scholarly Publishers Association (OASPA) made changes to their databases after the Bohannon sting operation (Davis 2013; see also Teixeira da Silva and others 2018). However, the sting operation also led to significant backlash against

Science, leading to questions about the journal's editorial practices. For example, in a blog post published on 3 October 2013, Michael Eisen responded to Bohannon's sting operation by drawing attention to a 2010 *Science* article that had previously sparked controversy and criticism of traditional peer review and publishing processes (Eisen 2013). In this situation, which has come to be known as the '#arseniclife' case, it was not so much an intentional hoax as a situation that raises questions about the changing nature of the relationship between science journalism and traditional peer-reviewed journals.

The '#arseniclife' case began with a 29 November 2010 press release from the National Aeronautics and Space Administration (NASA) that captured international attention with its announcement of a news conference scheduled for 2 December 'to discuss an astrobiology finding that will impact the search for evidence of extraterrestrial life' (Brown and Weselby 2010: 1). The 'astrobiology finding' to which the press release referred was from a research team that had purportedly discovered the existence of an organism that could use arsenic instead of phosphorus as a foundation for its DNA. If this had been true, it would have been the only organism of its kind and could have suggested that the organism came from a different planet other than Earth (Rosen 2012). On 2 December 2010, the day of the NASA news conference, a news story published on the NASA website (Phillips 2010) made even bolder claims about the study:

> NASA-supported researchers have discovered the first known microorganism on Earth able to thrive and reproduce using the toxic chemical arsenic. The microorganism, which lives in California's Mono Lake, substitutes arsenic for phosphorus in the backbone of its DNA and other cellular components. (para. 1)

This claim later turned out to be false and based on poor-quality science; the microorganism did require phosphorus, but the science was conducted in a way that did not make that apparent. However, NASA's press release was written and taken up in a way that suggested their scientists had discovered an organism that would cause us to expand the scientific definition of life in a way that would make the existence of extraterrestrial life much more likely. The *Science* publication (Wolfe-Simon and others 2011) was later refuted, as it was found in replication studies that the organism did need tiny amounts of phosphorus and that the arsenic was not actually incorporated into its genetic structure as the initial research team had reported (Vergano 2012).

In short, this case showed how even the most high-profile journals can publish science of questionable quality — ironically, in this case, it was the initial excitement and desire to be the first to break the news that led *Science* to publish these NASA findings too quickly, without good-quality peer review. In fact, a *USA Today* investigation later revealed that *Science* editors were so eager to be the ones to publish this breaking news that they purposely sent the article to peer reviewers whom they knew would not be too critical (Vergano 2013a). In other words, the desire for profit and the need to keep feeding the high-impact machine led to the same outcomes — publishing of substandard science — that critics love to point out in open access or so-called predatory journals.

One of the major problems in this situation, as critics observed, was that by 2 December 2010, when *Science* published online the actual peer-reviewed papers that had been the subject of all this hype, Internet chatter had largely debunked the paper's findings, so that when the paper was published in its final version after the initial embargo period, it was old news. In Rosen's (2012) opinion, this case should cause us to question the value of tried-and-true practices of withholding scientific evidence under journal embargoes and so on. Her stance is that allowing debate to play out freely as soon as evidence is available, in the manner that is allowed by online media, can result in better-quality science than the slower mechanism of traditional peer review and withholding findings until they make their way into print. As she says,

> Perhaps this is clear, but the reason to have 'proper' methods of engagement is because they ostensibly will produce better science and better science journalism. But in this one case study, we can see how the opposite is true: The 'proper' paths of engagement produced uninformed hype, poor science, and kept the sources – both human and paper – away from a conversation that was simmering with genuine enthusiasm and curiosity. The best science – and the best science writing – could come when we allow those natural levels of interest to have a field day with the research and researchers that are out there. (para. 21)

In short, the '#arseniclife' case, as it came to be known, exposed weaknesses in the kind of journal whose integrity is not typically called into question, proving that a high-impact subscription journal such as *Science* can be just as guilty of publishing substandard science as open access journals. As some have suggested, the important takeaway from the #arseniclife case was that, rather than focus the spotlight on open access publishing, or predatory journals, we should be taking a critical look at peer review, which is not always acting as the gatekeeper that we expect it to be, even at the most prestigious journals. As Eisen (2013) states in a commentary that addresses both the Bohannon sting operation and the #arseniclife scandal,

> First, and foremost, we need to get past the antiquated idea that the singular act of publication — or publication in a particular journal — should signal for all eternity that a paper is valid, let alone important. Even when people take peer review seriously, it is still just represents the views of 2 or 3 people at a fixed point in time. To invest the judgment of these people with so much meaning is nuts. And its far worse when the process is distorted — as it so often is — by the desire to publish sexy papers, or to publish more papers, or because the wrong reviewers were selected, or because they were just too busy to do a good job. If we had, instead, a system where the review process was transparent and persisted for the useful life of a work (as I've written about previously), none of the flaws exposed in Bohannon's piece would matter. (para. 14)

As Eisen's commentary suggests, it is worth noting that the 'legitimate' scientific article in the #arseniclife scandal, which was published at a top-tier journal, ultimately led to some of the same conclusions about the broken nature of our scientific publishing system as the intentional hoax and sting operations discussed above.

Concluding Thoughts and Some Practical Advice

Scientific hoaxes have a long history, originating long before the relatively recent concern about predatory journals. For example, well-known examples in the nineteenth century include Edgar Allan Poe's 1844 'balloon hoax', in which he published a hoax article in *The Sun* newspaper about someone making a three-day balloon trip across the

Atlantic in a gas balloon (Poe 1844), and Richard Adam Locke's 1835 'Moon Hoax', a six-day series in *The Sun* which made fabricated scientific claims about the discovery of life on the moon (Vida 2012). In more recent times, the 1996 Sokal hoax and a 2018 spin-off that has come to be known as the 'Sokal Squared' hoax were both published by high-profile journals that would not be considered predatory (Mounk 2018). These hoaxes were targeting a different aspect of academic publishing than Bohannon: their target was the tendency toward over-reliance on jargon, even in legitimate peer-reviewed journals. The original Sokal hoax, in particular, occurred well before the term 'predatory' was coined to refer to suspicious journals and publishing practices.

Even while acknowledging this long history, we might consider a different perspective on scientific hoaxes in the present moment given that, as explained in a recent Aspen Institute report, our information ecosystem in the twenty-first-century United States perpetuates a state of 'information disorder' that is especially harmful to those who live in 'marginalized communities' ('Final Report' 2021: 12). This harm is attributed to several factors, including the 'news deserts' in which 65 million Americans are reported to live (Simpson 2019) as well as the often-overlooked reality that many marginalized communities have valid reasons to mistrust expert information, based on the long history of scientific research that has abused them (Jaiswal and others 2020). An especially egregious example is a recent Senate report showing that black people were targeted more than other groups by Russians interfering with the 2016 election (Mak 2019).

Along these lines, some critics have questioned the ethics of scientific hoaxes and stings such as those enacted by Bohannon and Sokal. The criticism of Bohannon foregrounds multiple concerns: the fact that Bohannon's hoaxes wasted the time and resources of multiple journals, without issuing an apology, and the fact that he violated a basic principle of scholarly publishing ethics by submitting the same piece to multiple journals at that same time (Al-Khatib and Teixeira da Silva 2016; Teixeira da Silva and Al-Khatib 2016). By contrast, Sokal's hoax is criticized more generally for its deception and its potential to create mistrust of the academic enterprise (Fish 2000).

Even while acknowledging this long history of scientific hoaxes, we must also acknowledge that information and misinformation are able to spread more quickly now than ever before. In this context, if an idea resonates with something that audiences want to hear, it is going to spread even more quickly, regardless of the quality of the information. These trends are also related to other phenomena in scholarly communication such as the bias against publishing negative findings. The stakes have never been higher, and as academic researchers, or other professionals in the scholarly enterprise, we have a crucial role to play in safeguarding the knowledge produced by this enterprise.

Misinformation and disinformation are commonly depicted as phenomena that should concern us regarding public communication of scientific information (e.g., 'Final Report' 2021). Thus, when we hear about 'fake news', for example, we are usually talking about public audiences who seek out information that aligns with their beliefs, regardless of accuracy, or who do not possess adequate critical thinking skills to know the difference between accurate and inaccurate information. Far less attention has been paid to the potential for misinformation, disinformation, or 'fake news' in the context of expert discourse. As this chapter has demonstrated, this potential is significant, and it is not only something that we see in predatory journals but is occurring with some frequency in high-profile, seemingly credible, peer-reviewed journals produced by the major publishing companies. In all these ways, publishing hoaxes raise our awareness of the extent to which predatory journals should be understood as part of a complex ecology; these journals take advantage of the very same weaknesses that are often exposed by scientific hoaxes. Thus, publishing hoaxes have made an important contribution to the 'predatory paradox' that is this book's focus.

Practical Applications

Several mechanisms have been developed to guard against the various forms of scholarly misinformation addressed in this chapter. These mechanisms include the DOI to provide a unique identifier for published research texts and the 'Open Researcher and Contributor ID' (ORCID) to provide a unique identifier for authors and contributors to published research. Becoming familiar with these mechanisms is one strategy that researchers and other stakeholders can use to fortify themselves against scholarly misinformation and fraud (see Table 4.2). Although none of these systems is foolproof, understanding how they operate, what they mean, and their limitations, will make authors and other stakeholders in scientific research better informed and equipped to detect fake publications, whether they are published in journals considered predatory or not. The suggested activities below are designed to introduce these systems and provide some practice in using them.

Table 4.2 Systems to Guard Against Academic Fraud. © STEPP Research Team

Identifier Mechanisms

Mechanism	Definition and Purpose
DOI (digital object identifier)	Persistent and unique identifier of a digital object, sometimes described as the equivalent of a 'bar code' that is assigned to physical objects (Lammey 2014). Whereas a URL can change, the DOI should remain consistent, although it is the publisher's responsibility to ensure this consistency by maintaining DOIs that are assigned to digital texts that they publish. A DOI includes two parts: a prefix that is assigned to the publisher by Crossref, and a suffix that is assigned based on a system developed by the publisher.
Crossref	Crossref has been described as a 'digital switchboard' (Lammey 2014). Crossref began in 2000 as an association to connect publishers and publishing information and ensure accurate and consistent links to documents that are cited in a digital environment. It is an organization that publishers can join, and it provides benefits to members. The membership fee is dependent on the publisher's annual revenue. The most notable membership benefit is that Crossref allows linking of publications through a DOI; when a publisher joins Crossref, they are given a DOI prefix, and the publisher agrees to specific protocols for assigning and maintaining DOIs for their publications.

Identifier Mechanisms

Mechanism	Definition and Purpose
Crossmark	A service that allows authors or users of a published text, in .pdf or .html format, to determine whether sources cited are the current version. By clicking on the Crossmark link in a published document, one gets access to information on the status of each text that is cited. For example, if an article has been retracted, this will be indicated, or if a new version of an article has been published, that will be indicated and linked to as well.
Crosscheck	This service enables plagiarism detection for publishers who are Crossref members ('Crossref Announces CrossCheck' 2008). The originality of a submission is checked against all other texts in the Crosscheck database. Plagiarism detection is initiated through a tool that publishers can integrate into their submission processes.
Fundref	Provides a mechanism for standardized reporting of information on how research was funded ('Funder Registry' 2020). This is designed to be used in conjunction with Crossmark, but publishers do have the option of implementing Fundref independently from Crossmark.
ORCID (Open Researcher and Contributor ID)	Provides a unique identifier for authors and contributors to research articles ('Distinguish Yourself' [n.d.]). The ID is available at no cost to researchers, and the non-profit organization is supported by fees paid by member organizations. The ORCID ID is linked to a record that the researcher updates to include information on personal attributes such as their professional affiliations, publications, and research funding.

Key Takeaways

- Scientific hoaxes such as Bohannon's 'Chocolate' hoax have exposed weaknesses in the scholarly publishing ecosystem.
- Scientific hoaxes have served to expose fraudulent practices in both predatory and legitimate journals.
- Article retractions are supposed to correct the scientific record, but often do not, for a variety of reasons.
- Retracted articles often continue to be cited well after their retractions.
- Peer review, which should be the gatekeeping mechanism in scholarly publishing, often fails to detect hoaxes, or is not conducted at all by journals claiming to use peer review.
- Some critics question the ethics behind scientific hoaxes.
- Mechanisms such as DOIs and ORCID identifiers are intended to provide unique identifiers for authors and published research to help prevent unethical practices.

Discussion Questions

1. Look back at some of the news articles that cited Bohannon's 'Chocolate' study. At a casual glance, is there anything in the news articles that might make you suspicious about the science that was presented? Discuss why or why not.
2. What are some benefits that have come from Bohannon's 'Chocolate' hoax?
3. What are some of the ethical concerns related to scientific hoaxes?
4. Have you ever come across a retracted article while conducting research? What did you do? Would you still use it?

Activities

1. Johannes Bohannon was listed as the first author of the 'Chocolate with High Cocoa Content' hoax article. Search for 'Johannes Bohannon' in ORCID (https://orcid.org/). (Note: you can click on 'advanced search' to narrow your results by adding an institutional affiliation).

    a. Try searching for some of the other coauthors as well. What results do you find? How could a search like this have been helpful to each of the stakeholder groups who fell victim to the 'Chocolate with High Cocoa Content' hoax?

    b. Stakeholders who were addressed in this chapter include academics who cited the article and science journalists who reported on it. Can you think of other stakeholders who were potentially impacted by this hoax?

2. Try searching in ORCID (https://orcid.org/) for someone who is a well-known author in your discipline.

    a. Is this author indexed in ORCID? If not, try searching for names of other well-known authors in your discipline until you find someone who is indexed in ORCID.

    b. What types of information are you able to obtain from these authors' ORCID profiles?

    c. How might this type of information be helpful in assessing the legitimacy of a published text?

3. The DOI assigned to Bohannon and others' 'Chocolate' hoax article when it was initially published is 10.3823/1654.

    a. Try searching for this DOI in the DOI search tool (doi.org). What do you find?

    b. How could this tool have helped the various stakeholders who fell victim to the 'Chocolate with High Cocoa Content' hoax?

4. Table 4.1 lists articles that had cited Bohannon and others' hoax article according to a Google Scholar search carried out on 11 May 2022. Take a close look at each of these citations.

   a. Do these citations include a DOI for Bohannon and others' article, and if so, is it the same DOI listed in Question 3 (10.3823/1654)?

   b. Do you see evidence that the authors citing this article could have used any of the tools referenced here to screen out this bad citation and avoid citing it?

5. The *Open Ophthamology Journal* uses Crossmark for all its recent articles.

   a. Click on the Crossmark icon for a recent article in the journal. Here is one example of a recent article that uses Crossmark, but you will find several others to choose from: https://openophthalmologyjournal.com/VOLUME/14/PAGE/82/FULLTEXT/

   b. What information does this link provide about the article?

   c. How does Crossmark assist you in assessing the overall quality of this journal? Do you see any other cues on this journal's website that give you an indication of this journal's quality?

References

'About ACS'. [n.d.]. *American Chemical Society*, https://www.acs.org/content/acs/en/about.html?sc=180808_GlobalFooter_od

Akça, Sümeyye and Akbulut, Müge. 2021. 'Are Predatory Journals Contaminating Science? An Analysis on the Cabells' Predatory Report', *Journal of Academic Librarianship*, 47.4: 1–11, https://doi.org/10.1016/J.ACALIB.2021.102366

Alkalaj, Miso. 2017. 'Crisis of Confidence in Science, 2: Lies, Damned Lies, and Statistics', *Objektiv*, https://www.dnevnik.si/1042762387

Al-Khatib, Aceil and Teixeira da Silva. Jaime A. 2016. 'Stings, Hoaxes and Irony Breach the Trust Inherent in Scientific Publishing', *Publishing Research Quarterly*, 32.3: 208–19, https://doi.org/10.1007/S12109-016-9473-4

Arias-Castro, Ery. 2019. *Principles of Statistical Analysis: Statistical Inference Based on Randomization* (Cambridge, UK: Cambridge University Press)

Beall, Jeffrey. 2018. 'Scientific Soundness and the Problem of Predatory Journals', in *Pseudoscience: The Conspiracy against Science*, ed. by Allison Kaufman and James Kaufman (Cambridge, MA: The MIT Press), 283–99, https://doi.org/10.7551/mitpress/10747.001.0001

Berger, Monica, and Cirasella, Jill. 2015. 'Beyond Beall's List: Better Understanding Predatory Publishers', *College & Research Libraries News*, 76.3: 132–35, https://doi.org/10.5860/crln.76.3.9277

Bohannon, Johannes., Koch, Diana., Home, Peter and Driehaus, Alexander. 2015. 'Chocolate with High Cocoa Content as a Weight-Loss Accelerator', *International Archives of Medicine*, 8.55: 1–8, https://en.wikipedia.org/wiki/File:Chocolate_with_high_Cocoa_content_as_a_weight-loss_accelerator.pdf[4]

Bohannon, John. 2013. 'Who's Afraid of Peer Review?', *Science*, 342.6154: 60–65, https://doi.org/10.1126/SCIENCE.342.6154.60

——. 2015. 'I Fooled Millions Into Thinking Chocolate Helps Weight Loss. Here's How.', *Gizmodo*, https://gizmodo.com/i-fooled-millions-into-thinking-chocolate-helps-weight-1707251800

Bolland, Mark J., Grey, Andrew and Avenell, Alison. 2022. 'Citation of Retracted Publications: A Challenging Problem', *Accountability in Research*, 29.1: 18–25, https://doi.org/10.1080/08989621.2021.1886933

Bornemann-Cimenti, Helmar., Szilagyi, Istvan S. and Sandner-Kiesling, Andreas. 2016. 'Perpetuation of Retracted Publications Using the Example of the Scott

---

4   This manuscript is no longer available on the publisher's website, so the archived version is used instead.

S. Reuben Case: Incidences, Reasons and Possible Improvements', *Science and Engineering Ethics*, 22.4: 1063–72, https://doi.org/10.1007/S11948-015-9680-Y

Brown, Dwayne, and Weselby, Cathy. 2010. 'NASA Sets News Conference on Astrobiology Discovery; Science Journal Has Embargoed Details Until 2 p.m. EST On Dec. 2', *National Aeronautics and Space Administration (NASA)*, https://www.nasa.gov/home/hqnews/2010/nov/HQ_M10-167_Astrobiology.html#:~:text=WASHINGTON%20%2D%2D%20NASA%20will%20hold,of%20life%20in%20the%20universe.

Butler, Declan. 2013. 'Investigating Journals: The Dark Side of Publishing', *Nature*, 495: 433–35, https://doi.org/10.1038/495433A

Camps-Bossacoma, Mariona., Garcia-Aloy, Mar., Saldana-Ruiz, Sandra., Cambras, Trinitat., González-Domínguez, Raúl and others. 2019. 'Role of Theobromine in Cocoa's Metabolic Properties in Healthy Rats', *Journal of Agricultural and Food Chemistry*, 67.13: 3605–14, https://doi.org/10.1021/ACS.JAFC.8B07248

da Costa, Gabriel Gonçalves. 2021. 'Lowering the P-Value Threshold to Alleviate Information Crisis in Nutritional Epidemiology – a Possible Temporary Solution?', *OSF Preprints*, https://doi.org/10.31219/osf.io/ezmyj

'Crossref Announces CrossCheck Plagiarism Detection Service'. 2008. *Crossref*, https://www.crossref.org/news/2008-04-15-crossref-announces-crosscheck-plagiarism-detection-service/

Davis, Phil. 2013. 'Post Open Access Sting: An Interview with John Bohannon', *The Scholarly Kitchen*, https://scholarlykitchen.sspnet.org/2013/11/12/post-open-access-sting-an-interview-with-john-bohannon/

'Distinguish Yourself in Three Easy Steps'. [n.d.]. *ORCID*, https://orcid.org/

Editorial Office. 2015. 'Retraction Notice on 'Chocolate with High Cocoa Content as a Weight-Loss Accelerator', *International Archives of Medicine*, 8, http://imed.pub/ojs/index.php/iam/article/view/1087

Eisen, Michael. 2013. 'I Confess, I Wrote the Arsenic DNA Paper to Expose Flaws in Peer-Review at Subscription Based Journals', *It Is Not Junk*, https://www.michaeleisen.org/blog/?p=1439

Elkhateeb, Yomna Ali Moustafa Marzok, and Mohammed AL Harbi, Razan. 2018. 'Comparative Study on Health Knowledge about Biochemical Effect of Chocolate on Human Health among Females and Males of Hail University', *International Journal of Gastroenterology*, 2.1: 1–6, http://dx.doi.org/10.11648/j.ijg.20180201.11

Estruch, Ramón., Ros, Emilio., Salas-Salvadó, Jordi., Covas, Maria-Isabel., Corella, Dolores and others. 2013. 'Primary Prevention of Cardiovascular Disease with a Mediterranean Diet', *The New England Journal of Medicine*, 368.14: 1279–90, https://doi.org/10.1056/NEJMOA1200303

'Final Report: Commission on Information Disorder'. 2021. *The Aspen Institute*, https://www.aspeninstitute.org/publications/commission-on-information-disorder-final-report/

Finneman, Teri, and Thomas, Ryan J. 2018. 'A Family of Falsehoods: Deception, Media Hoaxes and Fake News', *Newspaper Research Journal*, 39.3: 350–61, https://doi.org/10.1177/0739532918796228

Fish, S. 2000. 'Professor Sokal's Bad Joke', in *The Sokal Hoax: The Sham That Shook the Academy*, 1st edn, ed. by Lingua Franca (Lincoln, NE: University of Nebraska Press), 81–84

'Funder Registry'. 2020. *Crossref*, https://www.crossref.org/services/funder-registry/

Gauthier, Benoît. 2016. 'Impact = Context × Influence: Evaluation, Evidence and Policy in Canadian Government Contexts', in *Evidence and Policy Symposium*, 1–14, https://digitalcollections.cdu.edu.au/nodes/view/4668

Giraldo, M., Toro, J.M., Arango, C.M., Posada, L.G. and Garcia, H.I.. 2017. 'Ensayo Clínico Aleatorizado y Controlado Del Efecto Del Consumo de Cacao En Pacientes Con Resistencia a La Insulina', *Acta Médica Colombiana*, 42.2: 90–96, https://doi.org/10.36104/amc.2017.988

Goldschmidt, Vivian. [n.d.]. 'Lose Weight, Get In Shape, And Build Your Bones With These 7 Scrumptious Foods', *Save Our Bones*, https://saveourbones.com/lose-weight-get-in-shape-and-build-your-bones-with-these-7-scrumptious-foods/

Grass, Robert N., and Stark, Wendelin J. 2015. 'The Dissipation Rate of News in Online Mass Media Evaluated by Chemical Engineering and Process Control Tools', *AIChE Journal*, 62.4: 1104–11, https://doi.org/10.1002/aic.15103

'How the "Digital Object Identifier" Works'. 2001. *Bloomberg*, https://www.bloomberg.com/news/articles/2001-07-22/online-extra-how-the-digital-object-identifier-works#xj4y7vzkg

Hyland, Ken. 1999. 'Academic Attribution: Citation and the Construction of Disciplinary Knowledge', *Applied Linguistics*, 20.3: 341–67, https://doi.org/10.1093/APPLIN/20.3.341

'International Archives of Medicine'. [n.d.]. *International Medical Publisher*, https://imedpub.jimdo.com/journals/list-of-journals/international-archives-of-medicine/

Jaiswal, J., LoSchiavo, C. and Perlman, D. C. 2020. 'Disinformation, Misinformation and Inequality-Driven Mistrust in the Time of COVID-19: Lessons Unlearned from AIDS Denialism', *AIDS and Behavior*, 24.10: 2780, https://doi.org/10.1007/S10461-020-02925-Y

Kawakami, Mark T. 2020. 'How (Not) to Search for the Truth and (Perhaps) Improve the Human Condition', *Toyohogaku*, 63.3: 291–319, http://doi.org/10.34428/00011523

Koerber, Amy., Starkey, Jesse C., Ardon-Dryer, Karin., Cummins, R. Glenn., Eko, Lyombe and others. 2020. 'A Qualitative Content Analysis of Watchlists vs Safelists: How Do They Address the Issue of Predatory Publishing?', *Journal of Academic Librarianship*, 46.6, https://doi.org/10.1016/j.acalib.2020.102236

Kyas, M., Springer, J. D., Pedersen, J. T. and Chkoniya, V. 2021. 'Data Analysis in the Shipping Industry: EShip Case Study–Problem Statement', in *Handbook of Research on Applied Data Science and Artificial Intelligence in Business and Industry* (Hershey, PA: IGI Global), 381–400

Lammey, Rachael. 2014. 'The Basics of CrossRef Extensible Markup Language', *Science Editing*, 1.2: 76–83, https://doi.org/10.6087/KCSE.2014.1.76

Lee, Younghyun, Hee Yang, Gihyun Hur, Jiwoo Yu, Sumin Park, and others. 2019. '5-(3′,4′-Dihydroxyphenyl)-γ-Valerolactone, a Metabolite of Procyanidins in Cacao, Suppresses MDI-Induced Adipogenesis by Regulating Cell Cycle Progression through Direct Inhibition of CDK2/Cyclin O', *Food & Function*, 10.5: 2958–69, https://doi.org/10.1039/C9FO00334G

Lowe, Derek. 2013. 'An Open Access Trash Heap', *Science*, https://www.science.org/content/blog-post/open-access-trash-heap

Mak, Tim. 2019. 'Senate Report Finds Russians Used Social Media Mostly to Target Race in 2016', *National Public Radio*, https://www.npr.org/2019/10/08/768319934/senate-report-russians-used-used-social-media-mostly-to-target-race-in-2016#:~:text=Senate%20Report%20Finds%20Russians%20Used,Target%20Race%20In%202016%20%3A%20NPR&text=Tiny%20Desk-,Senate%20Report%20Finds%20Russians%20Used%20Social%20Media%20To%20Target%20Race,to%20a%20new%20bipartisan%20report.

Malinowski, Grzegorz M. 2019. 'Uncertainty of Science and Decision-Making – Problems with Evidence-Based Policy', *Education of Economists and Managers*, 54.4: 9–29, https://econjournals.sgh.waw.pl/EEiM/article/view/1828/1988

——. 2020. 'Niepewność nauki a działanie, czyli – problemy z evidence–based policy', *Metody Ilościowe w Badaniach Ekonomicznych*, 21.1: 49–69, https://doi.org/10.22630/MIBE.2020.21.1.6

McCook, Alison. 2015. 'Chocolate-Diet Study Publisher Claims Paper Was Actually Rejected, Only Live 'for Some Hours.' Email, However, Says...', *Retraction Watch*, https://retractionwatch.com/2015/05/28/chocolate-diet-study-publisher-claims-paper-was-actually-rejected-only-live-for-some-hours-email-however-says/

Moore, D.A. 2016. 'Preregister If You Want To', *American Psychologist*, 71.3: 238–39, https://doi.org/10.1037/a0040195

Mounk, Yascha. 2018. 'What an Audacious Hoax Reveals About Academia', *The Atlantic*, https://www.theatlantic.com/ideas/archive/2018/10/new-sokal-hoax/572212/

Mukerji, N. 2017. 'The Third Commandment: Make Credible Assumptions', in *The 10 Commandments of Common Sense* (New York: Springer)

Müller, Phillip. 2021. 'Concerning Levels of Significance- Analysing Methods to Detect and Estimate P-Hacking' (Unpublished Bachelor's Thesis, Karlsruhe Institute of Technology), https://www.researchgate.net/profile/Philip_Mueller9/publication/352906629_Concerning_Levels_of_Significance_-_Analysing_Methods_to_Detect_and_Estimate_P-Hacking/links/60df2a3792851ca9449fd67a/Concerning-Levels-of-Significance-Analysing-Methods-to-Detect-and-Estimate-P-Hacking.pdf

'Open Access Publishing for the Scientific Community'. [n.d.]. *Hindawi*, https://www.hindawi.com/

Peck, Lori Nicole. 2021. 'Risk Portrayal and Actionability of Human Papillomavirus Coverage in Popular Magazines' (Unpublished Master's Thesis, Idaho State University)., https://www.proquest.com/docview/2621020323?pq-origsite=gscholar&fromopenview=true

Peng, Hao., Romero, Daniel M. and Horvát, Emoke Ágnes. 2022. 'Dynamics of Cross-Platform Attention to Retracted Papers', *PNAS*, 119.25: 16119–8, https://doi.org/10.1073/PNAS.2119086119

Perez, Carlos V. 2015. 'Public Disclaimer [Facebook Status Update]', *Facebook* [Group: International Archives of Medicine], https://www.facebook.com/groups/iamedicine/posts/10153415208752082/

Phillips, Tony. 2010. 'Discovery of "Arsenic-Bug" Expands Definition of Life', *NASA Science*, https://science.nasa.gov/science-news/science-at-nasa/2010/02dec_monolake/

'PMC Journal List'. [n.d.]. *NIH National Library of Medicine*, https://www.ncbi.nlm.nih.gov/pmc/journals/

Poe, Edgar Allan. 1844. 'The Balloon Hoax [Archived Full Text]', *New York Sun* (New York City), https://www.eapoe.org/works/tales/ballhxa.htm

Ponce, Ana Rita de Heaton Ayres. 2018. *O Papel Dos Comunicados de Imprensa No Sensacionalismo Em Notícias de Ciência* (Unpublished Master's Thesis: Universidada Nova De Lisboa), https://run.unl.pt/handle/10362/54180?mode=simple

Rahman, S. N., and Citrakesumasari, N. A. T. 2018. 'Effect of Cocoa on Body Weight, Waist Circumference and Visceral Fat Patient with Central Obesity', *International Journal of Science and Healthcare Research*, 3.1: 45–47, https://inrein.com/ijshr.com/IJSHR_Vol.3_Issue.1_Jan2018/IJSHR_Abstract.007.html

Ramezani, Tahereh., Behzadifard, Samaneh., Parvaresh, Nooshin., Jahani, Younes., Bakhtyari, Fahimeh and others. 2015. 'The Comparison of Resilience and Spirituality in Addicted and Non-Addicted Women', *International Archives of Medicine*, 8.55: 1–8, https://doi.org/10.3823/1654

Ramos, Sonia., Martín, María Angeles and Goya, Luis. 2017. 'Effects of Cocoa Antioxidants in Type 2 Diabetes Mellitus', *Antioxidants*, 6.4: 84, https://doi.org/10.3390/ANTIOX6040084

Reilly, Ian. 2020. 'Public Deception as Ideological and Institutional Critique: On the Limits and Possibilities of Academic Hoaxing', *Canadian Journal of Communication*, 45.2: 265–85, https://doi.org/10.22230/CJC.2020V45N2A3667

Rodríguez-Lagunas, Maria J., Vicente, Filipa., Pereira, Paula., Castell, Margarida and Pérez-Cano, Francisco J. 2019. 'Relationship between Cocoa Intake and Healthy Status: A Pilot Study in University Students', *Molecules*, 24.4: 812, https://doi.org/10.3390/MOLECULES24040812

Rosen, Rebecca J. 2012. 'The Case (Study) of Arsenic Life: How the Internet Can Make Science Better', *The Atlantic*, https://www.theatlantic.com/technology/archive/2012/07/the-case-study-of-arsenic-life-how-the-internet-can-make-science-better/259581/

Sauerwein, Tessa. 2019. 'Framework Information Literacy – Aspekte Aus Theorie, Forschung Und Praxis', *Bibliothek Forschung Und Praxis*, 43.1: 126–38, https://doi.org/10.1515/bfp-2019-2027

Schwitzer, Gary. 2015. 'Should the Chocolate-Diet Sting Study Be Retracted? And Why the Coverage Doesn't Surprise a News Watchdog', *Retraction Watch*, https://retractionwatch.com/2015/05/28/should-the-chocolate-diet-sting-study-be-retracted-and-why-the-coverage-doesnt-surprise-a-news-watchdog/

Secor, Marie, and Walsh, Lynda. 2004. 'A Rhetorical Perspective on the Sokal Hoax', *Written Communication*, 21.1: 69–91, https://doi.org/10.1177/0741088303261037

Simpson, April. 2019. 'As Local News Outlets Shutter, Rural America Suffers Most', *Stateline*, https://www.pewtrusts.org/en/research-and-analysis/blogs/stateline/2019/10/21/as-local-news-outlets-shutter-rural-america-suffers-most

Steel, E.A., Liermann, M. and Guttorp, P. 2019. 'Beyond Calculations: A Course in Statistical Thinking', *The American Statistician*, 73.sup1: 392–401, https://doi.org/10.1080/00031305.2018.1505657

Stoll, O. 1898. 'Zur Kenntniss Der Geographischen Verbreitung Der Ameisen', *Mitteilungen Der Schweizerischen Entomologischen Gesellschaft*, 10: 120–26

Stylianou, M. 2022. 'The Role of Dark Chocolate in the Diet and Consumer Sentiments' (Unpublished thesis, University of Thessaly), https://ir.lib.uth.gr/xmlui/bitstream/handle/11615/51872/19107.pdf?sequence=1

Teixeira da Silva, Jaime A., and Al-Khatib, Aceil. 2016. 'Questioning the Ethics of John Bohannon's Hoaxes and Stings in the Context of Science Publishing', *KOME*, 4.1: 84–88, https://doi.org/10.17646/KOME.2016.16

Teixeira da Silva, Jaime A., Dobránski, Judit., Alkhatib, Aceil and Pangiotis, Tsigaris. 2018. 'Challenges Facing the DOAJ (Directory of Open Access Journals) as a Reliable Source of Open Access Publishing Venues', *Journal of Educational Media and Library Science*, 55.3: 349–58, https://doi.org/10.6120/JoEMLS.201811_55(3).e003.BC.BE

'Top 10 Most Highly Cited Retracted Papers'. [n.d.]. *Retraction Watch*, https://retractionwatch.com/the-retraction-watch-leaderboard/top-10-most-highly-cited-retracted-papers/

Vergano, Dan. 2012. 'Discovery of an Arsenic-Friendly Microbe Refuted', *ABC News*, https://abcnews.go.com/Technology/discovery-arsenic-friendly-microbe-refuted/story?id=16737658

——. 2013. 'Glowing Reviews on "arseniclife" Spurred NASA's Embrace', *USA Today*, https://www.usatoday.com/story/tech/columnist/vergano/2013/02/01/arseniclife-peer-reviews-nasa/1883327/

——. 2013. 'Fake Cancer Study Spotlights Bogus Science Journals', *National Geographic*, https://www.nationalgeographic.com/pages/article/131003-bohannon-science-spoof-open-access-peer-review-cancer

Vida, István Kornél. 2012. 'The "Great Moon Hoax" of 1835', *Hungarian Journal of English and American Studies*, 18.1/2: 431–41

Wager, Elizabeth., Barbour, Virginia., Yentis, Steven and Kleinert, Sabine. 2009. 'Retractions: Guidance from the Committee on Publication Ethics (COPE)', *Maturitas*, 64.4: 201–3, https://doi.org/10.1016/J.MATURITAS.2009.09.018

Walsh, Lynda. 2006. *Sins against Science* (New York: State University of New York Press)

Wetterer, James K. 2006. 'Quotation Error, Citation Copying, and Ant Extinctions in Madeira', *Scientometrics*, 67.3: 351–72, https://doi.org/10.1556/SCIENT.67.2006.3.2

Wolfe-Simon, Felisa., Blum, Jodi Switzer., Kulp, Thomas R., Gordon, Gwyneth W., Hoeft, Shelley E. and others. 2010. 'A Bacterium That Can Grow by Using Arsenic Instead of Phosphorus', *Science*, 332.6034: 1163–66, https://doi.org/10.1126/SCIENCE.1197258

Wooven, L., and Snider, T. 2018. *Chocolate: Superfood of the Gods* (Detroit, MI: Lotus Press)

5. Avoiding the Pitfalls of Predatory Publishing
Guidance for Graduate Students and Junior Scholars

It almost happened to me... has it happened to you?

I was a postdoctoral fellow at the time of this incident, in the process of applying for tenure-track faculty positions. I was feeling the pressure to increase my publication count — I had been told that having more publications would increase my chances for landing the tenure-track position at an R1 institution I so dearly wanted.

At this point in my academic career, truth be told, I had never heard about predatory journals, and had no clue of the potential pitfalls awaiting me as I entered the academic publishing world. That is a large part of why I was so impressed when I was contacted by a journal editor, inviting me to submit a manuscript to a special issue.

Since I had not heard about the journal before, I did do some research: I googled the journal and looked through the website. It seemed like a professional website, and the articles I found seemed okay. I even recognized one author's name as someone in my field, so I started feeling more confident about the journal. But still, I wanted to make sure I was submitting to a good journal, so I looked up their editorial board and recognized a name or two. I was told there would be a fee for publication but given that I had never submitted (*by myself*) to an academic journal before, I assumed this was a normal part of the process. So far, everything seemed legitimate, and since the very notion of predatory journals was not something I was aware of yet, I had no remaining suspicions.

As I began working on the manuscript, which was a review of literature relevant to the special issue, I even invited a colleague to coauthor with me — someone who had experience publishing in other academic journals. We finished the manuscript and submitted it to the journal. Mentally, I was prepared to wait months to get a review back, and was merely hoping for a revise and submit, rather than a straight rejection. So, less than twelve hours after submission, I was shocked to see an email from the journal editor. Assuming that only a desk reject would come back that fast, I dejectedly opened the email, preparing myself for the harsh reality of having wasted my time. To my great surprise, it was an acceptance letter, with no suggested revisions, and in fact, no reviewer feedback at all!

This finally raised some red flags for me, and when I discussed this with my coauthor, we both agreed this was strange, and that we should remove our submission. I crafted an email to the journal editor, stating that as it turned out, I did not have the budget to pay the publication fee, so I needed to withdraw my submission. I had hoped this tactic would discourage them from harassing me — surely all they were after was my money, so if I told them I had none they would leave me alone. However, after a little back and forth with the editor, they said they would be willing to waive the fee if I would still just publish the manuscript with them. They were not giving up easily, which was odd. If they were not after my money anymore, what was their end game?

By this time, I had done a bit more research and learned that predatory journals were a thing I needed to guard against, and that this journal had been flagged on some of the predatory journal databases as engaging in less-than-scrupulous activities. I went on the attack and convinced the journal not to publish my manuscript. Luckily, they acquiesced, and I was saved from publishing in a predatory journal. Clearly, though, other scholars have not been so lucky, and to my knowledge, that journal still exists, publishing manuscripts with no peer review, and charging authors for non-existent services. While the journal's willingness to waive the fee places them in a grey area, the fact that they claimed to do the peer review, but then did not, makes them a direct threat to the credibility of scientific knowledge production.

Since that near miss with publishing in a predatory journal, I am extremely cautious about where I submit my manuscripts. I receive similar solicitation emails daily, as do all my colleagues. We have become accustomed to deleting them, barely letting them register in our minds now. I use a range of tools and critical thinking exercises to vet journals — many of which are outlined in the following chapter. Luckily, I avoided having my scholarly reputation ruined, because had that manuscript been published, I would have always had to explain it — removing the publication from my CV would have been unethical, yet any scholar who knew the field would have questioned the quality of my publications if they saw I published in that journal. This is a situation too many junior scholars now find themselves in.

It is my hope that my experience, and the tools I present in this chapter, will help others stay safe from the growing pitfalls of predatory publishers in the academic publishing world.

Introduction

Publishing in peer-reviewed scientific journals is the cornerstone of academic assessment and crucial for the communication of research findings (Christopher and Young 2015). In recent years, hundreds of thousands of researchers worldwide from research institutes, universities, and federal authorities published their papers in predatory (pseudo-scientific) journals (Boucherie 2018). This number includes researchers from even the most prestigious institutions, such as Harvard University (Clark 2018) and even a Nobel laureate (Boucherie 2018). While the problem is global (Beall 2016), some geographical regions are more prone to being targeted than others. (See Chapters 2 and 3 in this book for more detail.)

As explained in other chapters, controversy still surrounds the term *predatory* and how to define it. Nonetheless, there is some consensus on the practices that authors should be aware of as possible indicators that a journal is not trustworthy. For instance, authors should be suspicious of journals that offer quick acceptance times and cheap publishing fees that are not transparently explained in the submission guidelines. As revealed in the Bohannon hoax highlighted in Chapter 4, authors should be concerned if they receive an acceptance letter — and an unexpected invoice — from the publisher. Authors should also be aware of journals that do not provide peer review (Roberts 2016) or provide fake reviewer reports (Bowman and Wallace 2018), as in the example of two authors who submitted a manuscript to a predatory journal with only a repeated sentence containing expletives demanding they be taken off the journal's mailing list — and received an immediate and enthusiastic acceptance (Brezgov 2019). Finally, authors should be leery of journals that are not indexed in databases such as PubMed, do not conduct copyediting or other publication services, and do not have an archival plan to ensure the article is preserved in perpetuity as part of the published record (Roberts 2016).

Unfortunately, many researchers who submit papers to predatory journals fail to realize they are counterfeit journals until it is too late. In some cases when authors discover their error and seek to withdraw their papers, they cannot (Berisha Qehaja 2020), or else they do succeed, but only after a long struggle, or they are forced to pay a withdrawal fee (Leung and others 2020).

Predatory journals are a real threat to the credibility of science (Manca and others 2019). Students who lack the experience and credentials to recognize predatory journals may also be exposed to information published in predatory journals that may harm their education (Schira and Hurst 2019). Authors do not always understand the negative consequences of publishing their research in predatory journals, which may include consequences such as the loss of the manuscript, negatively scarring their publication records, and damaging their career (Al-Khatib 2016; Grudniewicz and others 2019; Teixeira Da Silva 2013). One of the interviewees in our study discussed the possible ramifications of publishing in a predatory journal: 'I think it reduces your credibility as a scholar [...] it can be sometimes even be hurtful to your career to publish in such journals' (P02).[1, 2] Previous research suggests that those who

---

1   Our Texas Data Repository Dataverse includes a table showing participant demographic information. See https://doi.org/10.18738/T8/QUBMLI ("Participant Occupation and Regional Demographics Table"). All quotations from interviews are reported without correction of grammatical errors or other irregularities. Some quotes were abbreviated using [...] to achieve clarity of the original message.

2   Coding to support this chapter's analysis was conducted in an early phase of the project, at a time when the transcripts had not yet been de-identified. Thus, we have not provided a published dataset specific to this chapter. However, readers may

publish their work in predatory journals and who are impacted the most are early-career researchers, including graduate students (master's and PhD students) and junior scholars (postdoctoral or pretenure faculty) (Darbyshire 2018; Larkin 2018).

This chapter combines the voices of participants in our interview study with the existing scholarly and mainstream literature to define some of the biggest pitfalls junior scholars and graduate students may encounter as they begin trying to publish manuscripts in the current academic publishing environment. Regarding graduate students, different training and funding models exist across departments and universities, and, as we demonstrate in this chapter, these models can impact graduate students' experiences with scholarly publishing and the type of mentoring they receive. For example, when a graduate student is accepted to a university and department they may be accepted and receive payment as a Research Assistant (RA), meaning they are fully committed to a known research project, based on a grant or budget their advisor has already obtained. Other students may be accepted as Teaching Assistants (TAs), meaning they are required to teach in their department in addition to performing their research. In some cases, when graduate students start their degree, they already have a designated advisor and a known research project. In other cases, students are accepted to programs or departments without an identified advisor or research topic, which they then select after the first year or two. In some institutions, graduate students are accepted to programs or departments without any financial support for their graduate degrees. Students may also be accepted to programs or departments with a fellowship that will support them; in many of these cases, the research project and identification of an advisor will be made in advance. In some institutions, publication in a peer-reviewed journal is a requirement for receiving a doctoral degree. All these factors influence the nature of mentoring that a graduate student receives and, ultimately, their experience with publishing as a junior scholar.

---

access the published dataset for Chapter 7, available at https://doi.org/10.18738/T8/3RZARP. This published dataset (see "NVivo file paradox theory 12.26.22.nvp") includes the full text of interview transcripts, de-identified to protect participants' anonymity, although the coding evident in this file was conducted at a later phase of the project.

Awareness of the Problem

Previous research suggests a lack of awareness among early-career researchers regarding predatory journals and the impact they might have. Lack of experience and knowledge to tell the difference between legitimate peer-reviewed journals and predatory journals (Christopher and Young 2015), along with the lack of formal institutional policies and intense pressure to publish, are suggested as the primary reasons why so many early-career researchers publish their work in predatory journals (Al-Khatib 2016). Therefore, there is a great need to raise awareness about the importance of selecting the right journals for publication, especially for young researchers who are in the early stages of building their academic careers (Kurt 2018). Echoing this previous research, many of our participants agreed there is a lack of awareness of predatory journals among early-career researchers, sharing comments such as, 'many students say they're not aware of [predatory publishing]' (P05) or 'when I started to write publications, I was not aware of how to do it, or where to publish. Some time I just rely on the journals of my classmate, where they publish [...] So I don't I didn't have like the idea to go and search for this feature journal of my area' (P03). Another participant noted that predatory journals actively look for ways to deceive inexperienced authors, such as using real people's names for their editorial board without their permission (P21). One of the ways authors are told to vet journals is to look at the editorial board, but if predatory journals are actively lying about their editorial board, then this seemingly straightforward way of determining a journal's credibility suddenly becomes much more difficult.

The Role of Mentors/Advisors

Academics involved in the mentoring process should warn and advise early-career researchers on where to submit their manuscripts for publication (Berisha Qehaja 2020). Therefore, research faculty in mentoring roles are the key to the future of science, as they are one of the most important influences on early-career researchers (Bankston 2017). An effective mentor-mentee relationship enhances the mentee's career and professional development (Ellis 1992; Gaff 2002; O'Neil and Wrightsman 2001), presents more academic opportunities (Busch 1985; Petrie and Wohlgemuth 1994; Wilde and Schau 2014), and can even develop into a more equal colleague-to-colleague relationship (Schlosser and others 2011). Therefore, the presence of an effective mentor for graduate students and junior scholars is an important aspect of their success and education (Foss and Foss 2008). A great mentor influence can be life-changing when ethics, drive, and skills for teaching and research are shared (Wrench and Punyanunt 2004).

Unfortunately, some graduate students and junior scholars may not get proper advice from their direct advisor or mentor and, in extreme cases, may not have any interaction with them at all. Even when there is a designated advisor or mentor, there could be a mismatch between the mentor and the mentee due to personality, communication style, relationship preference as well as career stage, and interest differences (Johnson and Huwe 2002). In addition, not all advisory relationships entail mentoring (Schlosser and others 2011), and not all advisors are relationally competent for the role (Johnson and Huwe 2002).

Suggestions for Improving Mentoring

According to Christopher and Young (2015), educational goals for early-career researchers, whether obtained through formal workshops or less formal mentoring, should include the following: (1) increased awareness of predatory journals, (2) ability to distinguish between legitimate and illegitimate open access journals, (3) understanding the similarities and differences between open access and subscription-based journals, (4) learning to evaluate journals and their processes, and (5) learning how to select the best journal for the scientific study.

Through mentorship and training programs, early-career researchers may be formally or informally educated on basic research concepts, including statistical methods, navigation of the institutional review board, and experience with the peer-review process through research conference presentations and publication (Leung and others 2020). Along these lines, one of our interview participants, a librarian from Africa who now works in the US, suggested bringing students into the research process early, encouraging them 'to look at the topic that are you working on, what journals that you find that fits this topic, [...] so you offer advisory services to them, and guidance and direction on how to publish' (P02). This corroborates other scholarly work that argues for the importance of educating early-career researchers on how to critically evaluate articles to help them avoid predatory journals and discern between legitimate open access publishers and predatory journals. This kind of training helps to safeguard the process of knowledge production (Christopher and Young 2015; Leung and others 2020). Furthermore, the mentor often guides the submission process by selecting the first and second target journals for submission, or providing lists of acceptable journals, as was shared by some of our participants when they noted things like, 'there are certain lists of journals that our promotion and tenure committee gave us' (P02), and 'my supervisor [...] had a list of journals that he recommended' (P10).

In some cases, the early-career trainee may be solely responsible for assessing a journal's submission requirements, gathering coauthor conflict of interest forms, creating a cover letter, and submitting the manuscript. However, trainees may unknowingly submit a manuscript to a predatory journal, resulting in consequences ranging from the simple loss of time to the loss of the manuscript and/or data, and in even more extreme cases, the loss of professional credibility. Therefore, it is important to mentor the trainees to educate them about predatory journals and their strategies and ensure proper manuscript submission (Leung and others 2020).

Institutional Differences in Mentoring and Publishing Expectations

Most junior scholars, especially graduate students and postdoctoral fellows, will have a faculty advisor with whom they will work directly. However, in some cases, mentoring may occur from other junior scholars, with no formal advising or mentoring. Mentoring also varies for pretenure faculty. In some cases, the department might assign a senior faculty member as a mentor as part of the tenure process, but often there is little oversight or accountability in the mentoring process.

In addition to vast institutional differences in mentoring, the path to tenure also varies greatly from institution to institution, which has direct implications on the research and publishing requirements for junior scholars (see Table 5.1), depending on whether they are at a research or teaching-focused institution.

Table 5.1 Differences in tenure track process (Research vs. Teaching Institutions) © STEPP Research Team

Research vs. Teaching Institutes

	Research Institutions	**Teaching Institutions**
Teaching Responsibilities	Undergraduate and graduate students, some institutions will only have graduate students.	Mainly undergraduate students.
Mentoring	Mentor undergraduate and graduate students, possibly postdoctoral fellows as well.	Work primarily with undergraduate students. Rarely work with graduate students.
Teaching Load	Low teaching load, varies from 1–2 classes per semester.	High teaching load, 3–4 classes per semester, possibly higher.
Research Load	High expectation for research, research work all year round.	Lower expectation for research work, research work mainly in the summer months.

Early-career researchers, including graduate students, postdoctoral fellows, and junior scholars, are expected to publish their research results as scientific papers to prove their research commitment and to achieve certain academic titles in higher education institutions (Berisha Qehaja 2020), and are therefore more likely to become victims of predatory journals and publishers (Al-Khatib 2016).

Junior faculty feel the pressure to meet their institutions' promotion and tenure requirements under the 'publish or perish' mantra, meaning they feel pressured to rapidly increase both the number of their publications as well as the visibility of those articles (Al-Khatib 2016).

Along these lines, a North American scholar we interviewed suggested the push for greater publishing numbers has increased in recent years, 'I'd say in the last ten years or so, there's been more emphasis on publishing' (P05), which may be driving the dramatic rise in the number of predatory journals trying to capitalize on this trend.

There is also pressure on graduate students, from different academic fields, to publish their work as part of their degree completion or long-term career success (Leung and others 2020), a notion corroborated by several of our interviewees, and exemplified by one European participant with decades of international publication experience: 'in many places it is expected that you publish paper before graduating' (P18). For example, Mills and Inouye (2021) mention that a master's student who needs a publication quickly to graduate or apply for an academic post might make a different choice at a subsequent career stage. There is insufficient attention to the processual dimensions of publishing across an academic career and the timing of individual choices in most accounts of predation (Mills and Inouye 2021). The following anecdote from an experienced scholar from Africa drives home the point that young, inexperienced researchers who are scrambling to get publications to find jobs may not fully understand the ethical (and career) ramifications of submitting their manuscripts to any journal that will take them:

> As a PhD at my university you need to publish two articles [before you can graduate]. So when you finish your work and [...] you submit [...] it is rejected, rejected [...] rejected. By that time [...] the student don't have too much time to wait. So they just find a journal and pay maybe $100 or $200 and publish it in one or two months. This is really common. Really common. Not because the work is not good [...] it is because they don't have too much time to wait for it. Because good journals sometime take time. Yes. And those who do their work, who have their own idea for their PhD work or their research work in [my country] sometimes face rejection with publication because the equipment sometimes it's not up to date. And [...] a good journal, they need publication with good equipment or up-to-date equipment. So, by this time [...] after a lot of rejection, people will just rely in predatory journal [...] knowing that they are predatory journal and they say, okay, I just want to finish and then I'll find time to do something good after. (P03)

As this quote illustrates, one of the biggest problems with predatory journals is that they take advantage of early-career researchers' desire to share their work; they bombard them with emails to invite them to submit a manuscript, attend a conference or become an editorial board member for a journal.

The desire to have your work be recognized by the field as important or impactful is a powerful drive for many researchers, as exemplified by interview participants who discussed the feelings they experienced when they began receiving solicitation emails early in their careers. A North American librarian surmised:

> [...] when you see a journal come up in your email, that's like, we here at the-journal-of-this-actually-sounds-very-reasonable-study says, 'You can publish with us and we'll get your work out there.' I can see how that is very tempting and it's probably very easy to get confused [when] those websites probably look exactly the same [...] and it's hard because you want the praise and you want to be told that your work is good. But [...] Yeah, it's absolutely a scam. And I have seen our own librarians fall for it (P07).

A South American academic researcher confirmed the widespread occurrence of receiving solicitations from suspicious publications, saying 'professors here and all over the world, it's not different here in [my country], we usually receive many invitations. The invitations are very strange because sometimes the English is not very good and they invite you to publish in journals that is nothing to do with your field' (P13). She continued her anecdote by noting she makes a point to share suspicious solicitations with her students, and to warn them not to fall prey once they defend their thesis, pointing out that publishers have mechanisms to find and target inexperienced researchers who may be the most desperate for publications as they enter the academic work force.

As these examples illustrate, for graduate students and junior scholars, getting these emails may seem like a great honor, but in many cases, these are sent by predatory journals and could lead to disastrous outcomes if a manuscript is submitted to one of these nefarious publications (Bowman and Wallace 2018; Roberts 2016; Wood and Krasowski 2020). Kurt (2018) stated that the pressure on early-career researchers to publish often causes them to fall prey to advertising used by predatory journals because they do not analyze the quality of the journal before sending the manuscript. Unfortunately, what many early-stage researchers do not understand is that when their work is published in a predatory journal, it not only condemns their work to obscurity, but also damages their reputation, academic credibility, and careers (Bowman and Wallace 2018; Darbyshire 2018). Additionally, the article they submitted has little or no validity, might not even be published at all, or it might be posted on a low-visibility site (Bowman and Wallace 2018).

Strategies for Avoiding Predatory Journals

The most important thing before submission of a manuscript is to educate yourself (or your students) about the journal. Knowing your field and taking the time to research a journal before submitting is key to avoiding predatory journals (Roberts 2016). The following sections provide insights into some additional strategies and resources to avoid falling prey to a predatory publisher and losing your work. Most of these strategies and resources have been addressed in scholarly literature, but we also supplement the findings of previous literature with insights from our interviewees, as appropriate. While some of the strategies listed below are rather straightforward (e.g., examining the journal scope and assessing the technical quality of the journal website), other strategies require more critical thinking and subjective judgement (e.g., knowing your field or determining the quality of individual articles), along with other strategies that may seem straightforward initially, but actually require critical thought (e.g., examining the editorial board, checking indexing sites and impact factors, or determining if a journal is known to colleagues). Although the mechanisms discussed in the following sections are not exhaustive, they do represent a series of indicators that can help authors determine whether a journal is legitimate or predatory.

Scope of the Journal

Shamseer and others (2017) note that an overly broad scope for a journal could be a warning signal, an indicator also used by our interview participants. For example, a North American librarian noted she examines 'whether or not what they claim the journal is matches what they've said they want my article for' (P04). Another participant, also located in North America, shared how he considers whether 'they have a focus in a certain field, or they just kind of like scattered?' (P08). Thus, paying attention to the declared scope of a journal and ensuring the articles they publish match that scope is one mechanism of determining credibility.

Technical Quality

Although Beall (2015) lists 'poorly maintained websites' (p. 5) as one of the features that could indicate a predatory journal, this criterion has also been called into question because it could place newer journals, or those being established in non-English-speaking countries, at a disadvantage and make it harder for them to break into the mainstream publishing area (Memon and Waqas 2018). Therefore, a careful look at several technical aspects of a journal may help establish whether it is a predatory journal, or just a startup publication that has not yet worked out all the errors and bugs in their website. Our interview participants offered several ways to examine the technical quality of a journal's website that may help determine its credibility. Clear statements of policies were one of the main components our interview participants pointed toward as a way to vet a journal (P03, P07), as exemplified by a South American senior researcher who argued that if 'the journal does not have explicit criteria and clear editorial policies' (P13), it could be a warning signal of predatory activity, especially if you 'can't tell where it's based [...or] if you can tell where it's based is different to where they claim it's based' (P09). On a more general level, a European publishing professional suggested taking a broader look at the digital presentation, and ask questions such as, 'Does the website look like a total mess? Is it full of stock photos? These kind of things. I've done this kind of analysis myself' (P09). Therefore, taking a critical look at the technical aspects of a journal's webpage can be an important aspect of the vetting process.

Know Your Field

Knowing your field will help researchers to select a journal that is topic-appropriate, within the scope of their research, respected among other researchers in their disciplines, and widely indexed and accessible to readers (Bowman and Wallace 2018; Christopher and Young 2015). Yet this is easier said than done, based on interview comments such as this one from a North American academic researcher who noted, 'you kinda have to have some expertise in the field to figure out if a journal is predatory' (P08). One way to begin acquiring this expertise is to talk to colleagues to make sure they have heard about the selected journal, and ask yourself questions such as, 'Do you know anyone who's published there? Do you actually read this journal? Would you cite the articles in this journal yourself?' (P09). It is also important to keep in mind that some predatory journals use similar names as legitimate journals. Thus, authors should examine any publication in question carefully and exercise caution before submitting to an unfamiliar journal (Bowman and Wallace 2018), and do not 'just go for journals that tell you they're going to give you a quick publication' (P23), as this can be a warning sign of predatory practices (and less-than-rigorous peer review).

Quality of Published Articles

One of the trickier mechanisms to detect whether a journal could be predatory is to examine the quality of the published articles. The quality of published articles is not always listed as a potential strategy for identifying predatory journals in the scholarly literature (e.g., Shamseer and others 2017) or from organizations aimed at assisting authors (e.g., Think. Check. Submit.), yet several of our participants indicated this was a component they examine when selecting a journal, as exemplified by the narrative shared by a North American researcher who regularly taught graduate students how to navigate academic publishing:

> [...] there's journals where I thought about publishing. And I'll pull a few sample papers from the journal, and [...] if I read it and I'm like,

wow, this thing has some gaping holes in it, you know it looks like the editing is not careful […] they just leave out blatantly obvious things like that and I'm like okay that's junk. Yeah, I'm not gonna publish there. So, that's a judgment call, that's not just charging a fee. (P08)

Therefore, examining individual articles from a journal can be a way to begin critically examining whether or not the journal seems to be vetting individual research and providing the expected services of peer review and copy editing.

Editorial Board

One of the strategies that some resources suggest for vetting a journal is to look at its editorial board (e.g., Shamseer and others 2017; Yucha 2014). However, this strategy has its limitations because, as predatory journals have grown more sophisticated in their deception, one of their tactics is to list individuals on their editorial board without their knowledge or consent (Ruiter-Lopez and others 2019). Despite the growing acknowledgement that editorial boards are relatively easy to fake, many of our interview participants suggested a good way to determine journal credibility was to 'look at the editorial board' (P23) and that 'if they recognize universities or the people who are on those boards, that's probably a sign that that journal is legitimate, generally speaking' (P07).

These recommendations, however, must now be couched with a caveat to look further than just whether prominent scholars are listed on the editorial board. For example, if there are other warning signals present when examining the journal, it would behoove the potential author to reach out to one or two of the editorial board members and ask them about the journal.

Indexing and Impact Factors

Checking whether a journal is indexed in a reputable database, along with assessing the impact factor of the journal through a credible external source (do not just trust what the journal says — stating false impact factors is now a common tool used by some predatory publishers) can be a good tool for vetting journals (Shrestha and others

2019). Despite some academic researchers and librarians viewing an overreliance on impact factors as a challenge to research quality (see Chapter 3), checking indexing (e.g., P04, P09, P13, P18) and impact factors (e.g., P09, P23) were some of the most common mechanisms mentioned by our interview participants as a way to determine whether or not a journal was credible.

In other cases, authors thought using an indexed list like PubMed Central® would be a good choice, but indexing does not guarantee that a given journal is legitimate (Misra and others 2017). The caveat to the reliability of some indexing mechanisms was addressed by one European researcher with decades of publishing experience who noted:

> Anybody can sign up for Crossref and the DOIs are given. So you'll find that all predatory journals have ISSNs and have DOIs. They might not be in ISI, but some other people are more careful. They won't be properly indexed, probably. There are exceptions. Some get into World of Science and also to Scopus, but not so many, but basically they can't usually get in properly indexed. [There are] all sorts of extraordinary organizations [...] Copernicus is one [...] (P18)

The Copernicus Indexing service, as mentioned by this interview participant, is one among a growing number of services that has contributed to the difficult terrain researchers must navigate as they prepare to submit their research for publication. Simply believing the journal or publisher when they list indices they are included on, or because they tout an impact factor, is no longer a valid method of vetting journals — one must also vet the index and impact rating organization to ensure they are not also promoting predatory journals.

Known to Colleagues

Another mechanism for vetting the credibility of journals mentioned by our interview participants was asking whether the journal was familiar to colleagues in the field. A North American Librarian suggested, 'doing a lateral reading about the journal [...] Can I Google it and find a real journal? What do other people say about that journal?' (P07) and a European publishing consultant concurred, suggesting inexperienced authors should 'look at whether people that you know in your subject area, or that you respect, or that are leaders in your area are publishing in that journal' (P23). While the mechanism of checking with colleagues can help steer junior researchers toward credible journals, there are constantly new journals (which may be entirely legitimate and credible) being added to each field, so simply asking colleagues who may not be up to date on the latest journal developments should be augmented with other vetting strategies.

Tools to Aid the Avoidance of Predatory Journals

As the diversity of strategies listed above indicate, it is becoming more and more complex to independently verify whether a journal is predatory or not. In response, several types of tools have been developed to help authors navigate the increasingly savvy attempts of predatory journals to lure authors into submitting their manuscripts. The anecdote below, shared by a publishing consultant working in eastern Europe, highlights the extent some predatory publishers go to deceive authors and exemplifies the need for additional tools to help avoid the ethical pitfalls of predatory publishing:

> If I was starting a predatory journal [...] I would pick a name that was similar to a journal in my field that was already well-known, so rather than *Annual Reviews of Ecology and Systematics*, I might call my journal *Annual Reviews of Systematics and Ecology*. Make a website that looks quite similar to the reputable one, and this is happening. It happens all of the time. There are millions of examples of this, especially in medical fields. I would put together an editorial board. I wouldn't necessarily even tell people that they were on the editorial board. This happens all of the time as well. Get some well-known names, put them on the website, and market that. Get some people to submit papers and keep the APC down so you can publish with us for $800 rather than $1500. Quick publication, the product looks good, but it's all about the money, and this is happening all of the time. There's millions of such journals. (P23)

In the increasingly deceptive environment of academic publishing, mentors and faculty in charge of training graduate students should be aware of the numerous tools available to help vet journals. There are three main types of tools available to help authors determine if a journal is predatory: watchlists (previously called blacklists), safelists (previously called whitelists),[3] and checklists.

Watchlists & Safelists

As detailed in earlier chapters, identification of potential predatory journals started in 2008 when Jeffrey Beall, a librarian at the University of Colorado Denver, created Beall's List, which contained a handful of journals and publishers that Beall identified as predatory (Beall 2012). The list, which was officially published in 2010, named 'potential, possible, or probable predatory scholarly open access publishers' (Quek and Teo 2018: 3). In 2017, due to legal pressure and increasing scrutiny about the methodology used for journal inclusion, Beall's List was taken offline. However, archived versions of the list are still available on the web, and these are supposedly being updated by scholars who wish to remain anonymous (e.g., 'Contact' [n.d.]). Cabells Blacklist, now renamed Cabells Scholarly Analytics, is another example of a watchlist. Although Beall's List was free of charge, access to Cabells list requires payment, which makes it unattainable for most individual scholars (unless their institutions purchase a subscription). Additionally, both scholars and institutions have begun to realize that, due to the ever-changing landscape of predatory journals, watchlists are outdated almost as soon as they are published, making them an unreliable source for vetting journals (Koerber and others 2020; Neylon 2017).

An alternative to watchlists is safelists — or lists that provide names of presumed legitimate journals that meet certain quality criteria (Umlauf and Mochizuki 2018). Examples of safelists include Web of Science (WoS), Scopus databases, Directory of Open Access Journals (DOAJ), and many others (Koerber and others 2020). Although these

---

3   In recent discourse, new terminology has been suggested instead of blacklists or whitelists, which have problematic symbolism in regard to racial relations. For example, Koerber and others (2020) use the term 'watchlist' to refer to lists that aim to identify predatory journals or publishers and 'safelist' to refer to lists that aim to identify legitimate journals or publishers. In the study, they highlight the commonalities and differences among the criteria of these lists to understand the broad contours of the controversies that underlie them.

watchlists or safelists might be helpful in some cases, new predatory journals will not appear on them, or the predatory journals might change their names and publishers. Therefore, some studies (e.g., Koerber and others 2020; Manca and others 2019) question the effectiveness of these lists. The issues with maintaining an updated watchlist or safelist were acknowledged by some of our interviewees. For example, an Asian publishing professional noted that 'not all predatory journals are on the blacklists' (P27), and a South American researcher shared that she is 'very careful when [using] a list [...] because I think there are mistakes in this list' (P13).

Additionally, some fields, institutions, or even countries provide their own lists of vetted journals. China and India were two specific countries listed by our participants (P17, P19, P23) where national lists were in place, and a Southeast Asian scholar (P39) indicated that his institution had an approved list of journals for his field.

Checklists

As an alternative to watchlists and safelists, a growing trend has been for scholars and institutions to develop checklists that can help authors determine whether a journal is predatory. For example, Rele and others (2017) created a checklist that authors could use to evaluate a journal and guided authors on how to consider specific criteria when evaluating a certain journal. These authors' recommendations include two steps: evaluation of the journal and evaluation of the publisher, where the total scores at the end of the evaluation will define whether the journal is a proper choice or not for publishing the work. Evaluation of the journal requires searching the internet for the journal name, then looking for the following content on the journal's webpage: editorial board, the review process, conflict of interest statements, revenue sources, archiving policies or procedures, publishing schedule, author fees, copyright information, indexing inclusion, access to past published articles, and information on the number of articles published by the journal. The second evaluation step includes a web search for the publisher and information about the publisher.

Some scholars have also taken a more field-specific approach to developing checklists. For example, Shamseer and others (2017) demonstrate that potential predatory journals may be distinct in some key areas from presumed legitimate journals and provides evidence of how they differ within the biomedical fields. The key points described by Shamseer and others (2017) are summarized below, and could be used as an author checklist for determining the credibility of a given journal, especially in the biomedical fields:

The scope of interest includes non-biomedical subjects alongside biomedical topics.

- The website contains spelling and grammar errors.
- Images are distorted/fuzzy, intended to look like something they are not, or are unauthorized.
- The homepage language targets authors.
- The Index Copernicus Value is promoted on the website.
- Description of the manuscript-handling process is lacking.
- Manuscripts are requested to be submitted via email.
- Rapid publication is promised.
- There is no retraction policy.
- Information on whether and how journal content will be digitally reserved is absent.
- The Article processing/publication charge is very low (e.g., $150 USD).
- Journals claiming to be open access either retain the copyright of published research or fail to mention copyright.
- The contact email address is not affiliated to a professional organization or to the journal (e.g., @gmail.com or @yahoo.com).

Although Shamseer and others (2017) recognize that these criteria are likely not sensitive enough to detect all potentially illegitimate, predatory journals, they feel they are a good starting point.

One of the most widely used and acknowledged checklist tools is Think. Check. Submit., which was established by scientific societies and publishers to guide authors through the publishing process (Grudniewicz and others 2019). Think. Check. Submit. provides simple guidelines that authors can use to assess a journal or publisher before submitting an article and was one of the most common tools mentioned by our interview participants (e.g., P09, P21, P23, P44). For example, using these tools, authors can distinguish between a predatory journal and a new journal that follows the principles and standards of ethical scientific publishing but has not built up its reputation yet (Larkin 2018). The key questions posed by Think. Check. Submit. are listed in Table 5.2.

Table 5.2 Evaluation Questions for Vetting Journals

'Think. Check. Submit' 2021

Think	Are you submitting your research to a trusted journal?	Is it the right journal for your work?
Check	Can you easily identify and contact the publisher?	Is the editorial board familiar with the specific field?
	Can you identify the peer review process?	Are articles indexed in a service you are familiar with?
	Are fees clearly stated, along with then they will be due?	Is the publisher a member of a recognized industry initiative (e.g., COPE)?
Submit	Only after you've answered all the above questions in a satisfactory manner.	

We created an additional tool following the Think. Check. Submit. tool. Our method does not require authors to be familiar with any existing list. Authors could follow questions that are similar to those mentioned above and will help provide an in-depth investigation of a questionable journal (See Figure 5.1).

Before submitting a paper to a journal answer the following questions:

Are you familiar with the journal and publisher?
YES / NO

Have you read any published articles from this journal?
YES / NO

Does the journal have information about their editorial board?
YES / NO

Are you familiar with people from the editorial board, can you find the journal on their professional website/CV?
YES / NO

Does the journal webpage provide information about the review criteria? / publication cost?
YES / NO   YES / NO

Is the quality of the journal's website written in clear, good English?
YES / NO

Is the journal indexed in known databases and have an impact factor?
YES / NO

Were you approached by the journal and received an invitation e-mail to submit your work, but the journal is far afield from your discipline?
YES / NO

If you answered YES to the last question and NO to most of the other questions, the journal is likely predatory

Fig. 5.1 Karin Ardon-Dryer. *Before submitting a paper to a journal, answer the following questions* (2022). © STEPP Research Team

Conclusion

Publishing in peer-reviewed scientific journals is the cornerstone of academic assessment and is crucial for the development of early-career researchers, including graduate students, postdoctoral fellows, and pretenure or junior faculty. Publishing papers in predatory journals, a common misstep among early-career researchers, could result in a series of negative consequences, such as the loss of the manuscript, negatively scarring the scholar's publication record, and even damaging the scholar's ability to be hired at certain institutions. Unfortunately, many of those who submit papers to predatory journals fail to realize the potential consequences until it is too late. Some of the issues come from the fact there is not enough awareness and experience among early-career researchers regarding predatory journals and the impact they might have. Advisors, mentors, and senior faculty have an important position in educating and providing guidance to early-career researchers. This chapter provides information mentors could use to guide graduate students and junior scholars to make sure they avoid the pitfalls of predatory publishing.

Key Takeaways

- Publishing in peer-reviewed journals is a crucial part of career development for faculty with research-related duties.
- In recent years, researchers at all stages in their careers, in all disciplines, and from countries in every region have fallen prey to predatory publishers, although graduate students and early-career faculty may be especially susceptible to falling prey to predatory publishers.
- While the term 'predatory' is somewhat controversial, there are certain markers that are broadly agreed upon which indicate less-than-ethical publication practices.
- Typically, once an author realizes they have submitted their work to a predatory publisher, it is too late to recover their work, and may damage their professional reputation.
- The range of institutional expectations and support for graduate students and early-career faculty means the levels of exposure and training related to ethical research practices and potential pitfalls varies greatly from institution to institution and even from department to department.
- Previous research suggests a lack of awareness among early-career researchers regarding predatory journals and the impact they might have.

- The role of mentors and advisors is crucial in educating graduate students and early-career faculty about the potential pitfalls of predatory publishing.
- The pressure to publish for early-career faculty and graduate students may contribute to the increasing trend of submissions to predatory journals, which often tout quick publication times and do not offer robust peer reviews.
- Three main tools are widely available to help determine if a journal is predatory: watchlists, safelists, and checklists.
- Numerous strategies can be used to help detect and avoid predatory journals, including the following: examining the scope of the journal, reviewing the technical quality and accuracy of their digital footprint, knowing the journals and researchers in your field, critiquing the quality of a journal's published articles, researching the editorial board, vetting claimed indexing and impact factor data, and determining whether a specific journal is known to your colleagues.

Discussion Questions

1. Have you or anyone you know fallen prey to a predatory journal? If not, discuss how you have avoided the pitfalls. If yes, discuss how you were deceived and what can be done to avoid it again.

2. Discuss some reasons why junior scholars, and especially PhD students who have publication requirements attached to their degree, might turn to predatory publishing.

3. Were you aware of predatory publishing before reading this book/chapter? If so, where did you hear about it?

4. Discuss the strategies in the chapter to help avoid predatory publishing. Have you used any of these strategies? Do you feel there are certain strategies you might use more than others? Why?

5. Examine some of the tools used to detect predatory publishers. Is there a different tool suggested or used in your institution/department? Do you feel a certain tool is more effective than others? Why?

Journal Assessment Activity

The purpose of this activity is to help junior researchers determine the quality of journals in their field. Assessment of the journal will be based on two factors: the quality of the journal itself, and the content of specific articles.

STEP 1: Divide the participants into groups of 2–4 people.

STEP 2: Each group will identify **5 journals** in their field. They should attempt to find journals that range in quality.

- Evaluate each of the journals to determine which ones are questionable and which ones are legitimate. Rank the journals as one of the following categories:
    - Predatory
    - Questionable
    - Legitimate
- Ask the group to list resources they used, and any other strategies they used to evaluate the journals.

NOTE: As a time-saving measure, the instructor may wish to find journals they feel fall into each of the above categories and begin the activity at STEP 3.

STEP 3: Have each group select one article from each identified journal. Then, have the groups exchange articles. The groups should then evaluate whether the articles come from predatory, questionable, or legitimate journals.

Use the provided worksheet to help facilitate the discussion afterward.

STEP 4: Have the groups share their assessment of the journals, based on the articles they reviewed. See if the different groups assessed the journals the same, or differently, and why that might be.

STEP 5: Show them the Think. Check. Submit. website: https://thinkchecksubmit.org/journals/

- Discuss whether they used some of those same strategies.
- If time permits, have them reevaluate the journals based on the Think. Check. Submit. rubric and see if they come up with the same journal categorization.

Discussion Questions

1. How confident do you feel determining which journals/articles are legitimate/predatory?
2. What factors helped you feel this way?
3. What is the main thing you learned from this exercise?
4. What is the first thing you might check the next time you are trying to determine whether or not a journal is credible?

Journal Assessment Worksheet

INSTRUCTIONS: Please use this worksheet to record the thought process of the group. It is **NOT** necessary to reach a consensus. Rather, note how many people felt the article met the criteria for each question and list a couple of reasons. (Example: 3 felt the journal was high quality because [reason 1] and [reason 2].)

The facilitator will screen share this document so everyone can see the responses as they are being entered to ensure the worksheet is correctly capturing your assessment of each of the articles.

ARTICLE 1: [please fill in title of first article assigned to you]
How would you assess the quality of this article? [high, medium, or low]
How would you assess the quality of the journal in which this article is published? [high, medium, or low]
Do you think this article is published in a predatory journal? [yes or no]
What are the factors you considered in responding to each of the questions above?

ARTICLE 2: [please fill in title of second article assigned to you]
How would you assess the quality of this article? [high, medium, or low]
How would you assess the quality of the journal in which this article is published? [high, medium, or low]
Do you think this article is published in a predatory journal? [yes or no]
What are the factors you considered in responding to each of the questions above?

References

Al-Khatib, Aceil. 2016. 'Protecting Authors from Predatory Journals and Publishers', *Publishing Research Quarterly*, 32.4: 281–85, https://doi.org/10.1007/S12109-016-9474-3

Bankston, Adriana. 2017. 'Needed: Flexible Mentors in Science', *Inside Higher Ed*, https://www.insidehighered.com/advice/2017/05/01/advice-how-research-scientists-can-best-mentor-those-who-work-their-labs-essay

Beall, Jeffrey. 2012. 'Predatory Publishers Are Corrupting Open Access', *Nature*, 489.7415: 179, https://doi.org/10.1038/489179a

——. 2015. 'Criteria for Determining Predatory Open-Access Publishers', *Scholarly Open Access*, https://crescent.education/wp-content/uploads/2017/09/Criteria.pdf

——. 2016. 'Essential Information about Predatory Publishers and Journals', *International Higher Education*, 86, https://doi.org/10.6017/IHE.2016.86.9358

Berisha Qehaja, Albana. 2020. 'Avoiding Publishing in Predatory Journals: An Evaluation Algorithm', *ERIES Journal*, 13.3: 154–63, https://doi.org/10.7160/eriesj.2020.130305

Boucherie, Sacha. 2018. '"Predatory" vs Trustworthy Journals: What Do They Mean for the Integrity of Science?', *Elsevier Connect*, https://www.elsevier.com/connect/predatory-vs-trustworthy-journals-what-do-they-mean-for-the-integrity-of-science

Bowman, Deborah E., and Wallace, Michael B. 2017. 'Predatory Journals: A Serious Complication in the Scholarly Publishing Landscape', *Gastrointestinal Endoscopy*, 87.1: 273–74, https://doi.org/10.1016/j.gie.2017.09.019

Brezgov, Stef. 2019. 'Bogus Journal Accepts Profanity-Laced Anti-Spam Paper', *ScholarlyOA*, https://scholarlyoa.com/bogus-journal-accepts-profanity-laced-anti-spam-paper/

Busch, Judith W. 1985. 'Mentoring in Graduate Schools of Education: Mentors' Perceptions', *American Educational Research Journal*, 22.2: 265, https://doi.org/10.2307/1162843

Christopher, Mary M., and Young, Karen M.. 2015. 'Awareness of "Predatory" Open-Access Journals among Prospective Veterinary and Medical Authors Attending Scientific Writing Workshops', *Frontiers in Veterinary Science*, 2.22: 111–22, doi.org/10.3389/fvets.2015.00022

Clark, Jocalyn. 2018. 'Letter to the Editor – Predatory Journals: Bad for All But Especially Authors from Low and Middle Income Countries', *Acta Medica Portuguesa*, 31.3: 181–85, https://doi.org/10.20344/amp.10489

'Contact'. [n.d.]. *Beall's List of Potential Predatory Journals and Publishers*, https://beallslist.net/contact/

Darbyshire, Philip. 2017. 'Fake News. Fake Journals. Fake Conferences. What We Can Do', *Journal of Clinical Nursing*, 27.9–10: 1727–29, https://doi.org/10.1111/JOCN.14214

Ellis, Henry C. 1992. 'Graduate Education in Psychology: Past, Present, and Future', *American Psychologist*, 47.4: 570–76, https://doi.org/10.1037/0003-066X.47.4.570

Foss, Karen A., and Foss, Sonja K. 2008. 'Accomplishing the Mission: Creating a Partnership with Your Advisor', in *Getting the Most from Your Graduate Education in Communication: A Graduate Student's Handbook*, ed. by Sherwyn Morreale and Pat Arneson (Washington, DC: National Communication Association), 59–70

Gaff, Jerry G. 2002. 'The Disconnect between Graduate Education & Faculty Realities', *Liberal Education*, 88.3: 6–13

Grudniewicz, Agnes., Moher, David., Cobey, Kelly D., Bryson, Gregory L., Cukier, Samantha and others. 2019. 'Predatory Journals: No Definition, No Defence', *Nature*, 576.7786: 210–12, https://doi.org/10.1038/d41586-019-03759-y

Johnson, W. Brad, and Huwe, Jennifer M. 2002. 'Toward a Typology of Mentorship Dysfunction in Graduate School', *Psychotherapy*, 39.1: 44–55, https://doi.org/10.1037/0033-3204.39.1.44

Koerber, Amy., Starkey, Jesse C., Ardon-Dryer, Karin., Cummins, R. Glenn., Eko, Lyombe and others. 2020. 'A Qualitative Content Analysis of Watchlists vs Safelists: How Do They Address the Issue of Predatory Publishing?', *Journal of Academic Librarianship*, 46.6, https://doi.org/10.1016/j.acalib.2020.102236

Kurt, Serhat. 2018. 'Why Do Authors Publish in Predatory Journals?', *Learned Publishing*, 31.2: 141–47, https://doi.org/10.1002/leap.1150

Larkin, Marilynn. 2018. 'To Thwart Predatory Publishing, We Need to Work Together', *Elsevier Connect*, https://www.elsevier.com/connect/to-thwart-predatory-publishing-we-need-to-work-together#reputable-journal

Leung, Jonathan G., Wieruszewski, Patrick M., Stee, LeAnn., Takala, Christopher R., and Palmer, Brian A. 2020. 'Predatory Journals: A Cautionary Tale and a Lesson in Copyright Transfer', *Commentary*, 95.3: 441–44, https://doi.org/10.1016/j.mayocp.2019.09.001

Manca, Andrea., Cugusi, Lucia and Deriu, Franca. 2019. 'Questioning the Efficacy of Predatory Journals' Blacklists', *BJPsych Advances*, 25.2: 120–21, https://doi.org/10.1192/BJA.2018.72

Memon, Aamir Raoof., and Waqas, Ahmed. 2017. 'Indexing by Bibliographic Databases of Journals Published in the Developing World', *Science and Engineering Ethics*, 24.4: 1371–75, https://doi.org/10.1007/S11948-017-9898-Y

Mills, David and Inouye, K. 2020. 'Problematizing "Predatory Publishing": A Systematic Review of Factors Shaping Publishing Motives, Decisions, and

Experiences', *Learned Publishing*, 34.2: 89–104, https://doi.org/10.1002/LEAP.1325

Misra, Durga Prasanna., Ravindran, Vinod., Wakhlu, Anupam., Sharma, Aman., Agarwal, Vikas and others. 2017. 'Publishing in Black and White: The Relevance of Listing of Scientific Journals', *Rheumatology International*, 37: 1773–78, https://doi.org/10.1007/s00296-017-3830-2

Neylon, Cameron. 2017. 'Blacklists Are Technically Infeasible, Practically Unreliable and Unethical. Period.', *Science in the Open*, http://cameronneylon.net/blog/blacklists-are-technically-infeasible-practically-unreliable-and-unethical-period/

O'Neil, James M., and Wrightsman, Lawrence S. 2001. 'The Mentoring Relationship in Psychology Training Programs', in *Succeeding in Graduate School: The Career Guide for Psychology Students*, ed. by S. Walfish and A. K. Hess (Mahwah, NJ: Lawrence Erlbaum Associates Publishers), 111–27

Petrie, Trent A., and Wohlgemuth, Elaine A. 1994. 'In Hopes of Promoting Cohesion among Academics: New and Established', *The Counseling Psychologist*, 22.3: 466–73, https://doi.org/10.1177/0011000094223009

Quek, Heng Chuan, and Teo, Eng Kiong. 2018. 'Predatory Publishing; Pressures, Promotions and Perils', *Proceedings of Singapore Healthcare*, 27.1: 3–5, https://doi.org/10.1177/2010105817749602

Rele, Shilpa., Kennedy, Marie and Blas, Nataly. 2017. 'Journal Evaluation Tool', *LMU Librarian Publications & Presentations*, 40, https://digitalcommons.lmu.edu/librarian_pubs/40/

Roberts, Jason. 2016. 'Predatory Journals: Think before You Submit', *Headache*, 56.4: 618–21, https://doi.org/10.1111/HEAD.12818

Ruiter-Lopez, Leon., Lopez-Leon, Sandra and Forero, Diego A. 2019. 'Predatory Journals: Do Not Judge Journals by Their Editorial Board Members', *Medical Teacher*, 41.6: 691–96, https://doi.org/10.1080/0142159X.2018.1556390

Schira, H. Rainer, and Hurst, Chris. 2019. 'Hype or Real Threat: The Extent of Predatory Journals in Student Bibliographies', *Partnership*, 14.1: 1–16, https://doi.org/10.21083/PARTNERSHIP.V14I1.4764

Schlosser, Lewis Z., Lyons, Heather Z., Talleyrand, Regine M., Kim, Bryan S. K. and Johnson, W. Brad. 2010. 'Advisor-Advisee Relationships in Graduate Training Programs', *Journal of Career Development*, 38.1: 3–18, https://doi.org/10.1177/0894845309358887

Shamseer, Larissa., Moher, David., Maduekwe, Onyi., Turner, Lucy., Barbour, Virginia and others. 2017. 'Potential Predatory and Legitimate Biomedical Journals: Can You Tell the Difference? A Cross-Sectional Comparison', *BMC Medicine*, 15.1: 1–14, https://doi.org/10.1186/s12916-017-0785-9

Shrestha, Jiban., Subedi, Subash., Shokati, Behzad and Chaudhary, Amit. 2019. 'Predatory Journals: A Threat to Scholarly Publishing', *Journal of Education and Research*, 8.1: 89–101, https://doi.org/10.3126/jer.v8i1.25482

Teixeira Da Silva, Jaime A. 2013. 'Predatory Publishing: A Quantitative Assessment, the Predatory Score', *Asian Aust J Plant Sci Biotechnol*, 7.1: 21–34, http://www.globalsciencebooks.info/Online/GSBOnline/images/2013/AAJPSB_7(SI1)/AAJPSB_7(SI1)21-34o.pdf

'Think. Check. Submit'. 2021. *Think. Check. Submit.*, https://thinkchecksubmit.org/

Umlauf, Mary Grace and Mochizuki, Yuki. 2018. 'Predatory Publishing and Cybercrime Targeting Academics', *International Journal of Nursing Practice*, 24.1: 1–7, https://doi.org/10.1111/IJN.12656

Wilde, Judith Busch, and Schau, Candace Garrett. 2014. 'Mentoring in Graduate Schools of Education: Mentees' Perceptions', *The Journal of Experimental Education*, 59.2: 165–79, https://doi.org/10.1080/00220973.1991.10806559

Wood, Kelly E., and Krasowski, Matthew D. 2020. 'Academic Email Overload and the Burden of "Academic Spam"', *Academic Pathology*, 7, https://doi.org/10.1177/2374289519898858

Wrench, Jason S., and M. Punyanunt, Narissra. 2004. 'Advisee-Advisor Communication: An Exploratory Study Examining Interpersonal Communication Variables in the Graduate Advisee-Advisor Relationship', *Communication Quarterly*, 52.3: 224–36, https://doi.org/10.1080/01463370409370194

Yucha, Carolyn. 2014. 'Predatory Publishing: What Authors, Reviewers, and Editors Need to Know', *Biological Research for Nursing*, 17.1: 5–7, https://doi.org/10.1177/1099800414563378

6. What's Being Taught about Predatory Publishing?
A Systematic Review of University Resources

> It's tempting to toss off a quick, 'Don't give them your work to publish. Problem solved!' It has the advantage of brevity, but it doesn't do much to address the very real fears of scholars who don't have the training and the experience to confidently evaluate the worth of a given publication. (Schlosser 2015)

The challenge of addressing threats from predatory publishing practices is not an easy one. As the above epigraph notes, the easy but simplistic suggestion of merely avoiding such outlets is not altogether helpful when many scholars across varied disciplines lack understanding of the phenomenon, its origins, and outcomes and consequences (AlRyalat and others 2019; Christopher and Young 2015; Maurer and others 2021; Swanberg and others 2020; Webber and Wiegand 2022). Although predatory journals are a relatively new development when one considers the broader history of scholarly publishing, their importance as a threat to the ethical conduct and dissemination of research is clear: Predatory publishers have the potential to undermine overall confidence in scholarly inquiry, both in terms of peer distrust in research output tainted by distribution in a potentially predatory outlet, as well as broader public distrust in the process of science and its outcomes (Eriksson and Helgesson 2018). To address this development, various stakeholders have worked to provide educational resources or opportunities that help educate uninformed scholars about this practice (Cukier and others 2020; Lopez and Gaspard 2020; Murphy 2019).

Although predatory publishing may be relatively new, efforts to educate the research community on other aspects of research ethics in general have a longer history. For more than thirty years, some form of research ethics education has been required by some federal funders of scholarly research (Heitman and Bulger 2006; Kalichman 2014). Efforts to satisfy these requirements may take a variety of forms, including in-person workshops, seminars, or for-credit courses, although many institutions rely on online training — and CITI training in particular — to satisfy federal requirements (DuBois and others 2010; Phillips and others 2018). Ostensibly, the macroscopic goal of such education is to ensure the responsible conduct of research, although more specific goals of training programs may be unclear, unstated, or unrealistic (Kalichman 2014; Kalichman and Plemmons 2007), which invites challenges in terms of assessing learning outcomes. Engagement in scientific misconduct may be the result of deliberate actions (e.g., falsification of data), normative perceptions, or mere ignorance — a fundamental lack of knowledge or awareness of ethical guidelines and practices about what exactly constitutes misconduct (Bouter 2015; Dubois and others 2013; Hofmann and Holm 2019; Resnik 1996; Steen 2010). With respect to the latter, training is offered (or mandated) as a vital tool to prevent misconduct in its varied forms and ensure the responsible conduct of research (Watts and others 2017).

We contend that the same is true in the area of predatory publishing. Scholars fall prey either due to a lack of knowledge on the subject or as willing participants for various reasons (see Chapter 5, this volume; Mills and Inouye 2021). As with other dimensions of the ethical conduct of research, training materials that explore predatory publishing may have the potential to play a vital role in informing scholars and providing a comprehensive knowledge base that aids decision making regarding potential outlets for their scholarly works. However, in order to identify gaps in training regarding predatory publishing, it is crucial to establish what current resources are available to others and most commonly used within scholarly research environments.

The purpose of this chapter is to provide an assessment of the publicly available training materials provided by universities on the topic of predatory publishing. This review examined resources provided by institutions with Carnegie classifications of 'very high research activity' ('Basic Classification Description' 2022) and systematically coded for a number of important variables that reflect the common elements provided within these training resources, topics covered by these resources, and the intended audience, among other things. The findings reveal that a wealth of materials is available, and they frequently describe or list characteristics that may be indicative of a predatory journal. Moreover, they reveal a network of other resources available to help researchers evaluate the quality of a journal and avoid potentially predatory outlets. However, online resources almost exclusively imply passive participation on the part of the reader and are rarely interactive or provide any means of assessing learning. Thus, educational materials on predatory publishing may not fulfill best practices for training the scholarly community (Watts and others 2017).

Background

The broader literature on research ethics education provides a useful lens for examining materials that explore the more focused topic of predatory publishing. Although funders may require research ethics education, the precise nature of that training varies (Kalichman 2013, 2014). Thus, the precise content, method of delivery, format, or means of assessment may differ across institutions or among researchers in different disciplines within an institution. Remarkably, scholars have variably decried either the inconsistency or general uniformity in research ethics education. For example, DuBois and his collaborators (2010) reported the results of a survey of research to assess how research ethics training was achieved among investigators with National Institutes of Health (NIH)-funded Clinical and Translational Science (CTSA) awards. Their data revealed that investigators employed a variety of training resources, such as online CITI training, textbooks or textbook chapters/selections, or original materials. They concluded that 'there is no unified approach to RCR [responsible conduct of research] training' (p. 110), and plans were inconsistent across or even within single institutions. For example, they noted that some survey respondents indicated that their university offered no RCR training, while colleagues at the very same institution correctly noted that such training was indeed offered.

On the other hand, some scholars have noted greater consistency within RCR training, at least with respect to topics of research ethics education and how universities satisfy federal training requirements.

The Office of Research Integrity within the Department of Health and Human Services identified nine core areas that should be included in RCR training (Steneck 2007). Kalichman (2013) noted that the specific topics addressed in RCR training have been fairly consistent through the various evolutions of federal guidance on education: 'While the wording has varied slightly, 5 topics (conflict of interest, data management, authorship and publication, research misconduct, and human and animal subjects) have been retained in all 4 versions of these requirements' (p. 385). In general, the materials and resources developed to meet these requirements directly reflect these topics.

Funder mandates stipulating some form of RCR training have spurred the rapid growth of materials and resources offered to satisfy these requirements (Kalichman 2013), and the systematic review or examination of courses, curricula, or other materials used in research ethics education represents a robust, ongoing body of scholarship (e.g., Phillips and others 2018; Pizzolato and others 2020) that can inform the broad assessment of resources developed to train scholars on the topic of predatory publishing. Furthermore, the curation of training materials has been the explicit focus of government-sponsored research as well as a goal of those types of reviews (Kalichman 2014). Thus, efforts to catalog training resources are not without precedent.

For example, Phillips and others (2018) examined publicly available training materials offered to satisfy RCR training requirements mandated by US federal funders. Specifically, their analysis focused on the nature and delivery format of these materials to determine if they reflected recommended best practices for research ethics training. As Phillips and others (2018) noted, these best practices were the result of a National Science Foundation (NSF)-funded workshop held by the National Academy of Engineering that was later summarized as an edited book (Hollander and Arenberg 2009):

> (1) noninstructor-led, online-only programs do not provide adequate instruction; (2) multiple formats of instruction are needed; (3) programs should be wide-ranging and cross-institutional, with content that varies by disciplinary areas and career stage; (4) ethics education cannot be administered in a single "dose"; and (5) principle investigators (PIs) should be positively involved in teaching RCR to their trainees. (Phillips and others 2018: 229)

To conduct their review, Phillips and colleagues examined publicly available training plans and materials from a sample of 108 US universities labeled as 'very high research activity' under the Carnegie classification system. Their review focused on a variety of attributes of the materials, including format (i.e., online versus in-person training), duration or frequency of training, and customization of the materials for researchers at different stages of their careers (i.e., undergraduate, graduate, or postdoctoral researchers). Among their varied findings, they reported that most university plans to satisfy NSF-mandated ethics training 'could be satisfied with online-only training' (Phillips and others 2018: 232). Of these, a large majority listed CITI training as the sole online resource for fulfilling this requirement. However, their findings also reflected an illuminating discrepancy between what was required versus what was offered. As they note, 'more than half the plans we reviewed *offered* more meaningful educational opportunities, but did not *require* that trainees engage in them' (p. 245). For example, in addition to the required online training, universities offered other optional opportunities for ethics training including seminars, brown-bag discussions, orientation sessions, or even for-credit coursework.

Moreover, their review also noted a lack of meaningful assessment or differentiation across the training materials reviewed. Indeed, Phillips and others (2018) noted that for a small handful of programs, undergraduate students could meet or fulfill research ethics training requirements by merely receiving a handout with no assessment of comprehension or retention. Furthermore, a majority of training programs had uniform requirements for undergraduate, graduate, or postdoctoral researchers.

In sum, Phillips and others (2018) concluded that most university-mandated trainings to fulfill NSF or NIH requirements do not live up to recommended best practices in terms of modality/format; variation of topic/content by discipline with a focus on the unique needs of a given field; variety as a function of the stage of one's research career; or PI-centered focus.

Although similar to the review by Phillips and others (2018), Pizzolato and colleagues (2020) conducted a systematic review that focused more squarely on the substantive content addressed in training materials. In their review, they examined 237 online resources on the topic of research integrity (RI) in order to capture twenty-one attributes or aspects of these resources, including topics examined, whether the content was tailored to specific disciplines or audiences, country of origin, or teaching approach (e.g., passive vs. active).

Among other things, they found that resources generally did not reflect disciplinary customization, and only implied passive participation of the learner (i.e., information was merely provided for review). Of particular interest to our discussion of predatory journals and publication ethics, they found that publication-related issues were among the top three most discussed topics, appearing on more than half (55%) of the resources examined. However, within the discussion of publication ethics, common topics were authorship or plagiarism, and no evidence was provided that predatory publishing was discussed within any of the resources they examined.[1] On the one hand, the fact that scholarly publishing is frequently included as an important ethical dimension of scientific research and associated training illustrates the importance of the effective (and ethical) dissemination of knowledge as part of the conduct of science (Heitman and Bulger 2006). However, the rise of predatory publishing models represents a new threat that could be included as a component of research ethics training.

With respect to the curation of resources, several of these studies have made their collections of training materials gathered in the conduct of their review publicly available. These resources could aid institutions in developing or implementing research ethics training, as well as individual researchers wishing to implement training within their own research groups, classrooms, or other venues by providing easy access to a single repository of materials. For example, as part of their systematic review of research ethics training materials, Pizzolato and others (2020) made these resources available online through their 'Embassy of Good Science' website. Furthermore, they created a grid that summarized these resources as a supplement file to their published manuscript.

---

1 Review of the supplementary document that accompanied their manuscript revealed no discussion of predatory publishing, although open access publishing was noted for two resources.

Guiding Questions

The present analysis was patterned after these models and sought both to examine the nature of the resources provided by universities and to curate extant educational materials or other resources on the topic of predatory publishing through a list of available resources. Specifically, the analysis sought to answer a number of questions. Given that training materials or other information on predatory publishing could take a variety of forms, what are the most common types of online resources available from universities? Moreover, do they reflect a stated audience, either as reflected by the content itself, or as a function of some explicit statement?

Cursory review of the myriad sources created to educate or inform the academic community about predatory publishing reveals a web of interconnected or commonly linked resources or materials. This begs the question, what resources are most commonly linked within materials that discuss predatory publishing? Among these resources, what topics are most commonly addressed within online resources that discuss predatory publishing? Lastly, the dynamic nature of online content affords tremendous flexibility in terms of the structural nature of these materials (e.g., text, videos, interactive features). As such, we ask, what are the formal characteristics of online resources in terms of content format or modality?

Method

Sample and Unitizing

Publicly available online resources from universities that provided information or training in the area of predatory publishing were examined. To collect this sample, a Google web search for universities in the United States categorized with a basic Carnegie classification of 'very high research activity' ($N = 131$) was conducted in July 2021 ('146 Results for Basic' 2022). To ensure that as many resources were captured as possible, separate searches were conducted using the university name and four search terms — predatory publishing, predatory publish, predatory journal, and library AND predator — to locate other publicly available resources, such as training or materials provided by discrete academic units or libraries.

Materials included in the sample were restricted to resources hosted or provided by the universities; thus, only resources under university URLs or domains were included. We attempted to capture all digital resources hosted by these universities that could be used as training or supplemental materials, including archived recordings of talks and lectures or slide decks of presentations. However, individual faculty scholarly publications on the topic, regardless of where they were hosted online (i.e., on a publisher's website or university's website) were not included as they did not constitute materials designed as training or educational materials. Similarly, pages simply announcing upcoming (or past) talks or lectures were not included for review, as these pages typically did not contain substantive information or training material that could be used as a durable resource. In addition, we did not include social media posts (e.g., Twitter posts) from university faculty on the topic as they did not represent training materials provided by the university.

One challenge in gathering materials for review was unitizing the resources identified through the search. For example, the search process described above often yielded multiple distinct URLs that included language on the topic of predatory publishing. However, upon closer inspection, these unique URLs may have been part of a single resource, such as a comprehensive library guide on scholarly publishing with multiple components or pages therein that referenced predatory publishing. As an analogy, these distinct URLs within a single resource could be compared to individual chapters within a single book. Counting the distinct URLs could have the effect of artificially inflating the amount or number of training materials provided. In order to provide a more conservative review of training materials that avoids this potential inflation, analysis of the materials was performed at the broader 'resource' level, rather than repeating the analysis on each individual page or part of a broader resource. This is analogous to Pizzolato and others (2020) who found that some educational tools were part of a single broader resource. For example, a guide on scholarly publishing from the University of Virginia library contained references to predatory publishing on two distinct pages within the guide. But for the purpose of analysis here, the guide was treated as a single unit.

Evaluation Criteria

Review of the characteristics of the materials examined twenty attributes and was patterned after suggested best practices in research ethics education or past research examining RCR training materials (Hollander and Arenberg 2009; Kalichman 2014; Phillips and others 2018; Pizzolato and others 2020). These attributes include both structural or formal features of the resources examined (e.g., the presence of video content; links to other resources or tools), as well as the substantive content of these resources in terms of the information provided (e.g., tailored or customized focus; definitions, descriptions, or common characteristics of potentially predatory publishers; discussion of the history of predatory publishing). Other attributes captured information about the creator of the content (e.g., an author was identified and contact information provided) and its currency (e.g., date of last update). These characteristics are summarized in Table 6.1 as an online supplement (Appendix A), along with a full copy of the coding scheme employed here.[2]

Coding

Resources identified through the aforementioned web search were examined between fall 2021 and spring 2022, and independently coded for the presence or absence of these structural and content characteristics by the first author of this chapter and a trained graduate student. Prior to formal coding, multiple rounds of training were conducted where coders reviewed the analysis scheme on a separate pilot sample of resources from programs identified as 'high research activity' by the Carnegie classification system. During this training,

---

2 Table 6.1 can be accessed at https://doi.org/10.11647/OBP.0364#resources. The full coding scheme ("STEPP Coding Scheme") and resultant data ("STEPP Systematic Review Dataset") are available in the Chapter 6 dataset: https://doi.org/10.18738/T8/D6RICU.

these pilot materials were coded, pilot reliability was reviewed, and the analysis scheme was revised in order to achieve satisfactory intercoder reliability on the study sample (Neuendorf 2017).

For the study sample, a commonly coded subsample of resources from 10% of the universities within the population was randomly selected to be examined by both coders and used for formal intercoder reliability assessment. For this study, simple percent agreement was employed due to the high incidence of select coding options within the sample and rare incidence of others (Zhao and others 2013). Intercoder agreement was >85% for all variables, and disagreements were reviewed by the first author of this chapter for final coding decisions.

Results

A total of 204 online resources comprised the study sample. Although most universities within the population provided some form of online information or resource on the topic of predatory publishing resource (e.g., library guide, informational newsletter article), for 17.5% ($n = 23$) of universities designated as very high research activity within the Carnegie classification system, the web search yielded no materials on the subject of predatory publishing. In addition, some online resources identified through the initial web search were no longer active once coders began examining them a short time later. This obviously speaks to the somewhat volatile nature of web content and challenges of examining online materials (McMillan 2000).

Resource Type and Source

One of the first questions we sought to explore through the analysis was the general nature of the training materials within the sample. As shown in Figure 6.1, among the resources gathered, the vast majority were library guides designed to provide a comprehensive understanding of the nature of predatory publications.

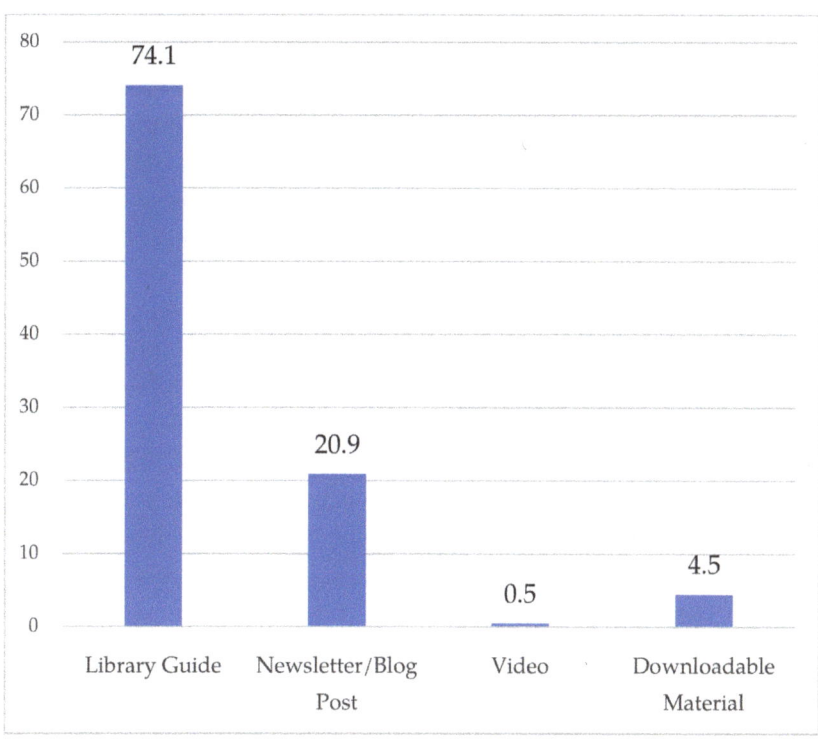

Fig. 6.1 R. Glenn Cummins. *Nature of Online Resources Regarding Predatory Publishing* (2022). © STEPP Research Team

Other newsletter articles, blog posts, or similar short discussions of predatory publishing varied in the depth and nature of the information presented. Some materials provided useful information that was designed to inform readers about the general nature of predatory publishing, review common characteristics of potentially predatory journals, and/or provide links to other useful resources. For example, the University of Illinois Chicago Graduate School provided a somewhat in-depth informational article on the topic ('Don't Fall Prey' 2020). However, other stories or posts merely mentioned predatory publishers in the context of other topics (e.g., managing email; Naegle 2016), or merely as personal opinion or discussion of events related to predatory publishing.

In addition, the web search discovered a small number of direct links to downloadable files, most typically Microsoft PowerPoint files or Adobe Acrobat/PDF versions of slide decks from a presentation on the topic. For example, an archived presentation on 'Author's Rights & Predatory Publishers' (Royster 2015) from a library staff member at the University of Nebraska-Lincoln provided a review of the nature of predatory publishers, a discussion of safe/watch lists, and potential warning signs.

Because library guides represented the most common type of online resource as well as the type of material most clearly designed to educate and inform regarding predatory publishing, the remaining analysis focused only on those guides ($n = 149$). Coders examined a number of descriptive characteristics of these resources, including whether they provided a contact person and an explicit date when the resource was last updated. With respect to contact person, the resources were evenly split, with a very slight majority not providing a specific person/point of contact should the reader request additional information or assistance ($n = 76; 51\%$). However, most of the resources did denote when they were last updated ($n = 121; 81.2\%$). Of those, almost all were relatively current, with only one resource providing an update date prior to 2020.[3]

Target Audience

Given the suggestion that educational resources or materials be developed for specific audiences, we examined whether materials in the sample reflected this suggestion. Two attributes of the resources were examined to determine the intended audience of the information. In terms of the tailored nature of the content, language or specific content within most of the resources was not focused on a specific discipline ($n = 126; 84.6\%$), while one-quarter did reflect some specialization, either through language within the page or specific resources linked within the materials. For example, a library guide published by the Texas Tech University Health Sciences Center included the explicit statement that 'This guide deals with predatory publishing in the health sciences'

---

3   Notably, that one resource has since been updated.

(Stuart 2021: para. 1). Other materials within the sample included links to resources with a disciplinary focus (e.g., MEDLINE, CINAHL Complete) with language that referenced the associated discipline or research area.

The specified audience was often not defined or presumed to be general ($n = 106$; 71.1%). When the intended audience was specified ($n = 43$; 28.9%), this was typically through language within the resource. For example, Cornell University library provides a resource titled 'MAE [Mechanical and Aerospace Engineering] Orientation for Graduate Students: Predatory Journals' ('Understanding and Avoiding' 2020). Likewise, the Ohio State University library provides a similar resource labeled 'General Resources for Graduate Students in the Physical Sciences and Engineering' ('General Resources' 2022).

Linked Resources

One distinguishing property of online content is the potential for interconnected content through shared hyperlinks. Thus, the analysis sought to examine the network of resources that characterize online materials on the topic of predatory publishing. Notably, all library guides examined in the sample provided at least some links to other resources external to the university, although there was considerable variability in the specific resources linked to within the guides. As seen in Figure 6.2, the Directory of Open Access Journals (DOAJ) was the most frequently linked external resource. Think. Check. Submit. was the second most frequently linked resource but was only found in roughly half of the guides. Likewise, as Figure 6.2 illustrates, almost half the guides also linked to scholarly articles or informational or blog posts on the topic of predatory publishing.

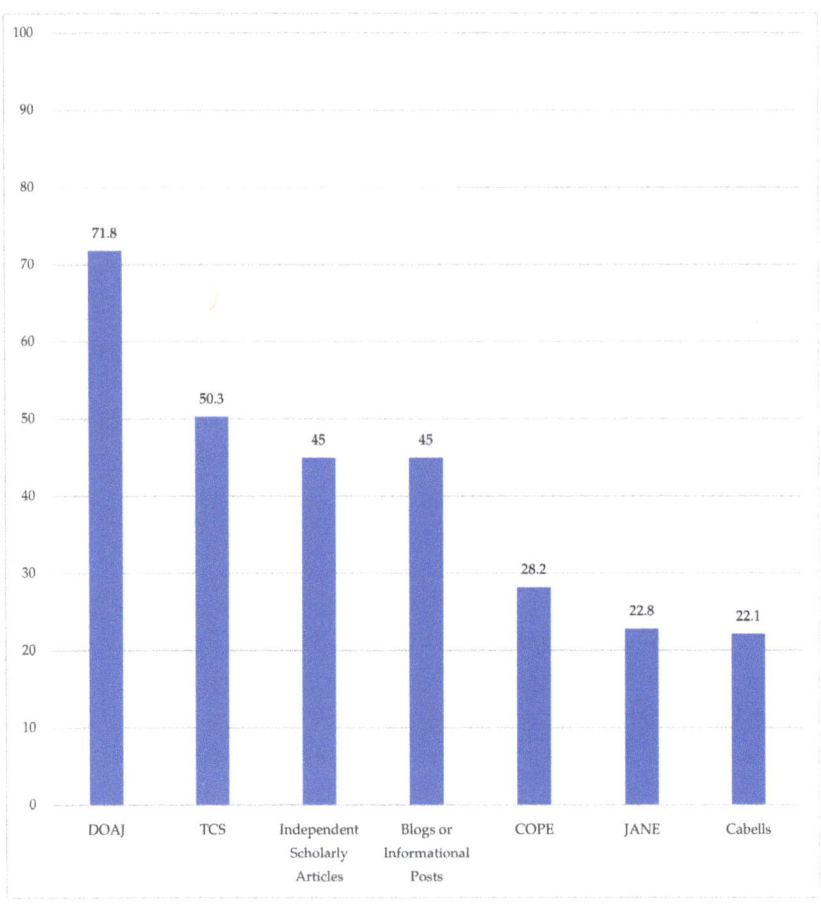

Fig. 6.2 R. Glenn Cummins. *Percentage of Library Guides that Provided Links to Common External Resources on Predatory or Open Access Publishing* (2022). © STEPP Research Team

Notably, although all library guides provided some links to external resources, a slight majority of those ($n = 81$; 54.4%) included at least some links that were password protected or behind some form of paywall that required a university subscription or credentials. Thus, although further information was provided, access was not freely available to all interested individuals.

Content Areas and Structural Attributes

Perhaps the most important elements examined within the systematic review of training resources was the actual substantive content of these materials, including discussion of the history of predatory publishing, characteristics of potentially predatory publishers, case studies describing individual experiences with predatory publishing, and more.

Notably, more than half of the resources provided did not offer a formal, explicit definition of predatory publishers ($n = 83; 55.7\%$). Often, resources would use the term 'predatory publisher' and then provide guidelines for selecting publishing outlets without explaining what the term means. For example, Stony Brook University library offers a guide that references solicitations to publish as well as pressure to produce published findings. It states, 'Some of these offers are legitimate but others turn out to be scams perpetrated by predatory publishers' ('How Do You Know' 2022: para. 1). But no further definition is offered to help guide the potentially uninformed reader. Likewise, one guide from the University of Houston library on 'Author Rights and Publishing Resources' briefly references 'so-called predatory publishers' in a section on publishing in open access journals before linking to DOAJ ('Take Control' [n.d.]). Again, no definition of the phenomenon is offered within that specific guide.[4]

Other resources provided more explicit definitions of predatory publishing. For example, the Health Sciences Library at the University of Utah provides a guide on 'Scholarly Publishing and Copyright' that defines the phenomenon: 'A predatory publisher is an opportunistic publishing venue that exploits the academic need to publish but offers little reward for those using their services' ('Predatory Journals' 2023: para. 1). Similarly, the University of Florida library provides a guide exclusively focused on predatory publishing that states, 'Predatory publishing typically refers to cases where individual journals or organizations intentionally deceive authors or readers by falsely claiming to offer publishing services or expertise' ('Predatory & Questionable Publishing' 2021: para. 1).

---

[4] It should be noted that other, separate guides from the university do offer an explicit definition.

Other guides draw upon consensus or published definitions of the term. For example, the Lane Medical Library at Stanford University provides a broad guide on 'Research Impact' that contains a subsection on predatory journals nested under a discussion of journal ranking ('Research Impact' 2023). It provides the consensus definition drafted by forty-three scholars who met in Ottawa, Canada, and was later published in the journal *Nature*: 'Predatory journals and publishers are entities that prioritize self-interest at the expense of scholarship and are characterized by false or misleading information, deviation from best editorial and publication practices, a lack of transparency, and/or the use of aggressive and indiscriminate solicitation practices' (Grudniewicz and others 2019: 211).

A relatively common element within the guides examined within the sample is some discussion of how to identify potentially predatory outlets. A majority of guides reviewed here ($n = 91$; 61.1%) provide either some discussion or an explicit checklist of these attributes. For example, a library guide from Virginia Commonwealth University titled 'Avoid Publishing Scams' provides a bulleted list of 'common qualities' of predatory publishers (Miller 2021). Other resources describe these characteristics in a more narrative form, such as the guide 'Navigating the Article Publication Process' from the Ohio State University libraries: 'Predatory publishers often aggressively solicit manuscripts from scholars, charge fees with no transparency about their purpose, and/ or have little or no quality control (peer review, editing, etc.) over their content' ('Navigating the Article' 2021: para. 2).

Library guides were much more likely to point to lists or directories providing information on so-called 'safelists' compared to 'watchlists'.[5] A majority of the resources examined provided links to other resources that contained information on journals that had been reviewed by some organization to ensure quality. The most common provider linked to was DOAJ. Indeed, of the 114 resources that provided links to 'safe lists', a large majority ($n = 91$; 79.8%) included a link to DOAJ, making it by

---

5   Until recently, many examining the topic of predatory publishing and lists of potentially problematic outlets employed the dichotomy of 'blacklists' and 'whitelists'. As noted in Koerber and others (2020), we follow the lead of Cabells International and adopt the phrase 'safelist' and 'watchlist' to avoid the 'symbolism inextricably tied to the idea of blacklists and whitelists' (Bisaccio, 2020, para. 1)

far the most common such resource. Links to UlrichsWeb Global Serials Directory were less common ($n = 39$; 24.2%), as were links to Cabells Journalytics ($n = 15.8\%$).

Although not referenced as a comprehensive list of safe publishing outlets, some resources also suggested checking to see if the journal publisher was a member of the Open Access Scholarly Publishers Association (OASPA). For example, the Himmelfarb Health Sciences Library at George Washington University provided a library guide on predatory publishing that contained a section on 'Qualities of Reputable Journals' ('Researcher Services and Support' 2022). It suggested checking to ensure that the journal was indexed in UlrichsWeb and DOAJ, as well as checking to see if the publisher was a member of the OASPA (see Figure 6.3).

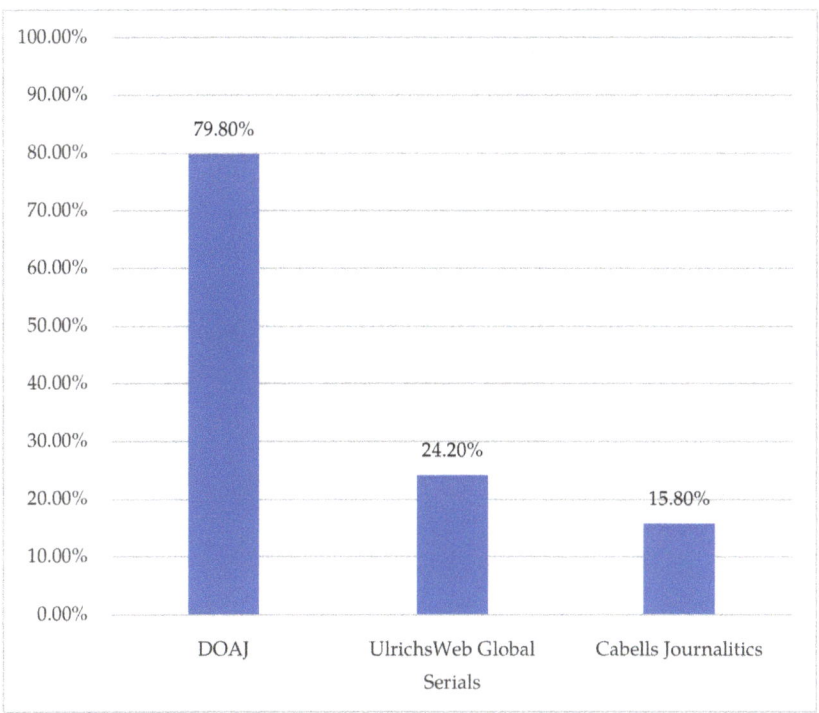

Fig. 6.3 R. Glenn Cummins. *Percentage of Library Guides that Link to Providers of 'Safe Lists' or Databases of Scholarly Journals Reviewed for Quality* (2022). © STEPP Research Team

Regarding watchlists of potentially predatory journals, these were relatively rare within any of the resources within the sample ($n = 49$; 32.2%). Of those that did provide links to lists of predatory journals, all linked to some archived (or dead) version of Beall's list of potentially predatory journals (Beall 2016).[6] However, some resources explicitly advise readers to not rely upon such lists. For example, the library at Northeastern University acknowledges Beall's list but instead encourages readers to rely on other tools to avoid potentially predatory journals ('Choosing a Publication Venue' 2022).

Multiple additional content attributes were also examined within the sample of resources (see Figure 6.4). The history of predatory publishing was all but ignored within the sample, appearing in only one material (0.7%). That resource, provided by the library at Georgetown University, gave a brief summary of the increase in open access publishing and noted, 'Due to the ease and low cost of publishing online, many of the new journals were from unknown publishers, some of which were labeled 'fake' or 'predatory' as they did not deliver the quality and service expected, while collecting substantial fees from authors' ('Journal Quality' [n.d]: para. 1). The resource then describes various attempts to address concerns surrounding this phenomenon, including links to various commentaries and other resources on the topic.

---

6   E.g., http://web.archive.org/web/20170111172306/https:/scholarlyoa.com/publishers/

6. What's Being Taught about Predatory Publishing? 219

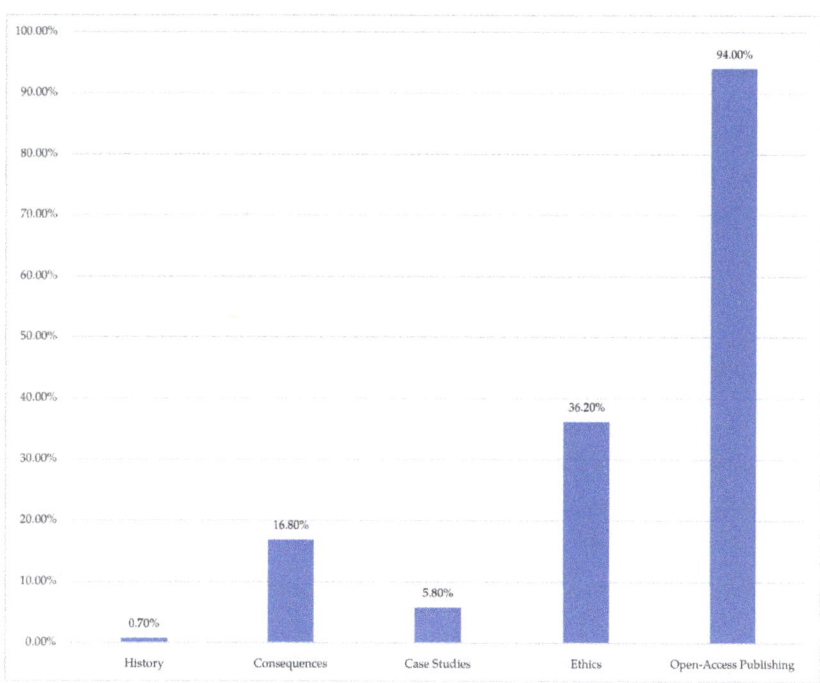

Fig. 6.4 R. Glenn Cummins. *Percentage of Library Guides that Include Discussions of Various Content Areas and Topics* (2022). © STEPP Research Team

A fairly small minority of resources ($n = 25$; 16.8%) provided discussion of the possible consequences associated with publishing in a potentially predatory publication. For example, the Brown University library provides a guide titled, 'Understanding Unethical Publishing Practices' that contains a section under the heading 'What's the harm?' The guide then describes various negative consequences of publishing in potentially predatory outlets such as sub-par peer review, the transitory qualities of some potentially predatory outlets, as well as possible stigmas associated with predatory outlets ('Understanding Unethical Publishing' 2020). But such discussions are rare, as a majority of materials do not discuss these consequences.

Likewise, discussion of specific case studies is uncommon and was found in only 5.8% ($n = 8$) of the sample. For example, as shown in Figure 6.5, the University of Pittsburg library's guide on 'Illegitimate and Predatory Publishing' provides a section under the 'Case Study' menu that provides an annotated example of an email solicitation indicative of a potentially predatory journal ('Case Study' 2021). In addition, it provides an image of a specific journal with annotations denoting potential concerns with the outlet. Similarly, the medical library at the College of Medicine at Florida International University provides a library guide on 'Where to Publish' ('Where to Publish' 2022). That guide also contains an annotated image of an email solicitation that notes potential concerns, such as lack of contact information for the journal and a false sense of urgency regarding the publishing opportunity. But again, these specific illustrations or examples were absent in the vast majority of training resources.

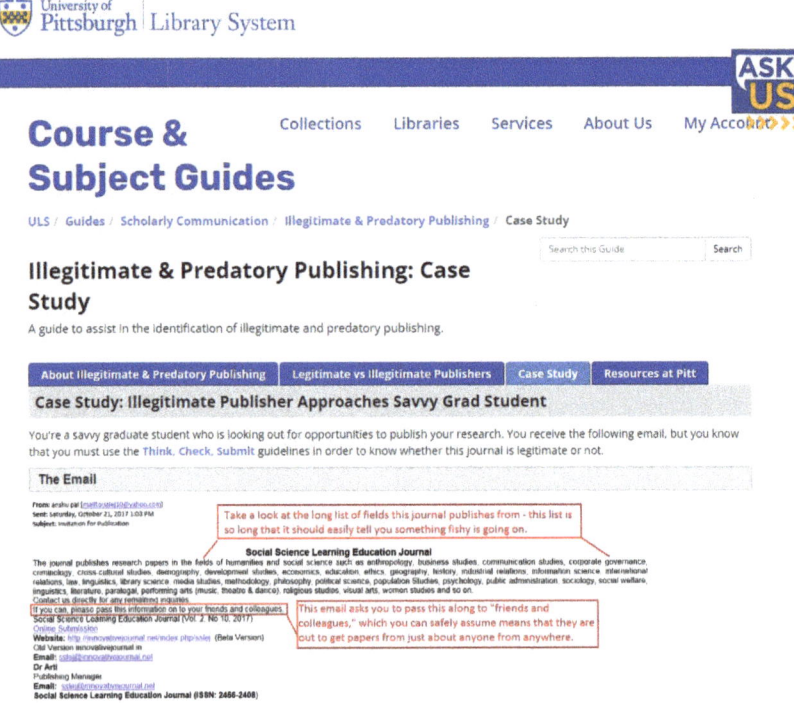

Fig. 6.5 R. Glenn Cummins. *Case Study from the University of Pittsburgh Library with Annotated Image of Potentially Predatory Solicitation Email* (2021). © University of Pittsburgh Library

With respect to the discussion of ethical aspects of potentially predatory publishing, a majority included no discussion or even reference to ethics (n = 95; 63.8%), and just over one-third of resources (n = 54;

36.2%) provided only a brief mention or simple link to the Committee on Publication Ethics (COPE). None provided a substantive discussion of the ethical dimensions of predatory publishing.

Lastly, the discussion of predatory publishing was almost universally placed within the context of or associated with some broader discussion of open access publishing ($n = 140$; 94.0%). For example, the University of Tennessee library provides a comprehensive guide titled 'Scholarly Publishing Toolkit'. Within this guide, one section focuses on open access publishing and also discusses predatory publishing, Beall's list, and other journal selection criteria ('Scholarly Publishing Toolkit' 2022).

Similarly, other resources place discussions of predatory publishing underneath the more macroscopic umbrella of open access publishing. As a case in point, the library at the University of California San Diego provides a guide explicitly focusing on open access publishing. Within the FAQ of that guide, predatory publishing is briefly defined and discussed, but primarily as a means of differentiating potentially predatory publishers from more transparent and reputable open access publishers ('What is Open Access?' 2022). Regardless, this reflects the potential confusion in differentiating open access from predatory publishing and long-standing relationships between the two (see Chapter 2).

Structural Features of Resources

Lastly, this systematic review sought to examine not only the content of the materials within the sample but the structural nature of that information, including the use of video, assessments, or other media or modalities. A small minority of resources employed only textual information ($n = 26$; 17.4%), whereas most resources within the sample employed various other forms of information including videos, graphics, or other elements.

Although not used in a majority of resources, videos were included in more than one-third of materials within the sample ($n = 59$; 39.6%). The source or creator of the videos varied considerably. Of those videos, most were from external sources ($n = 47$; 79.7%) and only 20.3% were created by someone within the university ($n = 12$). The most commonly linked or embedded videos were an overview from Think. Check.

Submit. ($n = 19$), and 'Open Access Explained!' from PhD Comics ($n = 12$), although a wide assortment of other videos were also found (e.g., an interview with Jeffrey Beall; a video on predatory publishing from a class titled 'Calling Bullshit' at the University of Washington; a video explaining the vanity press; an internally produced video explaining scholarly versus popular press sources).

In addition, many resources included downloadable Adobe Acrobat PDF documents ($n = 69$; 46.3%) as well as a scattered assortment of other types of files or modalities, including Microsoft PowerPoint files or information graphics. Notably, only three (2.0%) of the resources included within the sample were interactive beyond mere site navigation. Those two sources were library guides from Northwestern University and the University of Alabama at Birmingham, and both featured prompts or tasks that asked readers to review information from external sources (i.e., DOAJ; UlrichsWeb; Think. Check. Submit.) to answer specific questions.

For example, the resource from the University of Alabama at Birmingham contained a section labeled 'Evaluating Journals Practice' with links to four practice trials ('Predatory Publishing: Author Resources' 2022). Each link then asked users to find a specific journal or publisher within one of those external resources and answer questions about the source (e.g., 'Is the journal indexed in the Directory of Open Access Journals?'; 'Is the [journal] homepage free from language that targets authors? (ex. Prominently displays submission links and information, promotes quick peer review').

Lastly, learning assessments were also rare and were only found in two (1.3%) of the resources examined. One assessment was a question asking 'Was this information helpful?' with a simple yes/no response, and one was a forced-choice quiz in a resource from the Yale University medical library that asked a series of questions about the nature of open access publications ('Scholarly Communication' 2022).

Discussion

Inspired by previous assessments of learning materials and other resources regarding the responsible conduct of research (e.g., Phillips and others 2018; Pizzolato and others 2020), the present chapter systematically examined publicly available materials on the topic of predatory publishing from US universities receiving the highest research classification under the Carnegie system. Perhaps the most important finding from this review is that resources developed to educate the research community regarding predatory publishing are available. Almost all the universities included within the study sample provide at least *some* form of resource or training material on the topic of predatory publishing, with many universities providing multiple resources. Secondly, the majority of these materials were in the form of often quite comprehensive library guides on the subject. This reflects their role in leading efforts to inform the scholarly community about this phenomenon (Ciro 2021; Lopez and Gaspard 2020; Ojala and others 2020; Teixeira da Silva 2022). Thus, the challenge is determining how to encourage scholars — both emerging and senior — to engage with these materials in a meaningful way. As the opening epigraph from one resource provided by the Ohio State University notes, simply telling scholars not to publish in predatory journals does little to inform the academic community about why this problem exists or how to identify a potentially predatory journal — vital information if the threat of predatory journals is to be addressed.

Key Findings

Topics, Content, and Structure

In terms of topics, this analysis reveals a fair amount of consistency in terms of what is, and perhaps more importantly, what is not discussed. A majority of the resources examined here included some narrative description or bulleted list of common characteristics of potentially predatory publications (61%). Indeed, such approaches are a standard way to help authors identify potentially problematic scholarly outlets (Cukier and others 2020). Likewise, the present review also illuminated some consistency in terms of commonly linked resources that could be used to educate scholars. DOAJ was frequently linked as a tool authors could rely upon to evaluate the quality of open access journals. Moreover, many of the materials reviewed here also link to the tools and training provided by Think. Check. Submit. or even directly embed videos from that source designed to educate audiences on identifying quality publishing outlets.

The resources reviewed were also fairly consistent in what was not discussed. Broad discussion or even case-based review of the consequences of publishing in predatory outlets, the history of the phenomenon (see Introduction), and ethical aspects of predatory publishing (see Chapter 1) was less common and varied among the resources examined. Although these may be less pragmatic than simple checklists, discussions such as those in the present volume fill a demonstrated gap in terms of education surrounding predatory publishing, and the chapters and exercises provided herein can advance broader understanding of the potential threat posed by predatory publishing.

If one of the recommendations for research ethics training is to employ a variety of forms or modalities (Hollander and Arenberg 2009), the resources examined here on predatory publishing do achieve this to some extent. Few of the materials examined relied solely on text, and many embedded or linked to helpful videos. Again, the most common was a video from Think. Check. Submit. on the topic of evaluating publication outlets. Furthermore, many of the resources also provided additional documents that could be downloaded or reviewed.

Customization of Materials

Reviews of university resources available or efforts to satisfy these requirements have noted that such efforts are somewhat undifferentiated by both topic and audience and may not fulfill suggested best practices for providing such training (e.g., DuBois and others 2010; Pizzolato and others 2020). Such was somewhat the case here. This review of resources on the subject of predatory publishing found that a large majority of materials did not reflect any disciplinary focus (84.6%), and most materials (71.1%) did not state a specified audience (e.g., graduate students, junior faculty, etc.).

A common refrain among scholars focusing on research ethics is a stronger need to directly engage project principal investigators (PIs) in the effort to train emerging scholars regarding research ethics. For example, Phillips and others (2018) argue that challenges to ethics training may be more a function of PI awareness or engagement rather than a lack of university effort in creating training materials or opportunities. Mentorship has long served as a predominant model by which the practice of scientific research has been passed down, not unlike other trades or crafts (Kalichman 2013). One argument for the need for stronger efforts to engage PIs and provide education regarding predatory publishing is the (potentially false) assumption that knowledge on the topic is passed down through mentorship from senior to junior or emerging scholars (see Chapter 5).

Although research ethics education may be formally satisfied through courses or other activities, generating greater understanding and awareness may also take place through less formal means. For example, some scholars have noted the 'hidden curriculum', or 'the teaching that happens outside of the formal curriculum taking place in classrooms and lecture halls' that characterizes part of the mentorship experience (Fryer-Edwards 2002: 58). Here again, this emphasizes the importance of PI-driven efforts to combat against the potential pitfalls associated with predatory publishing. Although this hidden curriculum is certainly a function of peer-to-peer learning, mentors also play a strong role in this informal training in addition to more formal efforts, as is discussed in detail in Chapter 5 of this volume.

Together, this lack of disciplinary specialization along with the recognized potential for leveraging the hidden curriculum underscores the need for materials that have greater disciplinary focus. For example, training materials aimed at more senior faculty may emphasize specific methods of instruction for teaching regarding predatory publishing in formal classroom or informal lab settings, whereas materials aimed at student researchers or junior scholars may emphasize actual content (e.g., how to detect predatory journal solicitations). Likewise, although more generalized training may have some value (Watts and others 2017), development of discipline-focused resources can help inform and educate scholars in a way that has greater relevance (Gunsalus and Robinson 2018; Kalichman 2014).

Assessments

One noteworthy finding was a general lack of any form of assessment within the sample of materials examined. As previously noted, only two guides included any form of learning assessment, and materials most typically presented information without any attempt to determine their effectiveness. As with past reviews of research ethics training materials (Phillips and others 2018; Pizzolato and others 2020), there was very little evidence of active participation by the intended audience of the material. Despite being presented in a web-based format that could technologically afford dynamic, interactive content, information was provided with little to no input or engagement with the reader and implied only passive participation.

In their review of educational techniques employed in research ethics courses, Todd and others (2017) emphasized participation, student involvement, and case-based learning to facilitate more active learning styles and discouraged more passive educational approaches such as lectures. Likewise, Watts and others' (2017) meta-analysis of research ethics courses notes that 'courses appear to benefit most when training emphasizes individual-based, as opposed to group-based, activities that encourage at least a moderate degree of active participation' (p. 380). Thus, in many ways, the resources created to inform scholars about predatory publishing are much like many resources previously created to fulfill education on research ethics — they rely on educational approaches that are not necessarily the most effective.

Conclusion

In his review of the history of training in the area of the responsible conduct of research, Kalichman (2013) concluded with this pithy question and answer: 'With so many tools at our fingertips, it is fair to ask are they sufficient? Are they working? The answer is an unequivocal "We don't know."' (p. 389). Among the reasons offered for this uncertainty were that educational goals were diverse, requirements weren't taken seriously or were unclear, and 'nominal evidence of effectiveness' (p. 390). Although offered specifically regarding the responsible conduct of research, some of these could just as easily be applied to the topic of predatory journals.

Clearly, this systematic review illustrates the considerable energy devoted to creating materials designed to educate faculty and student researchers alike regarding the nature of predatory journals. However, these resources could be improved by integrating assessments that actually demonstrate learning. Moreover, these assessments should closely align with explicitly stated educational goals and provide sufficient nuance to distinguish precisely how well mentees understand varied aspects or dimensions of predatory publishing, its impacts, and potential perils. Such meaningful assessment then allows mentors, librarians, or other stakeholders to address specific areas where knowledge may be deficient (Keefer and others 2014).

Phillips and others (2018) noted that university web pages designed to provide links to training that fulfills NSF mandates may only list the specific tool used to fulfill or meet the requirement, and not include the broader array of additional opportunities for research ethics training and education above and beyond what was required. Likewise, the web search conducted to generate the study sample also yielded numerous public notices of workshops on the topic. As just a few examples, the University of California at Irvine hosted a workshop 'geared toward early-career researchers' on the topic of 'Predatory Publishing and Diversity in Open Access Publication'. The workshop synopsis noted the potential for power imbalances between non-Western researchers or institutions and US-based scholars (see Chapter 3, this volume). Likewise, the University of Illinois hosted a workshop, 'Evaluating Journals: The Good, The Bad, and the Predatory' that aimed to help attendees recognize characteristics of predatory publishers and aid decision making about publication outlets. Although these were not included in the analysis here (as they were merely persistent records or notices of past events and did not contain substantive information), they do provide evidence of university efforts to elevate the level of discussion around predatory publishing and help create a culture where the topic is addressed.

These workshops, when combined with the wealth of resources discovered and reviewed here, demonstrate that ample resources developed to inform others about the nature of predatory publishing exist. Although they certainly have value, mere safelists and watchlists (Koerber and others 2020; see Introduction), or static, noninteractive library guides like those reviewed here only reflect the beginning of what could be done to address the threat of predatory publishing. The next step is developing more interactive, tailored tools and encouraging thoughtful adoption and customization of these materials in courses and research lab environments to ensure widespread understanding of the ethical threat that predatory publishing models represents.

Key Takeaways

- Predatory publishers have the potential to undermine overall confidence in scholarly inquiry.

- To address the issue of ethical research practices, a variety of educational resources were developed to help scholars understand ethical practices, partially spurred by national or institutional funding requirements.

- This chapter assesses publicly available training materials related to predatory publishing that is provided by US universities who are ranked by the Carnegie classifications as having very high research activity.

- Two recent studies (Phillips and others 2018; Pizzolato and others 2020) found that most training materials currently available merely provided information, but did not have mechanisms to assess learning and retention of the materials.

- University libraries were the primary source of training and informational material related to predatory publishing, but the depth of information provided varied greatly.

- Most resources were not discipline specific, and instead targeted a broad academic audience.

- A majority of the resources linked to either DOAJ or Think. Check. Submit. as external sources for readers to get more information.
- More than half of the resources did not offer a formal, explicit definition of predatory publishers.
- Most resources offered suggestions on how to identify predatory outlets.
- The history of predatory publishing and the consequences for authors who submit their work to such publications was only discussed by a small minority of resources.
- Predatory publishing was almost always linked in some way to discussions about open access publishing.

Discussion Questions

1. Why might resources that invite passive participation not be the most effective means of educating scholars on predatory publishing?
2. What might some reasons be for the divide between researchers' perceptions of available training resources and the actual availability of such training resources?
3. What might be some benefits of creating educational resources that are field specific? What might some challenges be?
4. Consequences for publishing in a predatory journal were not often discussed in the reviewed training resources. Working individually or in groups, list some possible consequences for publishing in predatory journals.
5. Most training resources did not include case studies. Come up with a fictional case study that might help future researchers learn about the pitfalls of predatory publishing.

Activities

Activity One: Training at Your University?

This chapter provides links to a large assortment of training materials collected from universities across the US. Do a web search to see what types of resources you can find for your home institution.

Using the evaluation criteria/coding scheme described in this chapter, identify what elements are reflected in these training materials, and what elements are not reflected. How could they be improved?

- Who is the training material from? What unit on campus?
- Is there someone named that you could reach out to for collaboration or assistance?
- Do these materials link to any form of vetted 'safe' list of journals (or a third-party directory with such information)?
- Are these materials aimed at any particular audience? Any specific discipline?
- Are there any videos you could show in your classes/lab groups and discuss?
- What types or modalities of information are included, and can any of these be used in your lab in a piecemeal approach?

Activity Two: Integration Into Your Lab

In order for training programs to be successful, senior faculty or lab directors are strongly encouraged to explicitly integrate research ethics trainings into their lab discussions.

- Which aspects of the training resources examined here would be easiest to integrate into your lab for discussion?
- Which aspects of the training resources examined here would be most effective for educating your students about predatory publishing?
- What is the best way for you to assess that your lab students understand this phenomenon?

Activity Three: Examine A Predatory Solicitation Sent to You

One common way that potentially predatory publications solicit manuscripts is through direct email to authors. Find one that's been sent to you. (And be sure to check your Junk/Spam folder!) In our experience, they're not hard to find.

1. Share this email solicitation sent to you with students in your lab group, and ask them to help identify potential 'red flags' or warning signs. One of the more common elements of training materials reviewed here are checklists of the characteristics of potentially predatory publications. Use one of those lists to help walk through a specific solicitation sent to you.

2. Ask your students if they have ever received one of these. If so, ask them to share their own example and dissect it as well.

References

'146 Results for Basic = "Doctoral Universities: Very High Research Activity"'. 2022. *The Carnegie Classification of Institutions of Higher Education*, https://carnegieclassifications.acenet.edu/lookup/srp.php?clq=%7B%22basic2005_ids%22%3A%2215%22%7D&start_page=standard.php&backurl=standard.php&limit=0,50

AlRyalat, Saif Aldeen., Farah, Randa I., Shehadeh, Bara'., Abukeshek, A., Aldabbas, Leen and others. 2019. 'Biomedical Researchers and Students Knowledge about Predatory Journals', *The Journal of Academic Librarianship*, 45.5: 1–5, https://doi.org/10.1016/J.ACALIB.2019.102056

'Basic Classification Description: Doctoral Universities'. 2022. *The Carnegie Classification of Institutions of Higher Education*, https://carnegieclassifications.acenet.edu/classification_descriptions/basic.php

Beall, Jeffrey. 2017. 'Beall's List: Potential, Possible, or Probable Predatory Scholarly Open-Access Publishers [Web Archive]', *Scholarly Open Access*, http://web.archive.org/web/20170111172306/https:/scholarlyoa.com/publishers/

Bisaccio, Mike. 2020. 'Announcement Regarding Brand-Wide Language Changes, Effective Immediately.', https://blog.cabells.com/2020/06/08/announcement/

Bouter, Lex M. 2015. 'Commentary: Perverse Incentives or Rotten Apples?', *Accountability in Research*, 22.3: 148–61, https://doi.org/10.1080/08989621.2014.950253

'Case Study – Illegitimate & Predatory Publishing'. 2021. *University of Pittsburgh Library System*, https://pitt.libguides.com/c.php?g=718064&p=5375911

'Choosing a Publication Venue: "Predatory Publishers" and Deceptive Publishing Practices'. 2022. *Northeastern University Library*, https://subjectguides.lib.neu.edu/publishing/deceptivepublishing

Christopher, Mary M., and Young, Karen M. 2015. 'Awareness of "Predatory" Open-Access Journals among Prospective Veterinary and Medical Authors Attending Scientific Writing Workshops', *Frontiers in Veterinary Science*, 2.22: 111–22, https://doi.org/10.3389/fvets.2015.00022

Ciro, Jairo Buitrago. 2021. 'How Are Academic Libraries in Spanish-Speaking Latin America Responding to New Models of Scholarly Communication and Predatory Publishing?', *Journal of Librarianship and Information Science*, 54.3: 373–88, https://doi.org/10.1177/09610006211016533

Cukier, Samantha., Helal, Lucas., Rice, Danielle B., Pupkaite, Justina., Ahmadzai, Nadera and others. 2020. 'Checklists to Detect Potential Predatory Biomedical Journals: A Systematic Review', *BMC Medicine*, 18.1: 1–20, https://doi.org/10.1186/s12916-020-01566-1

'Don't Fall Prey to Predatory Journals'. 2020. *University of Illinois Chicago*, https://grad.uic.edu/news-stories/predatory_journals/

Dubois, James M., Anderson, Emily., Chibnall, John., Carroll, Kelly., Gibb, Tyler and others. 2013. 'Understanding Research Misconduct: A Comparative Analysis of 120 Cases of Professional Wrongdoing', *Accountability in Research*, 20.5–6: 320–38, https://doi.org/10.1080/08989621.2013.822248

DuBois, James M., Schilling, Debie A., Heitman, Elizabeth., Steneck, Nicholas H. and Kon, Alexander A. 2010. 'Instruction in the Responsible Conduct of Research: An Inventory of Programs and Materials within CTSAs', *Clinical and Translational Science*, 3.3: 109–11, https://doi.org/10.1111/J.1752-8062.2010.00193.X

Eriksson, Stefan, and Helgesson, Gert. 2017. 'Time to Stop Talking about "Predatory Journals"', *Learned Publishing*, 31.2: 181–83, https://doi.org/10.1002/LEAP.1135

Fryer-Edwards, Kelly. 2002. 'Addressing the Hidden Curriculum in Scientific Research', *The American Journal of Bioethics*, 2.4: 58–59, https://doi.org/10.1162/152651602320957619

'General Resources for Graduate Students in the Physical Sciences and Engineering'. 2022. *The Ohio State University Libraries*, https://guides.osu.edu/ScienceGrads

Grudniewicz, Agnes., Moher, David., Cobey, Kelly D., Bryson, Gregory L., Cukier, Samantha and others. 2019. 'Predatory Journals: No Definition, No Defence', *Nature*, 576.7786: 210–12, https://doi.org/10.1038/d41586-019-03759-y

Gunsalus, C. K., and Robinson, Aaron D. 2018. 'Nine Pitfalls of Research Misconduct', *Nature*, 557: 297–99, https://doi.org/10.1038/d41586-018-05145-6

Heitman, Elizabeth and Bulger, Ruth Ellen. 2006. 'Assessing the Educational Literature in the Responsible Conduct of Research for Core Content', *Accountability in Research*, 12.3: 207–24, https://doi.org/10.1080/08989620500217420

Hofmann, Bjørn and Holm, Søren. 2019. 'Research Integrity: Environment, Experience, or Ethos?', *Research Ethics*, 15.3-4: 1–13, https://doi.org/10.1177/1747016119880844

Hollander, Rachelle and Arenberg, Carol R. (eds). 2009. 'Ethics Education and Scientific and Engineering Research: What's Been Learned? What Should Be Done? Summary of a Workshop', *National Academy of Engineering* (Washington, DC: The National Academies Press), https://doi.org/10.17226/12695

'How Do You Know a Journal Is Legitimate?' 2022. *Stony Brook University Libraries*, https://library.stonybrook.edu/scholarly-communication/know-journal-legitimate/

'Journal Quality'. [n.d.]. *Georgetown University Library*, https://library.georgetown.edu/scholarly-communication/journal-quality

Kalichman, Michael W. 2013. 'A Brief History of RCR Education', *Accountability in Research*, 20.5-6: 380–94, https://doi.org/10.1080/08989621.2013.822260

——. 2014. 'Rescuing Responsible Conduct of Research (RCR) Education', *Accountability in Research*, 21.1: 68–83, https://doi.org/10.1080/08989621.2013.822271

Kalichman, Michael W., and Plemmons, Dena K. 2007. 'Reported Goals for Responsible Conduct of Research Courses', *Academic Medicine*, 82.9: 846–52, https://doi.org/10.1097/ACM.0B013E31812F78BF

Keefer, Matthew W., Wilson, Sara E., Dankowicz, Harry and Loui, Michael C. 2014. 'The Importance of Formative Assessment in Science and Engineering Ethics Education: Some Evidence and Practical Advice', *Science and Engineering Ethics*, 20.1: 249–60, https://doi.org/10.1007/S11948-013-9428-5

Koerber, Amy., Starkey, Jesse C., Ardon-Dryer, Karin., Cummins, R. Glenn., Eko, Lyombe and others. 2020. 'A Qualitative Content Analysis of Watchlists vs Safelists: How Do They Address the Issue of Predatory Publishing?', *Journal of Academic Librarianship*, 46.6, https://doi.org/10.1016/j.acalib.2020.102236

Lopez, Emme, and Gaspard, Christine S. 2020. 'Predatory Publishing and the Academic Librarian: Developing Tools to Make Decisions', *Medical Reference Services Quarterly*, 39.1: 1–14, https://doi.org/10.1080/02763869.2020.1693205

Maurer, Elke., Walter, Nike., Histing, Tina., Anastasopoulou, Lydia., El Khassawna, Thaqif and others. 2021. 'Awareness of Predatory Journals and Open Access Publishing among Orthopaedic and Trauma Surgeons – Results from an Online Survey in Germany', *BMC Musculoskeletal Disorders*, 22.365: 1–8, https://doi.org/10.1186/S12891-021-04223-7

McMillan, Sally J. 2000. 'The Microscope and the Moving Target: The Challenge of Applying Content Analysis to the World Wide Web', *Journalism & Mass Communication Quarterly*, 77.1: 80–98, https://doi.org/10.1177/107769900007700107

Miller, Hillary. 2021. 'Avoid Publishing Scams', *Virginia Commonwealth University Libraries*, https://guides.library.vcu.edu/predatory-publishing

Mills, David and Inouye, K. 2020. 'Problematizing 'Predatory Publishing': A Systematic Review of Factors Shaping Publishing Motives, Decisions, and Experiences', *Learned Publishing*, 34.2: 89–104, https://doi.org/10.1002/LEAP.1325

Murphy, Julie A. 2019. 'Predatory Publishing and the Response from the Scholarly Community', *Serials Review*, 45.1–2: 73–78, https://doi.org/10.1080/00987913.2019.1624910

Naegle, Kristen. 2019. 'Managing Email', *University of Virginia | Engineering*, https://engineering.virginia.edu/managing-email

'Navigating the Article Publication Process'. 2021. *The Ohio State University Libraries*, https://guides.osu.edu/article-publishing

Neuendorf, Kimberly A. 2017. *The Content Analysis Guidebook Second Edition*, 2nd edn (Los Angeles, CA: Sage Publishing)

Ojala, Marydee., Reynolds, Regina., and Johnson, Kay G. 2020. 'Predatory Journal Challenges and Responses', *The Serials Librarian*, 78.1–4: 98–103, https://doi.org/10.1080/0361526X.2020.1722894

Phillips, Trisha., Nestor, Franchesca., Beach, Gillian and Heitman, Elizabeth. 2018. 'America COMPETES at 5 Years: An Analysis of Research-Intensive Universities' RCR Training Plans', *Science and Engineering Ethics*, 24.1: 227–49, https://doi.org/10.1007/S11948-017-9883-5

Pizzolato, Daniel., Abdi, Shila and Dierickx, Kris. 2020. 'Collecting and Characterizing Existing and Freely Accessible Research Integrity Educational Resources', *Accountability in Research*, 27.4: 195–211, https://doi.org/10.1080/08989621.2020.1736571

'Predatory Journals: What Does it Mean?'. 2023. *University of Utah Health Sciences Library.*, https://campusguides.lib.utah.edu/scholarlypublishing/predatoryjournals

'Predatory & Questionable Publishing: Homepage'. 2021. *University of Florida George A. Smathers Libraries*, https://guides.uflib.ufl.edu/predatorypublishing

'Predatory Publishing: Author Resources'. 2022. *The University of Alabama at Birmingham - Libraries*, https://guides.library.uab.edu/c.php?g=826341&p=5922609

'Research Impact'. 2023. *Lane Medical Library - Stanford Medicine.*, https://laneguides.stanford.edu/researchimpact/journalimpact

'Researcher Services and Support: Predatory Publishing'. 2022. *Himmelfarb Health Sciences Library*, https://guides.himmelfarb.gwu.edu/researcher-services/predatory-publishing

Resnik, David. 1996. 'Data Falsification in Clinical Trials', *Science Communication*, 18.1: 49–58, https://doi.org/10.1177/1075547096018001003

Royster, Paul. 2015. 'Author's Rights and Predatory Publishers', *Library Conference Presentations and Speeches*, 118, https://digitalcommons.unl.edu/library_talks/118

Schlosser, M. 2015. 'How to Avoid Predatory Open Access Publishers', *Digital Scholarship @ the Libraries*, https://web.archive.org/web/20220221101626/https:/library.osu.edu/site/digitalscholarship/2015/12/04/predatory-open-access/

'Scholarly Communication'. 2022. *Yale University Library*, https://library.medicine.yale.edu/scholarly-communication

'Scholarly Publishing Toolkit'. 2022. *The University of Tennessee Knoxville Libraries*, https://libguides.utk.edu/c.php?g=369724&p=2497761

Steen, R. Grant. 2010. 'Retractions in the Scientific Literature: Do Authors Deliberately Commit Research Fraud?', *Journal of Medical Ethics*, 37: 1–5, http://dx.doi.org/10.1136/jme.2010.038125

Steneck, Nicholas H. 2007. 'Introduction to the Responsible Conduct of Research', *Department of Health and Human Services-USA*, https://ori.hhs.gov/ori-introduction-responsible-conduct-research

Stuart, Daniel. 2021. 'Predatory Publishing: Home', *Texas Tech University Health Sciences Center*, https://ttuhsc.libguides.com/PredatoryPublishing

Swanberg, Stephanie M., Thielen, Joanna and Bulgarelli, Nancy. 2020. 'Faculty Knowledge and Attitudes Regarding Predatory Open Access Journals: A Needs Assessment Study', *Journal of the Medical Library Association*, 108.2: 218, https://doi.org/10.5195/JMLA.2020.849

'Take Control of Your Research and Scholarship'. [n.d.]. *University of Houston Libraries.*, https://guides.lib.uh.edu/c.php?g=826609&p=5901634

Teixeira da Silva, Jaime A. 2022. 'Academic Librarians and Their Role in Disseminating Accurate Knowledge and Information about the Gray Zone in Predatory Publishing', *New Review of Academic Librarianship*, 28.4, 383–405 https://doi.org/10.1080/13614533.2022.2039242

Todd, E. Michelle., Watts, Logan L., Mulhearn, Tyler J., Torrence, Brett S., Turner, Megan R. and others. 2017. 'A Meta-Analytic Comparison of Face-to-Face and Online Delivery in Ethics Instruction: The Case for a Hybrid Approach', *Science and Engineering Ethics*, 23.6: 1719–54, https://doi.org/10.1007/S11948-017-9869-3

'Understanding and Avoiding Predatory Publishing: Home'. 2020. *Cornell University*, https://guides.library.cornell.edu/predatorypublishing

'Understanding Unethical Publishing Practices'. 2020. *Brown University Library*, https://libguides.brown.edu/unethical

Watts, Logan L., Medeiros, Kelsey E., Mulhearn, Tyler J., Steele, Logan M., Connelly, Shane and others. 2017. 'Are Ethics Training Programs Improving? A Meta-Analytic Review of Past and Present Ethics Instruction in the Sciences', *Ethics & Behavior*, 27.5: 351–84, https://doi.org/10.1080/10508422.2016.1182025

Webber, Nicole and Wiegand, Stephanie. 2022. 'A Multidisciplinary Study of Faculty Knowledge and Attitudes Regarding Predatory Publishing', *Journal of Librarianship and Scholarly Communication*, 10.1: 1–29, https://doi.org/10.31274/jlsc.13011

'What Is Open Access?' 2022. *University of California San Diego*, https://ucsd.libguides.com/oa/

'Where to Publish: Predatory Journals'. 2022. *Herbert Wertheim College of Medicine Medical Library*, https://libguides.medlib.fiu.edu/publish/predatory

Zhao, Xinshu., Liu, Jun S. and Deng, Ke. 2013. 'Assumptions behind Intercoder Reliability Indices', *Annals of the International Communication Association*, 36.1: 419–80, https://doi.org/10.1080/23808985.2013.11679142

7. Predatory Paradoxes
What Comes Next?

Many years after the demise of Beall's list, predatory publishing practices continue to be a concern for scholars, policymakers, research funders, and the general public (Elliott and others 2022; Linacre and others 2019; Xia 2021). Although most stakeholders agree on the seriousness of the problem, they disagree on how to solve it. The paradoxes we have highlighted throughout this book are at the heart of this complex situation. For example, as we have suggested, it is the same demands and changes to reform scholarly communication, such as the increased need for rapid turnaround from submission to acceptance to publication, that have created a situation in which the publishing practices often referred to as predatory have come to thrive. Along these lines, mainstream commercial journals and publishers have transformed themselves from opponents to beneficiaries of open access, in some cases seeking to dominate the lucrative open access game, and newer generations of scholars are facing challenges never imagined by the senior colleagues who are charged with training them.

In this closing chapter, we highlight some of the ways in which contradictions such as these play out for scholars and other stakeholders in scholarly communication, and we leave readers with some suggestions for moving forward. Our participants' responses, and other forms of research reported throughout this book, leave us with diverse and contradictory understandings of what it means for a journal or publisher to engage in predatory practices. These contradictions arise, in part, from the different positions that stakeholders occupy in the global scholarly publishing enterprise, and stakeholder perspectives, taken collectively, are far from optimistic. However, when considered through the lens of some insights offered by paradox theory (Smith and Lewis 2011; Waldman and others 2019), we can glean from these perspectives some productive ways forward for those who embrace paradox — both as a means toward individual publishing success and as a step toward sustainability for the scholarly publishing enterprise more broadly.

Paradox Theory

Management scholars Smith and Lewis (2011) define paradox 'as contradictory yet interrelated elements that exist simultaneously and persist over time' (p. 382). They identify two integral components of paradoxes that exist in organizations: 'underlying tensions – that is, elements that seem logical individually but inconsistent and even absurd when juxtaposed', and 'responses that embrace tensions simultaneously' (p. 382).

The research insights and practical recommendations we have offered in this book resonate with paradox theory in three important ways. Firstly, parallel to paradox theory in management studies, we have suggested that predatory publishing has emerged, in large part, as a response to 'contradictory demands' that are intensifying as 'environments become more global, fast paced, and competitive, and as internal organizational processes become more complex' (Smith and Lewis 2011: 381). Our chapters have highlighted numerous examples of such 'contradictory demands' in the context of scholarly publishing, including demands faced by authors, publishing professionals, and various other stakeholders in academic publishing. Corresponding with Smith and Lewis's observations, such demands are unquestionably intensifying as scholarly publishing becomes 'more global, fast paced, [...] competitive, [...] and complex' (p. 381).

Secondly, we have suggested that predatory publishing is a problem that defies one-time solutions. Specifically, as we have demonstrated, resources such as watchlists, safelists, or checklists can serve as useful heuristics for individuals who are fully educated on how to use them and aware of their limitations. However, no single list or set of instructions will ever provide an adequate solution to the complex assemblage of problems that exist beneath the surface of the deceptively simple term 'predatory publishing'. This insight resonates with Smith and Lewis's

(2011) assertion that paradoxes should be understood as 'tensions' that are 'embedded in the process of organizing' (p. 388) and 'persist over time' (p. 382). As such, they emphasize the need for long-term, rather than short-term, solutions: 'purposeful and cyclical responses to paradox over time enable sustainability — peak performance in the present that enables success in the future' (p. 382). Whereas other management theories, such as contingency theory, advise choice among competing demands, paradox theory postulates that the most effective organizations and leaders are those who find ways to embrace contradictions (Smith and Lewis 2011; see also Waldman and others 2019). Smith and Lewis summarize the advantages of paradox-based approaches as follows: 'Although choosing among competing tensions might aid short-term performance, a paradox perspective argues that long-term sustainability requires continuous efforts to meet multiple, divergent demands' (p. 381).

Thirdly, the contradictions that we foreground in this analysis constitute paradoxes that exist on at least two levels: (a) contradictions among different stakeholders in scholarly publishing that arise from their different experiences and locations, and (b) contradictions that exist in the larger system and are revealed through participant comments and other forms of research we have reported in this book. These two sources of contradictions echo Smith and Lewis's (2011) observations about the reasons why paradoxes exist in organizations. As they observe, paradox has been considered, on the one hand, as 'inherent — existing within the system', and on the other hand, as 'socially constructed — created by actors' cognition or rhetoric' (p. 388). They advocate an understanding that acknowledges both qualities: understanding organizational paradox as 'embedded in the process of organizing' but, at the same time, being 'brought into juxtaposition via environmental conditions' (p. 388). Echoing Smith and Lewis, Waldman and others (2019) observe that, in paradox theory, the tensions that exist in organizations involve 'multiple demands that are both contradictory, as well as interdependent' (p. 5).

In sum, although the term predatory publishing is relatively new, the phenomenon it describes must be understood as a set of problems that has many layers, has taken shape over many years, and that we can expect to exist for the foreseeable future. As such, it is a problem that demands long-term, flexible thinking and solutions that engage multiple stakeholders rather than quick fixes. The next section of this chapter summarizes the insights we have offered throughout the chapters of this book by foregrounding eight distinct but related paradoxes in twenty-first-century scholarly publishing that emerged in our research as reported in this book.

As demonstrated below, the paradoxes that we highlight can be understood through four categories of paradox that, according to Smith and Lewis (2011), 'represent core activities and elements of organizations' (p. 383). These categories include paradoxes of 'learning (knowledge), belonging (identity/interpersonal relationships), organizing (processes), and performing (goals)' (p. 383). (See Table 7.1).[1] While some of the paradoxes we highlight are squarely located in one of these four categories, others have elements of more than one.

Table 7.1 Categories of Paradox. Used with permission of Academy of Management, from 'Toward a Theory of Paradox: A Dynamic Equilibrium Model of Organizing', Wendy K. Smith and Marianne W. Lewis, *Academy of Management Review*, 36.2, 2011; permission conveyed through Copyright Clearance Center, Inc.

Adapted from Smith and Lewis 2011

Learning-Belonging	Learning	Learning-Organizing
Conflicts between the need for adaptation and change and the desire to retain an ordered sense of self and purpose (e.g., Fiol 2002; Ibarra 1999; O'Mahony and Bechky 2006)	Efforts to adjust, renew, change, and innovate foster tensions between building upon and destroying the past to create the future (e.g., March 1991; Senge 1990; Weich and Quinn 1999)	Organizational routines and capabilities seek stability, clarity, focus, and efficiency while also enabling dynamic, flexible, and agile outcomes (e.g., Eisenhardt and Martin 2000; Teece and Pisano 1994)

---

1 The codebook and complete NVivo file that support this analysis are included in the published dataset that accompanies this chapter: https://doi.org/10.18738/T8/3RZARP. (See "Codebook STEPP Interviews" and "NVivo file paradox theory".)

Belonging	Belonging-Organizing	Organizing
Identity fosters tensions between the individual and the collective and between competing values, roles, and memberships (e.g., Badaracco Jr 1998; Brewer 1991; Huy 1999; Markus and Kitayama 1991; Pratt and Foreman 2000)	Tensions between the individual and the aggregate, individuality vs. collective action (e.g., Murnighan and Conlon 1991; Smith and Berg 1987) **Learning-Performing** Building capabilities for the future while ensuring success in the present (e.g., Andriopoulos and Lewis 2008; Dweck 2006; Tushman and O'Reilly 1996)	Structuring and leading foster collaboration and competition, empowerment and direction, control and flexibility (e.g., Adler and others 1999; Flynn and Chatman 2001; Ghemawat and Ricart Costa 1993; Lüscher and Lewis 2008; Siggelkow and Levinthal 2003)
Performing-Belonging Clash between identification and goals as actors negotiate individual identities with social and occupational demands (e.g., Dukerich and others 2002; Kreiner and others 2006)	**Performing** Plurality fosters multiple and competing goals as stakeholders seek divergent organizational success (e.g., Denis and others 2007; Donaldson and Preston 1995; Jarzabkowski and Sillince 2007; Margolis and Walsh 2003)	**Performing-Organizing** Interplay between means and ends, employee vs. customer demands, high commitment vs. high performance (e.g., Eisenstat and others 2008; Gittell 2004; Kaplan and Norton 1996)

Paradoxes of Learning

In Smith and Lewis's (2011) scheme, 'learning paradoxes surface as dynamic systems change, renew, and innovate' (p. 383). Three sets of tensions that can be understood as learning paradoxes emerged in our research: (a) tensions between old and new publishing practices, (b) tensions between science as open and science as closed, and (c) tensions between restrictions and opportunities created by open access.

Tensions between Old and New Publishing Practices

Even though principles such as open access and open science are often presented today as big new ideas, our research reminds us that these principles align with what have long been presumed to be the core fundamentals of science. For instance, the scientific method was developed as a means of systematically questioning authority and encouraging a skeptical attitude toward accepted traditional beliefs, rather than acting on blind trust in religious or other sources of authoritative knowledge. This paradox can be explained through participant insights suggesting that a lot of the problems we currently face in scholarly publishing are a product of the immense growth in science and the globalized nature of knowledge production. According to this line of reasoning, our traditional scholarly communication infrastructure was built for a world in which scholarly communities were much smaller, and experts were writing for other experts who all knew each other, so there was an inherent trust and accountability. With the globalization and expansion of the scholarly enterprise, this trust and accountability is no longer automatic, and this is why we need to implement mechanisms such as open science, which paradoxically, is promoted as a 'new' principle but actually brings us back closer to the openness and transparency that was intended at the origins of science. As stated by one participant, 'an open science is an inherent and core commitment to the scientific mission' (P48).[2] Another participant elaborated on this point:

---

2   Our Texas Data Repository Dataverse includes a table showing participant demographic information. See https://doi.org/10.18738/T8/QUBMLI ("Participant Occupation and Regional Demographics Table"). All quotations from interviews

> Yeah. You want to achieve a situation in which the work you published can be used by other people to build on it. So it's really a question of reproducibility. That's the key thing. Now, what used to happen in the old days, which I can remember, is that if you had a group and you got interested in a piece or area of work in science, you would send one of your post-doctorals around and we all knew each other, of course, in those days, it was a much smaller business, and I'm talking about the '60s and '70s, last century. You'd get permission for one of your staff to work in the lab of the person who had done the paperwork, which you want to build on. This was all the gentlemanly sort of situation.
>
> But at the moment, just to read a paper, it's extremely difficult to understand how they did it, especially now as they tend to cut back on the method section. The method section is much smaller than it used to be. And so you need to have things like open data, but more important, actually, is the process. (P18)

Building on this participant's reasoning, another paradoxical aspect of these 'new' developments in publishing practices is that even though such developments made it possible for predatory publishing to emerge, they could also go a long way toward eliminating the motivations that have led to predatory publishing, if adapted in the right way. For instance, if open science principles were widely adopted to their fullest extent, some have argued, we may abandon the scientific article altogether. As stated by a European publishing professional:

> At some point, probably, I expect the article as we know it now won't exist anymore. People will just contribute to some kind of [...] Like Wikipedia, I suppose, but something that's a little more robust and scientific, but the same kind of thing, that's just added to by evolving research, discoveries, and contributions from people. (P29)

A communication researcher from Asia referred to a new development known as 'overlay journals', defining these as

> [...] journals that are organized either by departments or by groups of interested scholars that exist outside of the traditional publishing space, where there, you can have reviewers and a process for publication in these sorts of things that exists outside of the Elseviers and the Wileys of the world. (P45)

---

are reported without correction of grammatical errors or other irregularities. Some quotes were abbreviated using [...] to achieve clarity of the original message.

The goal of such alternative publishing formats is for science to become self-correcting. As a result, some have speculated, there would be no incentive to pay anyone to publish your article (see Chapter 2 discussion of Mellor and others 2020). According to this line of reasoning, the publishing formats that we have clung to for so many years — like the expectation of a detailed methods section, but also the natural length constraints of print publishing and the expectation that methods will be reported in a clean, sanitized manner — are the same formats that have led us to the replicability crisis.

An important manifestation of these tensions between old and new publishing practices in the lived realities of our research participants is that senior faculty and leaders in the academy may not be well informed about predatory journals, yet they are the ones charged with training younger scholars. As stated by a publishing professional working in Asia,

> Yeah, people in leadership positions, they don't know about this stuff [...] Most professors, when they become a professor, they don't publish. They stop reading. They just get people to do their work for them. So, they are not very well informed about the current specifics of things. They have to be educated so they can educate [...] If the top is doing something bad, the person, it will only get worse when you go to the lower levels. (P27)

This participant's comment succinctly captures the learning paradox — experienced in participants' lived realities as a tension between old and new publishing practices — that is at the heart of the intense confusion that surrounds predatory publishing in today's academy. As revealed in the next section, this tension between old and new co-exists with other tensions that arise from idealized expectations about science and the way in which science is practiced.

Tensions between Science as Open and Science as Closed

A separate but related paradox that emerged in our analysis is founded in a tension between scholarly research as an endeavor that is expected to be 'open', in many different senses of the word, and the reality that many aspects of science as it is practiced are 'closed', in the sense that audiences are expected to accept scientific findings on blind faith, trusting that processes such as double-blind peer review are being enacted rigorously and fairly, even though in traditional publishing, these processes are completely obscured from public view. This paradox is illuminated through various comments that participants made regarding open research practices. For example, as a European researcher now working in North American stated,

> Open science is essentially a commitment to accurately and honestly present research findings, and to assure the quality of science, to assure the mission of science. The mission of scientific investigation is that you don't have to believe me. I am not an authority. I cannot say, 'Oh, I'm the big [P48] or whatever, or the big [Interviewer 1]. And because I'm so smart and big and great and influential, you have to believe me.' This is anti-science. Science is about anti-authoritarian. Science is about, 'Show me the data and show me how you got the data. And if I can reproduce it and can repeat it, we come to the same conclusion and make the same true predictions.' (P48)

Along the lines of this participant's comments, it is often suggested that open science is a much-needed correction to the black-box nature of academic publishing. From this perspective, predatory publishers can do what they can because traditional publishers do everything in an opaque manner, so, as an academic community, we are all accustomed to this non-transparent approach, and we have no means to assess whether peer review has been conducted rigorously and fairly from looking at just the published version of an article. As stated by a North American communication or publishing consultant,

> Yeah, but I think you can't stop it. I think there's got to be a community-level responsibility. Publishers certainly play their part. As I've said before, I think not entirely, but to some extent predatory publishers have been able to do what they do because non-predatory publishers are not very transparent. In fact, [they are] often positively opaque about what they do. That allows that opacity to be accepted. (P21)

Building on this participant's observations, this paradox has another dimension as well: even though we idealize peer review as the primary means of validating scientific knowledge, it has a lot of shortcomings when we consider how it is actually implemented. For example, just because an article makes it through peer review does not mean the study can actually be replicated. From this perspective, the entire system that we use to validate knowledge is one that unfolds primarily behind closed doors, so we cannot really tell if it is happening or not; we just have to trust. And, as noted above, the whole idea of science is that it is supposed to move us away from blind faith and encourage us to be skeptical toward received wisdom. This is the paradox that motivates all the changes that are highlighted in the tensions between old and new that serve as a foundation for the learning paradox. Along these lines, another problem of traditional science that advocates claim can be solved with open science (specifically by preprints, preregistration, in particular) is the publication bias toward publishing only positive results.

On the one hand, we distinguish predatory journals from legitimate journals by saying the legitimate ones conduct peer review, but on the other hand, many participants point out that traditional peer review is not very effective. Furthermore, as we have addressed in a few high-profile examples in this book, even though we tend to focus all our negative attention on predatory journals, high-profile, well-established journals also sometimes publish bad research (see Introduction and Chapter 4 for examples).

As we have suggested, predatory publishers satisfy the desire that multiple stakeholders have expressed for faster scholarly publishing processes. However, at the same time, these publishers exploit the tendency that has long persisted in scholarly communication that the same processes we trust to ensure the quality and validity of scientific knowledge — such as peer review — take place behind closed doors, where audiences and other stakeholders simply have to trust the editors and journals that peer review is being carried out in a rigorous and trustworthy manner. Predatory publishers are able to satisfy this desire for quicker publishing by taking advantage of this long-standing trust in a system that carries out its means of legitimizing scholarly knowledge completely in a black box. If mainstream publishers were in the habit of practicing open peer review in some form (meaning that they would provide publicly available proof to document that peer review was rigorously conducted), predatory publishers would not be able to operate in the way that they do.

Tension between Restrictions and Opportunities Created by Open Access

Another example of a paradox that falls into the learning category is one that emerges in some of our participants' comments expressing mixed feelings about open access publishing. As many participants observed, open access publishing was developed as a means of leveling the playing field by ensuring that everyone, regardless of their financial resources, could have equal access to the research results produced by scholars across the globe. However, even as open access publishing addresses this problem, it creates new inequities, such as the fact that it often shifts the cost of publishing to researchers, and not all individuals or institutions have the funding to cover this cost. As stated by a European communication researcher:

> Yeah, seemingly, open access journals make the science communication more equal, but it is only for the side of the audience, only side of the readers, because we, without financial support and the appropriate resources, we can openly reach the articles. As readers, the market is more open for us, if the open access became mandatory, but as writers, as authors, it gives us more serious burdens. Additional burdens, because it's not likely that we can afford to pay these article processing charges. That's my main problem. (P35)

In addition to geographic disparities, disciplinary disparities also exist, with authors in less well-funded disciplines, particularly social sciences and humanities, less likely to have funding to cover author publication costs than those in well-funded disciplines (STEM). Thus, another important manifestation of learning paradox in the lived realities of our research participants is that open access is meant to level the playing field by expanding access to published research, but it also creates new inequities.

Paradoxes of Performing

In Smith and Lewis's (2011) scheme, 'performing paradoxes stem from the plurality of stakeholders and result in competing strategies or goals' (p. 384). Two examples of performing paradox have emerged in our research: (a) a tension between the need for top-down compliance measures and the expectation of individual responsibility, and (b) a tension between public benefit and profit as motivations for publishing scholarly work.

Tension between the Need for Top-Down Compliance Measures and the Expectation of Individual Responsibility

The whole system of scholarly communication is built around the assumption that people will do the right thing even when no one is watching. As discussed in the previous section, our existing system of scholarly communication places a lot of trust in authors, reviewers, and editors, and rests on the assumption that these individuals will do the right thing, even without any explicit monitoring. Furthermore, although we have a system in place that is supposed to include checks and balances, there is not any oversight or checks and balances on the system as a whole. As expressed by a STEM researcher in North America,

> Well, it's essential, and it isn't talked about as much as it probably should be. And um, it is challenging to you know enforce, I don't want to use the word enforce, but it is challenging to validate or look at you know because so much of the decision is that you make yourself, you know, and like I said, the moral value of honesty is essential for the scientific process to progress. (P08)

In the lived realities of scholars and other stakeholders, this performing paradox is experienced as a tension between the expectation of individual compliance with shared (but often implicit) ethical norms and a desire for regulatory efforts imposed by a top-down authority. Thus, a North American publishing consultant observed, 'I feel that's a difficult one, isn't it because I don't disagree, but I also think the author should be able to publish where they want as well' (P21) in response to a suggestion from the interviewer that funding agencies could possibly play a more active role in regulating predatory journals. As this quotation indicates, it is hard to regulate a phenomenon such as predatory journals because academic freedom suggests that scholars should be free to publish wherever they want.

Tension between Public Benefit and Profit as Motivations for Publishing Scholarship

Another important example of a performing paradox emerges from the tensions between the expectation of scholarly communication to report transparently on all findings — whether they correspond with our assumptions or not — and the very real pressure that publishers face to 'sell a product' — that is, to publish results that will get audiences excited, will achieve media coverage, and will accrue great numbers of citations.

This is the kind of paradox that is often highlighted in management literature. For example, as noted by Smith and Lewis (2011), it used to be assumed that organizations could be classified as either 'profit' or 'non-profit', but now these lines are becoming blurred as 'for-profit organizations are increasingly attending to social as well as financial outcomes' (p. 396). Although many scholars would like to believe they operate independently from profit motivations, the scholarly enterprise as a whole is sustained by publishing companies that reflect Smith and Lewis's observation about the need for successful organizations to attend to both kinds of outcome.

As for the lived realities of our research participants, these tensions are often evident in participant comments about the political dimensions of scholarly publishing — for example, the idea that 'who you know' can be just as important as the quality of research that a scholar conducts. This is also experienced, for some participants, as a tension between our idealized system of scholarly publication, in which only the best knowledge rises to the top, and the actual system in which sometimes research gets published in a prestigious journal, regardless of its quality, because of relationships, networking, or other forms of political activity. In the words of a European communication researcher, it is 'like the mafia' (P35).

The conflicting goals of scholarly publishing also emerge in participant comments about writing for different audiences, including those outside the academy. Some talk about science journalism, while others talk about textbooks. Some express the opinion that sometimes science journalists 'hype' too much, and when authors seek this kind of hype in publishing their research, it perpetuates a vicious cycle that can cause even the most prestigious journals to publish poor-quality work, as shown in the #arseniclife example in Chapter 4 of this book. A European publishing consultant described a conflict between their desire to make their research results widely available, by publishing open access, and the mandate to publish in a prestigious, high-impact journal, even if it is not open access:

> As a researcher, doing my PhD or working to get tenure or any stage of my academic career, and I saw this when I was working as an academic, I'd finish a piece of research and I understand the significance of it, like a new dinosaur or a new whatever. I have a choice, then, as a researcher to publish that in an open access fully accessible journal or to go through a journal with a high impact factor. For my career and for my university assessment and my chance of getting another grant, it doesn't matter how I feel and what I feel is best for the research. I'm not going to not publish it in *Nature* if it has the chance of getting published in *Nature*. (P23)

Other participants experienced this tension in different ways, such as a tension between their desire to publish in smaller regional journals that would reach local audiences more quickly and the realization that they would need to publish in larger international journals to gain recognition from their evaluators.

Paradoxes of Belonging-Organizing

In Smith and Lewis's (2011) schema, the belonging-organizing paradox emerges when 'belonging and organizing efforts intersect via tensions between the individual and the aggregate' (p. 384). This type of paradox emerged in our analysis as a tension between the responsibility of individual authors to avoid predatory publishing and the responsibility of the scholarly community. For example, when authors continue to cite articles that are published in poor-quality journals, we might hold the larger scholarly community accountable for allowing such journals to exist, but we also need to hold accountable the individual authors who continue to cite such flawed publications. As narrated in Chapter 4, in the case of the Bohannon hoax, authors continued citing this false article even after the DOI was broken and the original article had been replaced with a retraction notice.

In our interview data, we see this tension emerging in the comments of numerous participants who observed that predatory publishing is a direct outcome, or maybe unintended consequence, of the system of evaluation that we have created — a system that continues to exist because the larger community, as well as individuals who hold power within this community, continue to participate in it. As expressed by a North American consultant:

> I've been saying that for so long. First of all, they have to change the reward system. You can't have publication be a decider of tenure because then, and especially publication in certain journals, that's what drives the system. That is the basis of the current system. If universities change, that, that would be a seismic change in the industry. It would change everything. (P14)

In participants' discussion of journal impact factor and the commercialization of scholarly research as obstacles to reform of scholarly communication, we see further evidence of this tension between individual and collective responsibility for addressing the problem of predatory publishing, as expressed by a European publishing consultant:

> Oh, no. I think open research and open access is great, and that's what I'd like to see as the future of academic publishing, but until we get rid of this impact-factor-based assessment for academics, especially in STEM subjects, we're never going to see people pushing their research entirely into open access journals. There's always a commercial perspective to this as well. Somebody has to make money. (P23)

As these participant comments emphasize, a large part of scholarly publishing is the desire and need for an individual scholar to become part of a community; this is the aspect of our research data that aligns with both the belonging and organizing paradoxes as outlined by Smith and Lewis (2011). When we join the scholarly conversation, we are hoping to be taken seriously, to make an important contribution to that conversation with our novel research findings. A lot of tensions or contradictions arise as scholars attempt to achieve this task, which is becoming increasingly complex as scholars around the globe strive to join a conversation that is inherently biased against them. For example, as stated by a European communication researcher:

> Maybe at most parts of the developing world or the non-center world, they start to adopt the publish-and-perish paradigm without the quality control. That's why many, many journals can live, because many, many people want to publish, but the established journals are too much competitive. Then, of course, in [my country], for example, there are many institutions, 'Let's just fund our own journal in English, and then we can publish our stuff in this journal and we can make an appearance that we are publishing international.' This is absurd and this is a joke, because nobody reads these journals. Nobody reads these papers, but

they just, they can fulfill the administration. These journals are just low-quality journals, or fake journals, or substitutions of real publishing, but not predatory, in a sense. (P35)

As this participant's comments suggest, even though we like to think of scholarly communication as a global endeavor, it is quite localized when we view it from the perspectives of those who live in marginalized communities. Scholars who are most successful are those who find a way to embrace these contradictions: maybe they publish some of their work in prestigious English-only journals, but they also return to their native countries and assist in establishing local journals, bringing back with them the knowledge they have gained about so-called 'predatory' publishing and so on. We also have organizations such as AuthorAid and SciDev that are trying to level the playing field. Listening to people who are trying to be successful scholars in marginalized locations also emphasizes another important aspect of the belonging-organizing paradox: that the very same systems we use to evaluate scholars, to sort out the good from the bad, are the systems that are creating the demand for 'predatory' journals, and, viewed another way, large commercial publishers are arguably just as guilty of predatory practices as those journals that end up on watchlists.

Paradoxes of Performing-Organizing

The performing-organizing paradox, in Smith and Lewis's (2011) schema, arises through 'the interplay between means and ends or process and outcome, apparent in conflicts between meeting employee and customer demands [...] and between seeking high commitment and high performance' (p. 384). As an example of this form of paradox in scholarly publishing, when we measure research quality in the academy, we are often referring to abstract measurements that are far removed from the actual quality of the science that is reported in an article. As one North American publishing professional described it, when we rely exclusively on systems such as journal impact factor to assess research quality, we are 'maximizing a very poor proxy for quality, just because it's quantifiable' (P22).

Along these lines, a few participants noted that it is ultimately up to individual scholars to assess the quality of published research, and if everyone took the time to do this, rather than relying on metrics or other sources, then predatory publishers could not exist. For example, as noted by one European publishing professional,

> It does in terms of [...] Say if you're looking at a journal that you want to submit to, you look at a few of the other articles that they've published. Are they the types of articles that you would want to associated with? Maybe you could have some kind of assessment of quality by looking at the other articles. That is one measure, I think. Actually reading the full papers is probably the only way to assess quality in the articles anyway. (P29)

The problem is that assessing the quality of research as published in individual articles, without relying on metrics, would be time consuming. For instance, it would mean that to assess a journal's quality before deciding to submit one's work there, an author would need to look carefully at other articles published in a journal, rather than simply relying on someone else's assessment of the journal's quality.

In line with these participants' observations, in Chapter 4, we discussed a high-profile example of published scientific research that accrued a lot of citations but had been cited inaccurately. As also discussed in Chapter 4, there has been a great deal of research on retracted articles that continue to get cited for years after they are retracted. As these examples remind us, impact factor and H-index are abstract measurements that tell us little about the quality of the science that is reported in a published article. When research participants discuss quality, as noted in Chapter 3, they often refer to concrete and specific aspects of published research — not just citation numbers.

Along these lines, when our research participants talked about lists, such as that of Jeffrey Beall, or more recently developed lists, they often refer to the limitations and bias they perceive in lists. As stated by a North American publishing or communication consultant,

> I don't put much stock in those as a resource because I think there is a lot of bias that goes into those lists. That's definitely true of Beall's, who went all rounding on favela publishing, famously, or infamously, as the case may be. Again, a lot of the supposedly predatory journals come from global south venues, and I do think there's a lot of colonial bias that is in there. If it's not written in good English and produced in the global north, then there's something suspect about the quality of this output. (P25)

An Asian publishing professional offers a more scathing critique of Beall's list, based on their own personal experience as editor of a journal that was included on the list:

> I had a journal that was owned by university, and it was one of the most proper journals here. It was on there for no reason. So, we sent him an email. We explained the situation. Next day, the journal was off there. The other case was there was this journal we didn't publish, but the editor, through an author, they found out that they were included in that list. Again, the journal, the editor, he was probably one of the more involved editors in the field. They had no financial gain, and they were just doing proper vetting. We still don't know why the journal was on there. We sent him, now defunct a couple of emails. He didn't respond. I haven't checked the list of that journal again. But, yeah, I know from personal experience two journals were affected by that that were not predatory. But, I know that there are predatory journals here who are not on that list. (P27)

Many participants seem to agree with these participants' assertion that no list will ever be adequate, but some also suggest that safelists may be more feasible than watchlists. Many criticize Beall for his lack of transparency, but some also criticize Cabells for charging cost-prohibitive fees to access their lists. As an Asian publishing professional said, 'They [Cabells] have started a whitelist and a blacklist which is not helpful at all, because they are charging to see the list' (P27).

As noted in the previous section, participants also comment on larger changes to the system that would help address the problem of predatory publishing, sometimes suggesting that without these changes, the motivation to pursue a fast and easy publication will always be there, and some publishers will prey on it. Some also talk about the impact factor and the added pressure it creates, and some talk about the uneven playing field faced by scholars in the global south. As for distinguishing legitimate from predatory journals, participants mention cues like getting a solicitation email for a journal far outside their discipline. Others mention the gray areas and how hard it can be to discern predatory journals in some cases.

Productive Ways Forward

Even as we acknowledge the challenges that scholars, especially junior scholars, face because of the paradoxes that are confronted by these individuals on a daily basis, we offer several suggestions for moving forward in the context of these challenges. Firstly, faculty mentors in the research process have an opportunity to better prepare graduate students and early-career scholars for these challenges by increasing their transparency about the research processes they go through. Being increasingly open in their discussion of failed projects, rejections by journals, strenuous research collaborations, and ugly peer reviews can benefit graduate students who envision themselves stepping into research positions and make them better prepared when they begin faculty positions and begin their pursuit of tenure. This could be done both through ad-hoc discussions on an individual level and through department or college-level initiatives to integrate ethical research practices into graduate curricula. Part of this discussion should also focus on the perils of predatory publishing practices, along with candid conversations about the potential career ramifications of submitting research to predatory publications.

Secondly, given the unanimous agreement among scholars and the existing literature on the central importance of peer review, the scholarly establishment needs to make a more concentrated effort to educate future faculty on how to critique scholarly work. While there are numerous blog posts and web-based articles listing the attributes of quality peer review (e.g., Dhillon 2021; Stiller-Reeve 2018), these are suggestions aimed at junior faculty who have already entered the field of academia and who are now expected to learn these new skills in addition to performing their new professorial duties. Instead of leaving this essential component of the entire scholarly knowledge production process to on-the-job, self-guided training, there is an opportunity to integrate this type of training into graduate programs or other institutional structures. As one innovative example of this practice, a leading journal in the communication field has initiated a 'Third Reviewer Program', where a PhD student conducts a peer review of an article in their focus area under the guidance of a faculty mentor. Especially if it is complemented with formal classroom training, this apprenticeship model could go a long way toward offering junior scholars the support they need to understand what makes peer review effective. Given that, in traditional scholarly publishing, the only real 'gatekeeper' of the 'gatekeepers' (peer reviewers) in scholarly publications are the journal editors themselves, it seems logical to ensure that the peer reviewers have the best possible training before they enter into the arena of judging their peers' work. Yet, as was discussed in previous sections, there is almost no formal reviewer training in the academy — most junior researchers learn the skill on the fly — and often through receiving terrible reviews and swearing they will never commit the same grave mistakes. But an even more glaring problem is the fact that peer reviews are almost exclusively undertaken as 'volunteer' work — and little institutional recognition is awarded for those efforts. While there are some attempts to rectify this through initiative such as Publons or journals publishing an end-of-year 'thank you' that lists all the reviewers for the year, the work of reviewing our peers' work goes largely uncelebrated — despite being lauded as the cornerstone of all that is scholarly knowledge production. While our participants almost exclusively agreed that peer review is still the main way to ensure the quality of manuscripts being published in academic journals, several offered mechanisms to improve or expand the peer-review process to make it more open or credible. The primary suggestion was to use technology to better facilitate both finding reviewers (P05, P09), and assessing the quality of peer reviews (P28), using metadata to ensure peer-reviewed status (P44), or open-source platforms such as 'wiki journals' (P19). Reviewing data sets (P19) or even going to a fully blind system where not even the editor knows the identity of the author (P35) show the range of options that could be used to make the peer review process more transparent.

Thirdly, given the emphasis on transparency and rigor as markers of quality in the knowledge production process, one of the primary means of addressing the problems affiliated with predatory publishing is through the tools and solutions offered by the open science movement, as elaborated in Chapter 2. Some of the components of open science, such as preprints and registered reports, offer solutions for engaging peers in the earlier stages of research production, whereas open peer review offers transparency at the later stages of knowledge production and dissemination. In terms of actions individuals could take to improve the quality of their research output, one of the most frequently discussed mechanisms was the need to be critical of your own work, and to have a strong moral compass to do the right thing, even when no one is looking. To that end, integrating ethical research practices into all graduate courses and building internal networks for discussing research before it reaches the publication stage seems to be the best course for improving the quality of scholarly communication. In fact, transparency seems to be the biggest actionable item that stakeholders suggest could improve the scholarly publication process. Increasing levels of transparency — from how the research was conducted, to how it was reviewed, and how it can be disseminated — seems to be the primary recommendation of both the emerging literature on evaluating scholarly knowledge production and the participants in our study.

Fourthly, scholars who participated in our study, with the exception of a few, did not seem to view librarians as a source for determining journal or publisher credibility, but the librarians viewed themselves as having a critical role, and often expressed frustration at academics for not using them as the resource they are intended to be. This suggests that within institutions, there needs to be a more concerted effort to direct researchers — both new and experienced — to the librarians who can guide them through the increasingly complex publishing landscape. As discussed in Chapter 6, there is no shortage of training materials available (many of them free for any user, not just members of the institution) related to ethical publishing practices, yet researchers still submit their work to predatory journals, whether unknowingly or not. Among Euro-American scholars who participated in our study, there was a predominant view that it is easy to determine if a journal is predatory by spending a few minutes going through their website, looking at past publications, the editorial board, and doing a quick assessment of the quality of the journal's public face. These statements are often juxtaposed with comments that indicate researchers outside the more affluent Euro-American regions may not know to look at these things to determine publisher credibility, or that due to different (and often implied to be inferior) standards, it may not matter whether a journal is predatory, as long as the researchers get the expected numbers. Other tools, such as lists, indexes, and peers, were all mentioned as resources available for authors to take responsibility for avoiding publishing in a predatory journal and to protect or improve the quality in scholarly knowledge production.

In Closing

For a point of contrast to our present situation, we might consider the mid-nineteenth century, when citizens of England were trying to fight a cholera outbreak that was killing tens of thousands of people. Authorities were desperate to understand the origins of the outbreak, and their main strategy was to tell people they should avoid breathing in toxic vapors that were believed to travel through the air in certain parts of the city. This so-called 'Miasma Theory' was, at this time, the prevailing belief, and it could not be proven or disproven because it was based purely on superstition. By contrast, 'Germ Theory', providing an explanation closer to our contemporary understanding of disease, was still in its infancy and not widely accepted by the medical community at this time (Tulchinsky 2018). In this context, when John Snow published a report in 1849, 'On the Mode of Communication of Cholera', suggesting the disease was caused by contaminated water that people were drinking, no one believed him (Snow 1849). We might say this was an idea that emerged prematurely, before audiences were ready to accept it (Bynum 2013). It was not until several years later that Snow was able to support his theory by collecting extensive data on cases in a particular district of London and demonstrating that those who were getting sick had all been drinking water from a specific pump that drew water from a well that had been contaminated with sewage; in 1855, he published an extended version of the earlier report, incorporating all of this data (Snow 1855). His idea was accepted at this time, leading to removal of the contaminated Broad Street water pump, and the end of this particular cholera outbreak, after tens of thousands of lives had already been lost.

As this example indicates, the game of scientific knowledge production has been around for a long time, and the rules of the game are continually evolving and changing. However, one thing has remained constant amid these changes: as a global society, we benefit greatly from this game. Without it, we would still be making guesses, based purely on hunches and superstitions, that could never be substantiated with any amount of scientific evidence. We might think COVID-19 is caused by mysterious, invisible vapors in the air, without any idea where these vapors come from. Or we might still be thinking, as was the case for many centuries, that most of women's health problems can be attributed to the fact that the womb is a wild animal that wanders uncontrollably throughout the female body and can only be made to hold still by intercourse or pregnancy. So, in other words, even though our current system may not be perfect, at least it is a system.

In this book, we have highlighted the many complexities that surround the term predatory. We have offered insights and anecdotes based on our interviews with forty-eight individuals who are stakeholders of various sorts in the game of scholarly publishing — ranging from real-life stories of authors who have fallen 'prey' to predatory publishing practices to people involved in the publishing industry who feel their publications have been wrongly accused of being 'predatory' in some capacity. We have examined the misunderstandings and misperceptions that many people have about predatory publishing, and we hope we have provided readers with accurate and complete information to combat these misunderstandings and misperceptions. We advocate a view of predatory publishing that emphasizes gray areas and individual responsibility rather than lists or hard-and-fast distinctions between journals or publishers that are predatory and those that are not. As is the case for any qualitative study, the primary limitation is that our findings cannot be generalized to larger populations.

Another important limitation is that scholarly publishing is evolving so quickly that it is virtually impossible to keep up with every new trend or development. One glaring example is Artificial Intelligence (AI), which exploded in the popular imagination when ChatGPT became publicly available in November 2022, just as we were putting the finishing touches to this manuscript. Experts are beginning to speculate on the potential impacts of AI-generated writing for scholarly communication. Perhaps not surprisingly, some are optimistically touting its benefits as a writing aid, suggesting it could automate the drafting of routine components of scholarly writing, while others are expressing alarm about the extent to which such automation will exacerbate the "publish or perish" mandate, leading to even higher expectations about the quantity of publications and further diminishing concerns about quality (Kubacka, 2023). For these reasons, as suggested in the Epilogue to Chapter 1, the role of AI in scholarly communication will certainly be an important topic for future researchers to address, and it will likely have a profound impact on many of the other trends and phenomena we have explored in this book.

Despite these limitations, our interview population, in conjunction with the other forms of research reported throughout the book, is diverse enough to extend scholarly conversations about the complex array of factors that have enabled predatory publishing practices to emerge and flourish and to leave readers with some concrete suggestions for moving forward. Through these suggestions, supported with examples from textual analysis and interviews offered here, we hope to leave readers with a set of tools and knowledge that prepare them to succeed in the game of scholarly publishing and to mentor those who come after them to be similarly equipped.

References

Adler, Paul S., Goldoftas, Barbara and Levine, David I.. 1999. 'Flexibility Versus Efficiency? A Case Study of Model Changeovers in the Toyota Production System', *Organization Science*, 10.1: 43–68, https://doi.org/10.1287/ORSC.10.1.43

Andriopoulos, Constantine and Lewis, Marianne W. 2008. 'Exploitation-Exploration Tensions and Organizational Ambidexterity: Managing Paradoxes of Innovation', *Organizational Science*, 20.4: 696–717, https://doi.org/10.1287/ORSC.1080.0406

Badaracco Jr, Joseph L. 1998. 'The Discipline of Building Character', *Harvard Business Review*, 114–24, https://hbr.org/2006/01/the-discipline-of-building-character

Brewer, Marilynn B. 1991. 'The Social Self: On Being the Same and Different at the Same Time', *Personality and Social Psychology Bulletin*, 17.5: 475–82, https://doi.org/10.1177/0146167291175001

Bynum, William. 2013. 'In Retrospect: On the Mode of Communication of Cholera', *Nature*, 495.7440: 169–70, https://doi.org/10.1038/495169a

Denis, Jean Louis., Langley, Ann and Rouleau, Linda. 2007. 'Strategizing in Pluralistic Contexts: Rethinking Theoretical Frames', *Human Relations*, 60.1: 179–215, https://doi.org/10.1177/0018726707075288

Dhillon, Paraminder. 2021. 'How to Be a Good Peer Reviewer of Scientific Manuscripts', *The FEBS Journal*, 288.9: 2750–56, https://doi.org/10.1111/FEBS.15705

Donaldson, Thomas and Preston, Lee E.. 1995. 'The Stakeholder Theory of the Corporation: Concepts, Evidence, and Implications', *Academy of Management Review*, 20.1: 65–91, https://doi.org/10.5465/AMR.1995.9503271992

Dukerich, Janet M., Golden, Brian R. and Shortell, Stephen M. 2002. 'Beauty Is in the Eye of the Beholder: The Impact of Organizational Identification, Identity, and Image on the Cooperative Behaviors of Physicians', *Administrative Science Quarterly*, 47.3: 507–33, https://doi.org/10.2307/3094849

Dweck, Carol S. 2006. *Mindset: The New Psychology of Success* (New York: Random House)

Eisenhardt, Kathleen M., and Martin Jeffrey A. 2000. 'Dynamic Capabilities: What Are They?', *Strategic Management Journal*, 21.10–11: 1105–21, https://doi.org/10.1002/1097-0266(200010/11)21:10/11<1105::AID-SMJ133>3.0.CO;2-E

Eisenstat, Russell A., Beer, Michael. Foote, Nathaniel. Fredberg, Tobias and Norrgren, Flemming. 2008. 'The Uncompromising Leader.', *Harvard Business Review*, 86.7–8: 57, https://hbr.org/2008/07/the-uncompromising-leader

Elliott, Tracey., Fazeen, Bisma., Asrat, Asfawossen., Cetto, Ana María., Eriksson, Stefan., Looi, Lai Meng., and Negra, Diane. 2022. 'Perceptions on the prevalence and impact of predatory academic journals and conferences: A global survey of researchers.', *Learned Publishing*, 35.4: 516–28, https://doi.org/10.1002/leap.1458

Fiol, C. Marlene. 2002. 'Capitalizing on Paradox: The Role of Language in Transforming Organizational Identities', *Organization Science*, 13.6: 653–66, https://doi.org/10.1287/orsc.13.6.653.502

Flynn, F., and Chatman, J. 2001. 'Strong Cultures and Innovation: Oxymoron and Oppurtunity?', in *International Handbook of Organizational Culture and Climate*, ed. by C. Cooper, S. Cartwright, and C. Earley (Chichester, UK: Wiley), 263–87

Ghemawat, Pankaj and Ricart Costa Joan E.I. 1993. 'The Organizational Tension between Static and Dynamic Efficiency', *Strategic Management Journal*, 14.S2: 59–73, https://doi.org/10.1002/SMJ.4250141007

Gittell, Jody Hoffer. 2000. 'Paradox of Coordination and Control', *California Management Review*, 42.3: 101–17, https://doi.org/10.2307/41166044

Huy, Quy Nguyen. 1999. 'Emotional Capability, Emotional Intelligence, and Radical Change', *Academy of Management Review*, 24.2: 325–45, https://doi.org/10.5465/AMR.1999.1893939

Ibarra, Herminia. 1999. 'Provisional Selves: Experimenting with Image and Identity in Professional Adaptation', *Administration Science Quarterly*, 44.4: 764–91, https://doi.org/10.2307/2667055

Jarzabkowski, Paula, and Sillince, John. 2007. 'A Rhetoric-in-Context Approach to Building Commitment to Multiple Strategic Goals', *Organizational Studies*, 28.11: 1639–65, https://doi.org/10.1177/0170840607075266

Kaplan, Robert S, and Norton, David P. 1996. 'Using the Balanced Scorecard as a Strategic Management System', *Harvard Business Review*, 74.1: 75–85, https://hbr.org/2007/07/using-the-balanced-scorecard-as-a-strategic-management-system

Kreiner, Glen E., Hollensbe, Elaine C. and Sheep Mathew L. 2006. 'Where Is the "Me" Among the "We"? Identity Work and the Search for Optimal Balance', *Academy of Management Journal*, 49.5: 1031–57, https://doi.org/10.5465/AMJ.2006.22798186

Kubacka, Teresa. 2023. '"Publish or Perish" and ChatGPT: A Dangerous Mix.' https://lookalikes.substack.com/p/publish-or-perish-and-chatgpt-a-dangerous?subscribe_prompt=free

Linacre, Simon., Bisaccio, Michael and Earle, Lacey. 2019. 'Publishing in an Environment of Predation: The Many Things You Really Wanted to Know, but Did Not Know How to Ask', *Journal of Business-to-Business Marketing*, 26.2: 217–28, https://doi.org/10.1080/1051712X.2019.1603423

Lüscher, Lotte S., and Lewis, Marianne W. 2008. 'Organizational Change and Managerial Sensemaking: Working Through Paradox', *Academy of Management Journal*, 51.2: 221–40, https://doi.org/10.5465/AMJ.2008.31767217

March, James G. 1991. 'Exploration and Exploitation in Organizational Learning', *Organization Science*, 2.1: 71–87, https://doi.org/10.1287/ORSC.2.1.71

Margolis, Joshua D. and Walsh, James P. 2003. 'Misery Loves Companies: Rethinking Social Initiatives by Business', *Administrative Science Quarterly*, 48.2: 268–305, https://doi.org/10.2307/3556659

Markus, Hazel Rose and Kitayama, Shinobu. 1991. 'Culture and the Self: Implications for Cognition, Emotion, and Motivation', *Psychological Review*, 98.2: 224–53, https://doi.org/10.1037/0033-295X.98.2.224

Mellor, David T., Nosek, Brian A. and Pfeiffer, Nicole. 2020. 'Conflict between Open Access and Open Science: APCs Are a Key Part of the Problem, Preprints Are a Key Part of the Solution', *Center for Open Science Blog*, https://www.cos.io/blog/conflict-between-open-access-and-open-science-apcs-are-key-part-problem-preprints-are-key-part-solution

Murnighan, J. Keith and Conlon, Donald E.. 1991. 'The Dynamics of Intense Work Groups: A Study of British String Quartets', *Administrative Science Quarterly*, 36.2: 186, https://doi.org/10.2307/2393352

O'Mahony, Siobhan and Bechky, Beth A.. 2006. 'Stretchwork: Managing the Career Progression Paradox in External Labor Markets', *Academy of Management Journal*, 49.5: 918–41, https://doi.org/10.5465/AMJ.2006.22798174

Pratt, Michael G. and Foreman, Peter O. 2000. 'Classifying Managerial Responses to Multiple Organizational Identities', *Academy of Management Review*, 25.1: 18–42, https://doi.org/10.5465/AMR.2000.2791601

Senge, P. 1990. *The Fifth Discipline: The Art and Practice of a Learning Organization* (New York: Currency Doubleday)

Siggelkow, Nicolaj and Levinthal, Daniel A. 2003. 'Temporarily Divide to Conquer: Centralized, Decentralized, and Reintegrated Organizational Approaches to Exploration and Adaptation', *Organization Science*, 14.6: 650–69, https://doi.org/10.1287/ORSC.14.6.650.24840

Smith, Kenwyn K. and Berg, David N. 1987. *Paradoxes of Group Life: Understanding Conflict, Paralysis, and Movement in Group Dynamics* (San Francisco CA: Jose-Bass)

Smith, Wendy K. and Lewis, Marianne W. 2011. 'Toward a Theory of Paradox: A Dynamic Equilibrium Model of Organizing', *Academy of Management Review*, 36.2: 381–403, https://doi.org/10.5465/amr.2009.0223

Snow, John. 1849. *On the Mode of Communication of Cholera*, 1st edn (London, UK: John Churchill)

——. 1855. *On the Mode of Communication of Cholera*, 2nd edn (London, UK: John Churchill)

Stiller-Reeve, Mathew. 2018. 'How to Write a Thorough Peer Review', *Nature*, https://doi.org/10.1038/D41586-018-06991-0

Teece, David and Pisano, Gary. 1994. 'The Dynamic Capabilities of Firms: An Introduction', *Industrial and Corporate Change*, 3.3: 537–56, https://doi.org/10.1093/ICC/3.3.537-A

Tulchinsky, Theodore H. 2018. 'John Snow, Cholera, the Broad Street Pump, Waterborne Diseases Then and Now', *Case Studies in Public Health*: 77–99, https://doi.org/10.1016/B978-0-12-804571-8.00017-2

Tushman, Michael L. and O'Reilly, Charles A. 1996. 'Ambidextrous Organizations: Managing Evolutionary and Revolutionary Change', *California Management Review*, 38.4: 8–30, https://doi.org/10.2307/41165852

Waldman, David A., Putnam, Linda L., Miron-Spektor, Ella and Siegel, Donald. 2019. 'The Role of Paradox Theory in Decision Making and Management Research', *Organizational Behavior and Human Decisions Processes*, 155: 1–6, https://doi.org/10.1016/j.obhdp.2019.04.006

Weich, Karl E. and Quinn, Robert E. 1999. 'Organizational Change and Development', *Annual Review of Psychology*, 50.1: 361–86, https://doi.org/10.1146/ANNUREV.PSYCH.50.1.361

Xia, Jingfeng. 2021. *Predatory Publishing* (London: Routledge), https://doi.org/10.4324/9781003029335

Index

#arseniclife 152, 154, 249

academic administrators 8, 13
academic freedom 38, 42, 66, 248
academic knowledge production 7–8, 66
academic misconduct 12
acceptance letter 170–171
accessibility 25, 75–76, 95
accountability 77, 81, 95, 125, 176, 242, 250
accountability mechanisms 43
Africa 73, 108, 175, 178
American Chemical Society 146
analysis
  content 10, 27
  legal and policy 10, 43
Antioxidants 145
ant scientists 147
archive 39–41, 49, 137, 162, 186, 208, 212, 218
artificial intelligence (AI) 61–63, 65–66, 259
  ChatGPT 61–63, 259
  generated writing 259
artisan's guild 38
Asia 73, 86–87, 116, 122, 243–244
  Southeast 85, 87, 108, 187
Aspen Institute 155
astrobiology 152
Atlantic Islands of Madeira 147
attributes 15, 61, 97, 121, 126, 132, 158, 205–206, 209, 212, 216, 218, 255
AuthorAid 252
authoritative knowledge 242

authors 10, 12–17, 19–23, 26–31, 39–41, 44, 47, 52–53, 57, 64, 66–67, 74–75, 79, 81–84, 86, 89, 91, 98, 106, 112–113, 115, 124–125, 128–129, 138, 140, 145, 147–149, 156–161, 169–172, 174, 180, 182–185, 187–189, 191, 209–210, 215, 218, 222–223, 229, 231, 238, 247–250, 253–254, 256–257, 259, 271
authorship 31, 37, 45, 204, 206
Avery, Oswald 8–9

Beall, Jeffrey 10–13, 15, 19, 49, 54–55, 58, 73–74, 84, 86, 144, 150–151, 171, 181, 186, 218, 221–222, 237, 253–254
Bentham, Jeremy 42
bias 17, 73, 107–108, 110, 115, 124, 156, 246, 253
Big Pharma 51, 65, 67
biomedicine 188
black box 28, 81–82, 84, 246
blacklist 10, 186–187, 216, 254
blind faith 28, 81, 244, 246
blog posts 15–16, 83, 152, 211, 213, 255
Bohannon, Johannes 137–142, 144–152, 154–155, 159–161, 171, 250
Bohannon, John. *See* Bohannon, Johannes
Broad Street water pump 258
Brown University 219
business model 13, 19, 40, 44, 46, 49, 52, 61

Cabells 186, 216–217, 254
Canada 74, 216
cancer 148–149

Carnegie classifications 202, 205, 207, 209–210, 228
case study 10, 28, 31, 41, 153, 215, 219, 229
cease and desist 51, 53
Center for Open Science 83
central nations 74
cheating 20–21
checklist. *See* safelists, watchlists, checklists
China 187
chocolate 137–138, 148
cholera outbreak (19th century England) 258
citation 19, 30, 60, 82, 97, 103, 114, 116, 128, 131, 140, 143–148, 161, 249, 253
  milling 114
CITI training 202–203, 205
civil penalties 41–42
Clarivate's Journal Citation Reports 128
Clinton-Gore administration 39
Coalition for Diversity & Inclusion in Scholarly Communications (C4DISC) 25
cocoa 145–146, 148–149
code of ethics 38, 41–43, 59–60, 63, 66–67
Cold War (and post-Cold War) 44, 48
collaboration 7, 75–76, 78, 80, 95, 127, 130, 133, 241, 255
commercial journals and publishers 237. *See also* journals; *See also* publishers
Committee on Publication Ethics (COPE) 43, 67, 128, 140–141, 189, 221
communication
  scholarly 8, 10, 12–13, 25, 139, 156, 237, 242, 246, 248, 251–252, 257, 259
  reform of 251
  technologies 39, 43, 48–49, 60
compliance measures 247
conference presentations 175
Conference Series LLC 51–52, 54–56
conflict of interest 37, 176, 187, 204
contingency theory 239
contradictory demands 238

Copernicus Indexing service 184
copy editing 143, 183
Cornell University 213
COVID-19 9, 23–24, 89, 258
Crick, Francis H.C. 8–9
criminal penalties 58
criteria 84, 124, 151, 181, 186–188, 195, 221, 230
CrossRef 145–146
crowd-sourcing 82
cultural capital 75
customers 23, 48, 61, 241, 252
CVs 66, 74, 91, 106, 171
cyberspace 37, 39–43, 48–49

databases 37–41, 43, 54, 61–64, 98, 110, 151, 158, 170, 172, 183, 186
data management 204
deceptive 11, 37, 41, 43, 50–51, 53, 55–60, 64, 85–86, 91, 185
defamation lawsuit 55
de-identification of research data 27, 76, 172–173
deterritorialization 42
diffusion 88
Digital Object Identifiers (DOI) 30, 89, 141, 145, 147–148, 156–157, 159–161, 184, 160
digitization 38–41, 43, 49
Directory of Open Access Books (DOAB) 47
Directory of Open Access Journals (DOAJ) 47, 67, 128, 150–151, 186, 213, 215–217, 222–223, 229
disciplinary 247
disciplinary differences 109
Discover 17
disinformation 156
diversity, equity, and inclusion 25–26, 47, 68, 75–76, 80, 95, 106, 115, 151, 185–187
  epistemic diversity 107, 111, 125
DNA, double-helix model 8–9

Earth 152

editorial board 16, 52, 54, 56, 64, 122, 142, 169, 174, 179–180, 183, 185, 187, 189, 192, 257
editors 7, 11–12, 14–15, 18–22, 39, 42, 54–55, 73, 78–79, 81, 87–88, 93, 112, 114–115, 123–124, 127, 138–142, 149, 153, 169–170, 246, 248, 254, 256, 269, 272
Elsevier 150
embargo 153
Embassy of Good Science 206
epistemic constraints 38
error 78, 140–141, 172, 181, 188
   grammatical 85, 105, 143, 172, 243
   quotation 147
ethical challenges 104
ethical norms 248
ethical or moral reasoning 42
ethical principles 37, 91, 130
Europe 40, 47, 87–88, 109–110, 116, 178, 181, 184–185, 243, 245, 247, 249, 251, 253
experimental psychology 76, 94
extraterrestrial life 152

Facebook 141–142
fake news 23, 156
fear 73, 82–83, 89, 92, 126, 130
federal requirements 41, 43, 53–54, 58, 60, 65, 202–204
Federal Trade Commission (FTC) 28, 41–43, 51, 53–59, 63, 65, 67
   v. OMICS case 53–58
female body 25, 259
fields of knowledge production 7–8, 20, 24–25, 29, 38, 43, 51, 57, 64, 66, 68, 89, 103–113, 116–118, 120–121, 125–126, 129–132, 170, 176, 242, 255–258
Florida International University 220
fraudulent 14, 18, 21, 23, 29, 50, 106, 140, 146, 159
Frontiers 11, 125
funder mandate 204

game 8–10, 12, 19–20, 22, 25, 28, 31, 116, 128, 170, 237, 258–260

gatekeeping, gatekeeper 79–81, 89, 112, 126–127, 130, 132, 154, 159, 256
Gedela, Srinubabu 54
generalizability 76–77, 94, 259
Georgetown University 218
George Washington University 217
Germany 138
germ theory 258
globalization 48, 59–60, 67, 242
Global North and Global South 47, 105
global publishing enterprise 103
Google 40, 61, 63, 184, 207
   Scholar 128, 143, 146, 161
graduate advisor 96, 117–119, 126, 132, 173, 175–176, 192
graduate student training/mentoring 29, 92, 117–120, 126, 130, 173–177
guest editors 21

heuristics 93, 238
hidden curriculum 225
higher education 43, 52, 104–105, 108, 177
Hindawi 150
H-index rankings 253
hoax 22, 29, 30, 58, 63, 137–141, 143–149, 152, 154–156, 159–161, 171, 250. *See also* Bohannon, Johannes
   balloon (Edgar Allan Poe) 154
   moon (Richard Adam Locke) 155
   scientific hoax articles 29
   Sokal 155
   Sokal Squared 155
human resources 109, 118
Hyderabad, India 51, 53
hydroxychloroquine, chloroquine 23–24
hypothesis 17, 79, 94, 112

iMedicalPublisher.com 143
iMedPub LLC 51–52, 54–56
impact 9, 12, 39, 42, 45, 59, 65, 77, 90, 106, 109, 112, 116, 150–154, 173–174, 184, 191–192, 249, 251, 260
   factor 12, 16, 48, 54, 56, 60, 103, 106, 111, 114, 180, 183–184, 192, 250–254
incentives 73, 82, 84, 109, 244

India 28, 51–54, 57, 65–66, 187
  government 28, 65
individual responsibility 31, 119, 247, 259
inequity 110, 247
information disorder 155
information ecosystem 29, 139, 155
infrastructure 90, 242
innovation, innovative 18, 24, 30, 38–40, 43–45, 48, 255
Institute of Diet and Health 137
institutional culture 92, 105, 130, 133
Institutional Review Board (IRB) 120, 138
integrity 9–11, 17, 29, 38, 45, 75–76, 80, 85, 87, 95, 104, 111, 120, 124, 141, 154, 206
intellectual property 37, 41, 46, 51, 53, 63
intercoder reliability 210
International Archives of Medicine 137–138, 140, 142–143, 145
International Communication Association (ICA) 110
International Science Council 90
internet 39–41, 48–49, 62, 66, 187
interview 10, 13–14, 27, 29, 31, 84–85, 90, 92, 105, 120, 172, 242, 259–260
invitation 14, 23, 74, 169–170, 179, 229
Iran 73
ivory tower 8, 104

John Snow 258
journal index 19, 106, 142, 172, 180, 182–184, 257
journalists, science 13, 137, 139, 142, 148, 160, 249
Journal of Agricultural and Food Chemistry 145
Journal of Nanoparticle Research 21
journal quality 123
journals 10–16, 18–21, 23, 26–27, 29–31, 37–43, 45–58, 64–68, 73–76, 79, 82–92, 96, 104–112, 114–115, 122–124, 126–130, 132–133, 138, 140, 145–157, 159, 169–188, 191–194, 201, 206, 211,
  215–216, 218, 223, 227, 229–230, 237, 243–244, 246–257, 259
  English 73
  hijacked 22
  international 73, 75, 250
  overlay 243
  Western 25, 73–75, 87–88, 90, 93, 105, 109–110
journal scope 180–181, 192
junk-science diet industry 137

kairos 8, 139
knowledge capitalism 47

laissez-faire principles 38, 40, 42
Lancet 123, 146
Latin America 110–111
law, legal aspects of scholarly publishing 10, 27–28, 38, 41–43, 50–51, 53–55, 58–60, 62, 65, 186
learning assessments 222, 226
learning outcomes 105, 202
legitimacy 20, 30, 81, 143, 146, 160
Lexis-Nexis 40
librarian 10, 55, 87, 106, 117, 175, 179, 181, 184, 186, 227, 257
library 27, 37, 39–41, 44, 49, 208–210, 212–223, 228, 271
  guide 208, 210, 212–214, 216–217, 220, 222–223, 228
lichen 148–150
linguistic capitalism 40
long-term/short-term solutions 239
low- or middle-income nations 26

Malaysia 74
management scholars, studies 238, 249
media 9, 23, 89, 92, 103, 106, 137–139, 153, 249
medical and pharmaceutical research industries 51–52, 66
medieval craft 38
mercantilist 42, 48, 58
methodology 79, 96, 110–111, 124, 186
metrics 12, 18–19, 60, 106, 253
miasma theory 258

Mihaila, Delia 15
Miller, Carolyn R. 8–9
misinformation 155–157
Molecules 145
Multidisciplinary Digital Publishing Institute (MDPI) 15–18, 145–146

National Academies of Sciences, Engineering, and Medicine 11
National Academy of Engineering 204
National Aeronautics and Space Administration (NASA) 152–153
National Institutes of Health (NIH) 43–44, 51, 53–54, 203, 205
National Science Foundation 10, 27, 44, 204
Nature 8, 12, 123, 216, 250
negative publication bias 17
New England Journal of Medicine 146
news deserts 155
newsletter articles 210–211
Nigerian government 73
Nobel laureate 44, 171
non-peripheral nations 27
North America 87–88, 109, 117, 129, 178–179, 181–182, 184, 245, 248, 250, 252–253
Northeastern University 218
Northwestern University 222

Office of Research Integrity (Department of Health and Human Services) 204
Ohio State University 213, 216, 223
Oldenburg, Henry 19
oligopolistic 38, 44–46, 54, 59–60
OMICS International 28, 37, 41–43, 51–60, 63, 65–68
opaque/non-transparent 77, 245
open access 8, 10–11, 13, 15, 17–18, 23, 25–26, 41–50, 53–54, 58–60, 62, 64–65, 75–76, 83–85, 87–88, 90–91, 94, 105, 149–151, 153–154, 175–176, 186, 188, 206, 215, 218, 221–223, 229, 237, 242, 247, 249–251
  gold 46
Open Access Books | InTech 47

Open Access Publishing in European Networks (OAPEN) 47
open data 78, 80, 90–91, 93–97, 243
'open' movement 75, 82–83, 87–88, 90–92
openness 28–29, 76, 78, 80–81, 83–84, 91, 94, 119, 150, 242
open science 17, 25–28, 75–84, 87–88, 90–94, 96, 98, 242–243, 245–246, 256
ORCID 30, 156, 158–160

pandemic 23–24, 89
paradigm shift 41, 44
paradox 14, 18–19, 30, 89, 107, 156, 237–240, 242, 244–252, 255
  theory 238–239
peer review 7, 10, 16, 19–24, 28, 46–48, 50, 52, 54–56, 58, 64–65, 74, 78–79, 81–84, 89, 94, 103, 105–106, 108, 111–115, 122–127, 130–133, 138–139, 143, 147–148, 152–154, 159, 170, 172, 182–183, 189, 216, 219, 222, 245–246, 255–256
  blind 80–82, 84
  double-blind 19–20, 28, 81–82, 84, 113–115, 130, 245
  fake 20–21
  open 78, 81–82, 90, 94, 124, 133, 246, 256
peer-to-peer learning 225
periodicals 40
peripheral nations 27, 74, 90–93
phosphorus 152–153
plagiarism 31, 37, 158, 206
PLOS 26, 150
policy 10, 28, 39, 43, 52, 91, 124, 174, 181, 187–188
policymakers 11, 13, 237
politics of publishing 74
postdoctoral fellow 169, 176–177, 191
preliminary injunction 55
preprints 24, 84, 88–89, 121, 246, 256
preregistration 78–79, 88, 90–91, 93–96, 246
press release 137, 152
prey 13, 23, 26, 31, 52, 68, 73, 86–87, 179–180, 191, 193, 202, 254, 259

principal investigators (PIs) 204, 224–225
professional self-regulation 37–38
profits 10, 28, 105
pseudo-scientific 171
publication cost 10, 26, 54–55, 64, 75, 218, 247, 254
publication fee 23, 84, 138, 170
public benefit of research 247
publishers 7, 10–11, 14, 16–20, 24, 26–29, 31, 37–38, 40–52, 54, 58–60, 63–64, 75, 104, 107, 111, 114, 129, 140, 149–151, 157–158, 171, 176–177, 179, 183, 185–187, 189, 191, 193, 201, 209, 211–212, 215–216, 218, 221, 227–229, 237, 245–246, 249, 252–254, 259
publishing
  commercial 27, 46, 49, 64, 252
  for profit 48, 52, 153, 247, 249
  industry 24, 31, 43, 47–50, 55, 63, 259
  legacy 38, 45–46, 48
  predatory 9–14, 18–19, 22, 26, 28–29, 31, 47, 49, 51, 55, 63, 65, 74–76, 78–80, 82–85, 90, 94, 106–107, 126, 129, 132, 174, 185, 191–193, 201–204, 206–213, 215–218, 220–230, 237–239, 243–244, 250–251, 254–256, 259–260
    characteristics of 215–216
    consensus definition of 216
      Ottawa summit 216
    history of 215
  scholarly 9–14, 18–19, 23, 25–26, 28–31, 38, 41–50, 54, 59–60, 63, 65–66, 68, 74–76, 83–85, 91, 103, 117, 130, 139, 148, 155, 159, 173, 201, 206, 208, 237–240, 242, 246, 249, 251–252, 256, 259–260
  STM 39
publishing cultures 109
publishing professionals 7–8, 13, 88, 181, 187, 238, 243–244, 252–254
publish or perish 52, 108, 177, 259
Publons 133, 256
PubMed Central 53–54, 142–143

qualitative research methods 92, 95–97, 121, 259
quantitative research methods 95, 121

R1 institution 169
Raoult, Didier 23
readership 103, 116
registered reports 78, 256
regulations 37–39, 41, 57, 59–60, 62–63
rejection 16, 78–79, 108, 111, 115, 125–126, 130–132, 141–142, 150, 170, 178, 255
  desk reject 170
replication 78, 94, 152, 245
  crisis 76–77, 79, 83–84, 88, 90–91, 94
repository 47, 89, 91, 206
reproducibility (replicability) 17, 37, 76–77, 94, 121, 243–244
research assistant 93
researchers 7–10, 12–13, 16, 22, 26, 28, 37, 39, 44–45, 47, 49, 51–55, 58, 60, 63–64, 66, 68, 73–80, 82, 85–93, 95–96, 98, 105, 108, 110–111, 114, 116, 119, 122, 127–130, 132, 141–142, 146, 148, 152–153, 156–158, 171–182, 184–185, 187, 191–193, 203, 205–206, 225, 227, 229, 243, 245, 247–251, 256–257, 259, 271
  Arab 73
  non-Western 74, 93, 227
  Turkish 73
research ethics education 202–204, 209, 225
research ethics training 203–206, 224, 226–227
research fraud 80
research integrity 11, 17, 111, 120, 206
research misconduct 140, 204
research quality 30, 80, 106, 129–130, 140, 184, 252
responsible conduct of research (RCR) 31, 42–43, 48, 202–203, 222, 226
retraction 21, 30, 85, 137, 140–143, 145–148, 158–159, 188, 250, 253
Retraction Watch 21, 141–142, 146

reviewers 15, 20–21, 28, 39, 42–43, 62, 74, 79–82, 86, 93, 112–115, 122–125, 127–128, 130, 145, 153–154, 170, 243, 248, 256
  fake reviewer reports 172
revision 74, 89, 98, 138, 170
  revise and submit 170
rhetorical
  acts 139
  features 139, 146
rigor, rigorous 16, 24, 29, 74, 80–82, 112, 121–123, 126, 130, 182, 246, 256
rule utilitarianism 42, 52, 60

safelists, watchlists, checklists 18, 107, 151, 186–189, 192, 216, 218, 224, 228, 231, 238, 252, 254
Sage Open 18
sample size 79, 138
scam 21–22, 179, 215
scholarly reputation 171
SciDev 252
Science 123, 148–149, 151–154
scientific protocol, method 8, 120–121, 130, 242
scientific record 91, 140, 146, 149, 159
Scimago 128
Scopus 184, 186
sensationalizing 108, 112, 130
Smith and Lewis (2011) four categories of paradox 14, 238–240, 242, 247, 249–252
social justice 25
social media 62, 208. *See also* Facebook
social sciences and humanities 87, 247
solicitation 179, 215–216, 225, 231
  email 14, 219–220, 231
South America 85, 179, 181, 187
special issue 16, 21–22, 169–170
Springer Nature 17, 21, 46
stakeholders 8, 10–15, 25, 29, 31, 37, 84–85, 103–104, 148, 157, 160, 201, 227, 237–240, 246–248, 257, 259
Stanford University 216
statistical significance 77, 79

STEM 86–87, 247–248, 251
Stony Brook University 215
subjects
  animal 204
  human 37, 138
subscription costs 27, 38–39, 44–46, 54, 59, 65, 75, 151, 154, 175, 186, 214
Supreme Court 40
survey 77, 83, 96, 203
sustainability 11, 46, 105, 238–239
Sustainability 16
systematic review 31, 204–206, 215, 221, 227

Taylor & Francis 15
technical quality 180–181, 192
telecommunications networks 39
television reality show 7–8
tenure 7, 74, 109, 116, 169, 176–177, 250–251, 255
Texas Data Repository 14, 27, 85, 92, 105, 172, 242
Texas Tech University Health Sciences Center 212
textbooks 203, 249
Think. Check. Submit. 182, 189, 194, 213, 221–224, 229
Third Reviewer Program 255
threats 9–11, 31, 55, 60–61, 65, 89–90, 103–104, 130, 170, 172, 201, 206, 223–224, 228
trademark infringement 53
training 20, 29–31, 68, 86, 91, 103–105, 118–120, 126, 129–130, 173, 175–176, 185, 192, 201–210, 215, 220, 223–231, 237, 244, 255–257
transparency 28–29, 50, 67, 75–78, 80–81, 94–95, 107, 121, 123, 126, 130, 216, 242, 254–257
truth/untruth 120, 139, 169
Turkey 73

UlrichsWeb Global Serials Directory 217
United States 28, 39–41, 43, 48, 51–52, 54–59, 64–65, 73, 155, 207

United States Court of Appeals for the 9th Circuit 56, 58
United States Department of Defense 48
United States District Court for the District of Nevada, Las Vegas 54–55
university-based curriculum 30, 204, 225, 255
University of Alabama 222
University of California Irvine 227
University of California San Diego 221
University of Colorado, Denver 10–11, 55, 186
University of Florida 215
University of Houston 215
University of Illinois Chicago Graduate School 211
University of Nebraska-Lincoln 212
University of Pittsburgh 220
University of Tennessee 221
University of Utah 215
university press 38, 44–45, 59
USA Today 153
US Department of Health and Human Services 43, 204
US Department of Health and Human Services (DHHS) 43, 51, 53
US Treasury 57

vaccination 9
vaccine 9
vapors 258
Virginia Commonwealth University 216

wandering womb 259
watchlist. *See* safelists, watchlists, checklists
Watson, James D. 8–9
Web of Science (WoS) 46, 186
wisdom of the crowd 82
withdrawal fee 172
World of Science 184
World War II 43
World Wide Web 39

Yale University 222

Zen and the Art of Motorcycle Maintenance 103, 107, 117

About the Team

Alessandra Tosi was the managing editor for this book.

Lucy Barnes and Anja Pritchard performed the copy-editing and proofreading.

The index was created by Rosalyn Sword.

Jeevanjot Kaur Nagpal designed the cover. The cover was produced in InDesign using the Fontin font.

Jeremy Bowman typeset the book in InDesign and produced the paperback and hardback editions. The text font is Tex Gyre Pagella; the heading font is Californian FB.

Cameron Craig produced the EPUB, PDF, HTML, and XML editions.

The conversion was made with open-source software such as pandoc (https://pandoc.org/), created by John MacFarlane, and other tools freely available on our GitHub page (https://github.com/OpenBookPublishers).

This book has been anonymously peer-reviewed by experts in their field. We thank them for their invaluable help.

This book need not end here...

Share

All our books — including the one you have just read — are free to access online so that students, researchers and members of the public who can't afford a printed edition will have access to the same ideas. This title will be accessed online by hundreds of readers each month across the globe: why not share the link so that someone you know is one of them?

This book and additional content is available at:

https://doi.org/10.11647/OBP.0364

Donate

Open Book Publishers is an award-winning, scholar-led, not-for-profit press making knowledge freely available one book at a time. We don't charge authors to publish with us: instead, our work is supported by our library members and by donations from people who believe that research shouldn't be locked behind paywalls.

Why not join them in freeing knowledge by supporting us:

https://www.openbookpublishers.com/support-us

Follow @OpenBookPublish

Read more at the Open Book Publishers **BLOG**

You may also be interested in:

Whose Book Is it Anyway?
A View from Elsewhere on Publishing, Copyright and Creativity
Janis Jefferies, Sarah Kember (editors)

https://doi.org/10.11647/OBP.0159

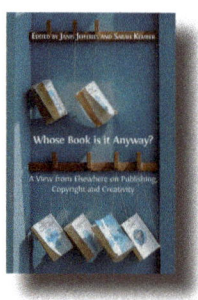

From Handwriting to Footprinting
Text and Heritage in the Age of Climate Crisis
Anne Baillot

https://doi.org/10.11647/OBP.0355

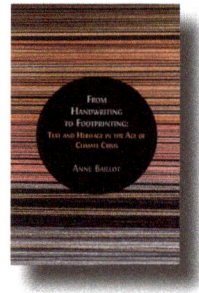

Digital Scholarly Editing
Theories and Practices
Matthew James Driscoll, Elena Pierazzo (editors)

https://doi.org/10.11647/OBP.0095

www.ingramcontent.com/pod-product-compliance
Lightning Source LLC
Chambersburg PA
CBHW061251230426
43664CB00025B/2925